Language and Other Abstract Objects

Language and Other Abstract Objects

Jerrold J. Katz

Basil Blackwell • Oxford

Copyright © 1981 by Jerrold J. Katz

First published in the United Kingdom 1981 by
Basil Blackwell Publisher Ltd
108 Cowley Road
Oxford OX4 1JF
England

British Library Cataloguing in Publication Data

Katz, Jerrold J.
   Language and other abstract objects.
   1. Language—Philosophy
   I. Title
   401   P106
ISBN 0-631-12946-4
      0-631-12954-5 Pbk

Printed in the United States of America

To the particular VVV, with all my love,
Platonic and otherwise.

Contents

Acknowledgments

One enjoyable duty of an author is to thank those who helped with the book. D. T. Langendoen, William Lycan, Robert Nozick, Paul Postal, Harris Savin, and Virginia Valian have been of much help, and I thank them warmly. I also thank Alan Berger, Thomas Bever, Richard Boyd, Robert Fiengo, Hans Herzberger, Fred Katz, Arnold Koslow, Robert Matthews, Richard Mendelsohn, James Murphy, John Pittman, Peter Stamos and a couple of anonymous reviewers.

Introduction

In the first half of the twentieth century, philosophy took a linguistic turn.[1] The idea behind this turn was that philosophical problems are basically about language and can be solved or dissolved linguistically. Logical empiricism (logical positivism) sought their solution or dissolution in the rational reconstruction of language. Ordinary language philosophy sought them in a better understanding of the use of language in ordinary life.

Both approaches showed themselves, over the years, to have serious drawbacks. Rational reconstruction tended to ignore the facts about natural languages and description of the ordinary uses of words made little or no attempt to construct theories of linguistic structure.[2] Thus, although logical empiricism went in for theory construction, its theories were only distantly and dubiously related to the basis of classical philosophical problems in natural language, and although ordinary language philosophy occupied itself with careful description of natural language, its descriptions stayed at the linguistic surface and failed to reveal the deeper, philosophically more significant principles of grammar.

It was in the light of these inverse strengths and weaknesses that the new theory of generative-transformational grammar developed in the fifties and early sixties seemed philosophically promising. The new theory promised an alternative approach with the strengths of logical empiricism and ordinary language philosophy but without their weaknesses. This approach, at least in the form it took in Chomsky's work, had a genuine scientific commitment to theory construction *and* to faithful, painstaking description of the grammatical facts about natural languages. Hence, the attractiveness of the new theory in linguistics for philosophers with a linguistic orientation was that the new theory offered a form of linguistic analysis that could not be criticized for resting solutions to philosophical problems on arbitrary formal constructions or for failing to reveal principles of linguistic structure deep enough to shed real light on philosophical problems.

1

It had the further appeal of a scientific treatment of philosophical problems. The lure of scientific philosophy has always been strong for philosophers, based as it is on their experience of the interminable and inconclusive controversies that characterize much philosophical discussion. Such a linguistically oriented philosophy of language promised the possibility of solutions to philosophical problems based on scientific theories, evaluated on objective evidence, using standard canons of scientific methodology.

This, then, was the appeal of the new theory of grammar for the philosophers who joined with the M.I.T. linguists in the early sixties to push generative-transformational theory to the point where it would provide solutions or parts of solutions to some traditional philosophical problems. This promise was, for example, behind my belief, which I expressed at the time,[3] that, to whatever extent philosophical problems really are at bottom problems about language, the most fruitful way to tackle them is on the basis of the best available scientific theory of natural language in linguistics.

No question was raised at the time about what kind of science linguistics is. Almost everyone involved in either the philosophical or the linguistic side of the enterprise assumed, and still assumes with Chomsky, that linguistics is a branch of empirical psychology. It was apparently not noticed, or if noticed not taken as a matter of much concern, that the linguistic turn in philosophy coupled with the scientific turn in linguistics coupled with the Chomskian view that linguistics is a branch of empirical psychology implies that philosophy, too, is at least in part empirical.

This equation of the scientific with the empirical was a consequence of Chomsky's central doctrine that grammars are theories of an aspect of human psychology. Acceptance of this doctrine was due, principally, to two factors. First, there seemed no alternative to this doctrine except the discredited doctrine of structuralist linguistics that grammars are tabulations of the noises produced in speech. Second, Chomsky's doctrine occupied a central place in the thinking that brought about the Chomskian revolution. Once Chomsky demonstrated the enormous advantages of his conception of grammar over the taxonomic conception, in particular the advantages of his psychological interpretation of grammars in achieving more abstract and comprehensive theories of natural languages, it would have seemed an extreme of blind conservatism to try to hang on to the taxonomic conception of structuralist linguistics. The psychological view was thus generally accepted and handed down to new generations of linguists and philosophers over the last two decades. The one-time revolutionary doctrine thus became a comfortable dogma.

I had been one of the strongest defenders of this view of what grammars are theories of.[4] Aside from the two reasons already mentioned for adopting Chomsky's view that grammars are about human psychology, I had a special reason for defending it. Since meaning could not be reduced to physical features of utterances and could not be defined operationally or behavioristically, it had no place in the structuralist's taxonomic grammar. In replacing the American structuralist view that grammars are about noise, the psychological view made it possible for semantics, the area of linguistics holding the greatest promise of philosophical contributions, to become a part of grammar. Because Harris's transformational theory, out of which Chomsky's developed, was constructed within the American structuralist tradition, there was, at this point in the development of the new theory, no conception of how to represent the meaning of sentences as part of their grammatical description. None had as yet been provided in the recently developed theory of generative-transformational grammar, but Chomsky's replacement of taxonomic theory made it possible to incorporate semantics in grammar. If grammars are theories of the tacit principles that constitute the speaker's grammatical competence, then semantic rules in a grammar can be a theory of the tacit principles that constitute the speaker's semantic competence.

The present book marks a radical change in my outlook on the nature of linguistics and the philosophy of language. Although I still think that some philosophical problems are about language and that constructing scientific theories in linguistics is the proper way to approach them, I no longer accept the equation of the scientific with the empirical and the view that the study of grammar is a part of psychology. I now realize there was all along an alternative to both the American structuralists' and the Chomskian conception of what grammars are theories of, namely, the Platonic realist view that grammars are theories of abstract objects (sentences), and I now think that this alternative is preferable to both. Acceptance of Platonic realism in this day and age does not, of course, come easy, but I found accepting the full implications of an empirical philosophy harder still.

The main purpose of this book is to lay out my conception of the study of grammatical structure in natural language as an *a priori* discipline like mathematics and my reasons for thinking it preferable, and then to carry my approach to the philosophy of language a step further by using this conception and the reasons for it to construct a solution to the classical ontological problem of universals.

My aim in this introduction is to explain these purposes more fully. I will try to do this by using my own change of outlook as an example. I will explain how this change took place and what line of thinking led to rejecting the psychological view of grammars and accepting a realist view.

Had I been solely a semanticist, I might have remained a staunch supporter of the view that grammars are psychological theories. But being also a philosopher I was brought to doubt this view. My primary interest in using theories in linguistics to solve philosophical problems forced me to take the philosophical implications of those theories far more seriously than they are taken in linguistics. The two philosophical problems to which I thought work in linguistics might make an important contribution were the rationalist-empiricist controversy and the issue of the existence of an analytic-synthetic distinction. Chomsky had argued that the problem about innate ideas can be cast in a new form within the theory of generative-transformational grammar.[5] He argued that the problem can be put, in part, as the question whether the speaker's knowledge of the grammar of a language can be acquired on the basis of inductive generalizations from linguistic experience or whether the acquisition of such knowledge depends on innate schemata expressing the form of the mature grammatical knowledge and the substance of the principles for its acquisition. The advantage of putting the problem in this specialized form is that the findings of comparative linguistics can be brought to bear on the problem of innate ideas and a strong case can be made on such findings for a solution along the lines of Cartesian rationalism.[6]

The other problem was one that concerned me even more directly. I had argued that the problem of distinguishing analytic and synthetic propositions can be cast as a question about the nature of semantic representation within a generative grammar of a natural language,[7] and that, so cast, a solution could be given that overcomes the objections to Kant's version of the distinction.[8] I argued that such a formulation of the problem eliminates Kant's metaphorical notion of containment (replacing it with a formal notion of the inclusion of representations at the semantic level of grammars), extends the Kantian distinction beyond subject-predicate sentences to relational sentences generally, and makes the division of sentences into analytic and synthetic a defensible matter of factual evidence and scientific methodology on a par with other grammatical distinctions.

The first sign of trouble came in connection with Chomsky's treatment of the rationalist-empiricist controversy. Cooper published a paper criticizing Chomsky's "new rationalism" on the grounds that it differs too substantially from classical philosophical rationalism for Chomsky's position to be thought of as being genuinely along classical rationalist lines.[9] Classical rationalism, Cooper argued, concerned itself with full-blooded necessary truth while the new rationalism concerns itself only with psychological or biological constraints on how children learn a language. At first it seemed this criticism could be easily handled. Chomsky and I replied to Cooper with a reasonable response from within the conception of grammars and linguistic theory as psychological theories.[10] However, as I came to realize later, our reply did not deal adequately with Cooper's central point about necessary truth—that Chomsky's rationalism comes to no more than nativism, and nativism offers no account like that which classical rationalists tried to give of the existence and nature of necessary truth.

In reflecting on my own work on analyticity, I reached the conclusion that even this criticism does not go far enough. This work led to a semantic theory, as part of linguistic theory, in which analyticity is explicated in terms of structural relations internal to senses of sentences and in which the logical interpretation of such relations secures all analytic sentences against falsehood and some, such as generics like "A nightmare is a dream" or conditionals like "If there are nightmares, then there are dreams," are necessarily true. Another feature of this work was that, because it bases the analytic-synthetic distinction on the Kantian distinction between explicative and expansive logical forms, it draws a sharp line between language and theory, classifying analytic truth as a matter of language but logical, mathematical, physical, and other non-analytic truth as matters of theory.[11] From this feature together with the fact that analytic sentences express necessary truths, it follows that natural languages, independent of theory, determine one species of necessary truth. Thus, a theory of natural language is responsible for explaining how language determines that species of necessary truth. At the very least, such a theory ought not preclude the possibility of necessary truth in natural language.

Therefore, my work in semantics brought me to a position on necessary truth and language closely paralleling the classical rationalist position on necessary truth and logic and mathematics. Up to this point, it had not seemed of critical importance that Chomsky's new rationalism could provide no account of necessary truth like that developed by the old rationalism. For one thing, the traditional rationalist doctrines applied to logic and other areas outside language, and for another, the old and the new rationalism were linked by a common nativism. But now the question arose of whether Chomsky's rationalism, committed as it is to treating language as a matter of the nature and functioning of a contingent object, the human mind or brain, could, in principle, account for necessary truth.

The answer seemed clearly that Chomsky's rationalism could not account for necessary truth. But it seemed clear also that, rather than being just a matter of leaving open the question of the existence of necessary truth, Chomsky's psychologism actually denies the possibility of genuine necessary truth in natural languages. Given Chomsky's treatment of grammars as theories of the psychological makeup of speakers, the strongest notion of compulsion that is possible on Chomsky's conception of language is a notion of the natural or biological limits humans work under in evaluating the truth of their beliefs. The grammatical principles underlying analytic truth, on Chomsky's view, only express laws of human mental or neural processes, and hence, can only determine what human beings have, on the basis of the nature of their linguistic capacities, to *conceive* of as true no matter what. Nothing can follow about what *is* true no matter what. There is no way to exclude the possibility that humans are innately programmed to conceive a set of contingent statements to be necessary, no way to preclude the possibility that humans conceive of statements as expressing necessary truths when they do not. Just as the fact of the matter in connection with the physical world *could* be different from what the true physical laws assert, so on Chomsky's psychologized account of language the fact of the matter in connection with grammar *could* be different from what the analytic truths assert. Thus, the best that Chomsky's rationalism offers is the notion of something's being necessary relative to the laws of human cognitive processes, which falls short of a bona fide notion of necessary truth, that is, one that is not relative at all but absolute (and hence, one that is the same for *any* rational creature no matter how radically different its cognitive processes from ours). Therefore, the claim that Chomsky's theory makes to being the true theory of language brings the theory into conflict with traditional rationalism, or rather, the linguistic parallel constructed with analyticity in place of logical and mathematical truth.

Having convinced myself on the basis of reflections like these that Chomsky's position prevents linguistics from doing justice to the logical character of natural language, I undertook an investigation into how a rationalist position that is fully in the spirit of traditional rationalism might be constructed. The result of this investigation was the conviction that rationalism requires Platonism if it is to rise above mere nativism. The psychological conception of grammars and linguistic theory has to be replaced with a conception of them as theories of the sentences of a language taking the sentences as abstract objects like numbers. Only a Platonist conception can succeed where psychological conceptions fail, that is, only a Platonist conception offers a theory of language consistent with and capable of explaining the existence of absolute necessary truths in natural languages.

But it is one thing to reach the conclusion that contemporary linguistic rationalism requires Platonism in order to be fully in the spirit of traditional rationalism and another to accept it. The initial resistance to Platonism in the present climate in philosophy and the behavioral sciences is formidable. I shared the common reluctance to accept Platonism and the temptation to suppose that if rationalism requires Platonism then perhaps this is a *reductio* of rationalism. However, the opposition toward Platonism turned out not to have its source in some knockdown argument against Platonism but rather in philosophical, particularly empiricist bias, in serious underdevelopment of the Platonist position, particularly in the area of language, in mistaken attempts to erect epistemological foundations on the part of Gödel and other contemporary Platonists, and in an anti-metaphysical attitude, particularly on the part of analytic philosophy. In the course of this book, I deal with each of the components of the opposition to Platonism.

There is, however, a more general aspect of the unwillingness to entertain a Platonist conception of natural languages that has to be dealt with at the outset. This is the widely held view that, in the words Quine uses to open *Word and Object*, "Language is a social art."[12] How critical this view is can be seen from the fact that it is Quine's basis for restricting linguistic evidence in questions of meaning to intersubjectively available behavioral stimuli. As Quine puts it: "Hence, there is no justification for collating linguistic meanings, unless in terms of men's dispositions to respond overtly to socially observable stimulations."[13] The restriction, as students of Quine's work know, is what enables him to construct the situation of the field linguist so that nothing beyond the behavioral effects of "dispositions to respond overtly to socially observable stimulations" counts as evidence for hypotheses about translation.[14]

Quine can introduce his book with the sentence "Language is a social art"—that is, he can say it without support—because this view is so widely held. We see it endorsed across the spectrum from popular writers on language to sophisticated linguists. Sapir expresses it in the following way:

Speech is a human activity that varies without assignable limit as we pass from social group to social group, because it is a purely historical heritage of the group, the product of long-continued social usage. It varies as all creative effort varies—not as consciously, perhaps, but nonetheless as truly as do the religions, the beliefs, the customs, and the arts of different peoples. Walking is an organic, an instinctive, function . . . speech is a non-instinctive, acquired, "cultural" function.[15]

On this view, natural languages, like governments and etiquette, wouldn't exist if there weren't people or speakers of some sort to

create it. Thus, it seems outlandish to think of a natural language as a
set of abstract objects, like numbers, whose existence is independent
of us.

Sapir makes it clear that the thrust of this view is that language is a
cultural artifact, a historical heritage of a community, not an instinctive
function like walking. Although at the time Sapir wrote, during the rise
of the social sciences in the first part of this century, this must have
seemed obvious, since Chomsky's revival of nativism in the past two
decades this feature has come to seem highly controversial. Chomsky
calls attention to factors that are completely overlooked in arguments
like Sapir's: the possibility of ethological models of instinctive behavior which contain hypotheses about releasing mechanisms, the
introduction of the theory of universal grammar with its substantive
and formal universals limiting the variability of languages, and the
restoration of the Port-Royal conception of deep grammatical structure
with its emphasis on the unobservable structure of sentences. The first
of these factors undermines Sapir's principal argument. He had argued
that humans are biologically predestined to walk but not to talk. The
sense people sometimes have that

. . . the individual is predestined to talk, but that is due entirely to the circumstance that he is born not merely in nature, but in the lap of a society
that is certain . . . to lead him to its traditions. Eliminate society and there
is every reason to believe that he will learn to walk, if, indeed, he survives at
all. But it is just as certain that he will never learn to talk.[16]

The force of this argument disappears once the speech the child
encounters in its social environment is cast in the role of a releasing
stimulus. The second factor makes Sapir's once readily accepted claim
that "Speech varies without assignable limit as we pass from social
group to social group" problematic. The third factor de-emphasizes the
significance for the nature of language of the surface aspects of sentences which most reflect cultural and historical accretions. The social
conception of language is seriously challenged by these factors and
hence cannot any longer be taken as obvious.

But this does not eliminate the objection. Whether language is
biological, social, or a mixture, there is a feeling that we are more
intimately related to our language than we are to mathematical entities
or truths. We feel our language is more a part of us than it would seem
to be on a Platonist conception of natural languages. The feeling is real
enough, but there is a question of whether it is a language—English,
French, etc.—about which we have that feeling or something else
closely related to language and as yet not distinguished from it.

Whatever it is that we have these feelings about is what we acquire in the process we call "language learning". Since in this process we do not acquire English itself but rather knowledge of English, what we feel to be a part of us, what we feel intimately related to, and what, in fact, depends on us is our *knowledge* of a language. There is a distinction between a speaker's knowledge of a language and the language itself—what the knowledge is knowledge of.

I am suggesting, then, that the facts about language learning, speech, and our emotional responses to them are compatible with a Platonist conception of language, and that the apparent incompatibility is due to a confusion between a language and knowledge of the language. The language is a timeless, unchangeable, objective structure; knowledge of a language is temporal, subject to change, and subjective. Someone becomes a speaker of a language by virtue of acquiring a set of tacit beliefs or principles that stand in the relation 'knowledge of' to a member of a set of such linguistic structures. On this conception, our feelings of intimate relation to a language and of its dependence on us are actually associated with the internalized beliefs or principles that constitute our knowledge of the language and are mistakenly construed as being about the language itself.

Let me take this conception a step further to make clear that it is coherent and squares with the relevant facts just as well as the social conception of language. There is a tendency to think that only the social conception can explain language change. This is not true. Language change can be understood in the Platonist conception as taking place when speakers within a certain line of linguistic development come to have a system of grammatical knowledge so different from the system of their predecessors that these two systems constitute knowledge of two different sets of abstract objects. Platonism faces no special problem about what counts as sufficiently different. The line-drawing problem is a problem for everyone. Relative to a solution, Platonism can group idiolects as a dialect and dialects as a language in terms of conditions for set membership over classes of abstract objects (sets of sentences so construed). There is an infinite range of such classes, including English, French, Sanskrit, Engrench (i.e., a class of sentences with English syntactic structure but an anglicized French vocabulary), and infinitely many other languages, living, dead, unborn, conceivable, and inconceivable. Language acquisition and language change thus involve changes in people's knowledge of languages, with concomitant changes in their relationship to the linguistic structures in this infinite range. The study of languages is the study of these linguistic structures. As such, this study is distinguishable from the study of human (or other) knowledge of them, its acquisition, use, or change. The former study is linguistics; the latter psychology.

Some of the wariness about Platonism in linguistics can be chalked up to unfamiliarity. Even though suggestions for interpreting theories of language to be about abstract objects have from time to time been put forward, they have not led, on the one hand, to an acquaintance with the main ideas of Platonism on the part of linguists generally, or, on the other, to a well-articulated formulation of linguistic Platonism. There is no formulation of linguistic Platonism that is even comparable to the highly articulated formulations of linguistic nominalism (in the structuralist tradition) or of linguistic conceptualism (in the tradition of generative grammar). The problem is that such suggestions have often been made outside linguistics, particularly in philosophical discussions, and that when they have been made in linguistics or found their way into linguistics, as in the case of Montague grammar, they have been tied to one particular approach.[17] The suggestion to interpret grammars Platonistically thus seems to be a move required only by the special features of the approach. Moreover, the advocates of the approach have not developed Platonism systematically, that is, into a full-fledged ontological framework for linguistics.

Therefore, one major aim of this book is to develop a systematic Platonist position for linguistics. The book is, therefore, at one level, an essay in the philosophy of or foundations of linguistics. The subject does not exist as yet in the full-blown form in which there are now well established subjects of the philosophy of mathematics and the philosophy of physics, although there are various discussions of a seemingly diverse nature that have examined questions in the philosophy of linguistics and that could be pulled together to establish such a subject. Hence, a related aim of the book is to encourage the establishment of the philosophy of linguistics as a well-defined, independent research discipline.

Developing a systematic Platonist position is principally a matter of formulating a comprehensive defense of the position in linguistics. This means working out what Platonism has to say about all the issues concerning the interpretation of theories in linguistics that can arise between it and nominalism or conceptualism. In particular, it means saying how Platonism answers conceptualist objections and what objections it makes to conceptualism, since nominalism, as I shall show, can be taken care of *en passant*. I have chosen to construct the Platonist case against conceptualism in linguistics as a case against a particular conceptualist position, which I take as representative. I made the choice for two reasons. First, it pins down the discussion in terms of actual doctrines, thereby avoiding the ethereal quality of a purely abstract discussion, and second, it helps us to make sure that we will take into consideration the full range of issues that arise in

controversies about the interpretation of theories in linguistics. There
is nothing like an examination of the actual to make sure that we have
not overlooked too many important possibilities.

The particular conceptualist position I have chosen is Chomsky's
theory of grammars and linguistic theories, and I have done so for a
number of reasons. First, Chomsky's theory undeniably occupies
center-stage in discussions of psychologism in linguistics. It was
Chomsky who refuted the nominalism of the structuralist tradition,
who made conceptualism the dominant position in linguistics, and who
today stands as the chief proponent of the view that linguistics is
psychology. Not to direct anti-conceptualist arguments against
Chomsky would be as bizarre as not to direct criticisms of the theory
that human behavior has unconscious determinants against Freud.

Second, Chomsky's theory, being by far the best worked out form of
conceptualism, serves us best as a means of making sure that our
Platonist argument does not overlook important issues.[18] It is,
moreover, and this is also important in our choice of a theory to focus
on, the best known of the various theories available outside linguistics,
particularly in philosophy.

I wish to make clear that I am aware of the fact that support in
linguistics for conceptualism does not come solely from Chomsky and
those sympathetic to his way of thinking. Conceptualism has for the
moment swept the field. Most linguists, including those hostile to
Chomsky's theories, are strong and outspoken supporters. For example, critics of Chomsky such as Lakoff and McCawley, who once led
the generative semantics counterrevolution against Chomsky's approach to grammar and who still oppose this approach in its newer
forms, now criticize Chomsky for not being psychologistic enough.
Thus, McCawley has recently written of Chomsky:

While I disagree strongly with a lot of his ideas, I think his influence on the field
generally has been very favorable. He has rehabilitated the human mind as an
object of study. To a large extent my criticisms of Chomsky are simply that he
hasn't gone far enough in that direction; I've said in public on a number of
occasions that Chomsky is not mentalistic enough to suit me.[19]

Furthermore, Chomsky's theory, conveniently, already has an
explicit ontological policy on the interpretation of theories in linguistics. This makes my task both easier and less open to objections
concerning the implications of conceptualism in Chomsky's sense for
theories in linguistics.

Finally, the choice of Chomsky's theory permits a continuity in the
line of argument from Chomsky's own arguments against the

nominalism in American structuralism through the arguments in the present book against Chomsky's and other forms of conceptualism. This offers the advantage of using Chomsky's arguments against nominalism, particularly in their form as criticisms of Harris's conception of transformational theory, as the first step in my own argument for Platonism in linguistics. Thus, it will be unnecessary to construct an independent argument to show that Platonistically interpreted theories are preferable to nominalistically interpreted theories. The entire emphasis of the book can then be placed on arguing that Platonistically interpreted theories are preferable to conceptualistically interpreted theories.

Although a major aim of the book is to develop a well-articulated Platonist position, it is only an instrumental aim and not the principal aim. The principal aim is to solve the philosophical problem of whether abstract objects exist. The problem is to determine whether there are objects whose existence is independent of mind and matter but which must count as real along with mental and material objects. The development of a well-articulated and well-defended Platonist position in linguistics is the basis for my solution to this problem. I first formulate this ontological problem as a question within the philosophy of or foundations of linguistics concerning the proper interpretation for grammars and linguistic theory. Such a formulation is possible because the Platonic realist thesis that abstract objects exist can be established if there is at least one science in which the proper interpretation of theories takes them to be about abstract objects. Given the formulation, I shall argue, on the basis of the Platonist position that I have developed, that Platonistically interpreted grammars and linguistic theories. If the argument shows that it is preferable, on scientific grounds, to interpret theories of a natural language and theories of language Platonistically (as theories of abstract objects) rather than nominalistically (as theories of disturbances in the air) or conceptualistically (as theories about the human mind or brain), then, assuming there is a true theory of each natural language and a true theory of language in general, we can infer that abstract objects exist.

Having sketched the approach, I should try to make clear how my formulation of the ontological problem and my argument for Platonism in linguistics constitute a solution to the problem of universals as it is ordinarily understood in philosophy. There are, I think, two things to explain in saying why I think a metaphysical question can be fruitfully approached in this way. One is to explain what it is about these ontological doctrines that enables them to be approached in this way, and the other is why such an approach can expect to settle ontological controversies non-arbitrarily and without begging philosophical questions.

Ontology and metaphysics have been the objects of a prolonged positivistic attack in this century which have left them under a cloud of suspicion. Although logical positivism is now gone as a philosophical movement, its distrust of metaphysics together with some of its arguments against metaphysics are still with us. One that seems to have survived is the argument that ontological controversies cannot, in principle, be settled because there is no agreed upon method for answering the questions at issue. Carnap expressed this criticism in its most influential form.[20] He claimed that questions about whether to accept one ontological framework rather than another, so called "external questions", are cognitively meaningless because they must be understood as not relative to any more encompassing framework. A method for answering any question, he argued, depends on there being a more encompassing framework.[21]

As an argument based on the claims of logical empiricism, it has little weight. Not only have logical empiricists generally failed to make their case for a criterion of cognitive significance, but the position Carnap takes on the cognitive status of external questions is itself paradoxical. Either the position is intended to stand on its own or to rest on logical empiricism. In the former case, it is directly paradoxical since the position constitutes an answer to an external question (about the possibility of justifying ultimate principles) and, there being no broader framework within which to determine its answer, must be cognitively meaningless. In the latter case, the position is indirectly paradoxical. There is a framework (logical empiricism) that provides a method for answering this and other questions about whether something is cognitively meaningful (the criterion of cognitive significance), but now the question of justifying this framework is the external question. Carnap's position on ontology rests on there being a rationally drawn distinction between cognitively meaningful and cognitively meaningless theses of the sort that logical empiricists sought to construct, and such a distinction, as is clear from Carnap and Hempel,[22] presupposes an answer to the question of whether the linguistic framework for science and philosophy is empiricist or rationalist. Since the justifiability of this presupposition is an external question if anything is, the logical empiricist framework is cognitively meaningless, and hence there is no rational method for answering questions about meaningfulness, and as a consequence, Carnap's position on ontology is cognitively meaningless.[23]

But as an argument disengaged from logical empiricism, Carnap's argument seems to strike a responsive cord. It reflects a commonly held view about the limits of justification that makes many think ontological questions not worth pursuing. The view is that justification works by subsuming a thesis under a more abstract one and hence such subsumption must eventually terminate in principles that are so abstract that they cannot be subsumed under anything else. It is also supposed in this view that there are alternative sets of such maximally abstract principles, and hence, that there are "ultimate dis-agreements", disagreements between alternative sets of fundamental principles. Disengaged from logical empiricism, the argument is not that such principles are cognitively meaningless, but only that the issue between them cannot, in principle, be settled by rational methods (showing one set to be justified over the other).

There is, however, no compelling reason to adopt this picture of justification. We need accept neither the supposition that justification proceeds exclusively by subsumption under more and more abstract principles nor the supposition that there are alternative sets of ultimate "ontological axioms" between which no rational choice is possible. There has always been another account of justification in philosophy (given by Plato, Aristotle, Kant, G. E. Moore, and numerous others). It is a picture of justification in which the justification of principles proceeds downward toward less abstract but more objective and secure foundations in the facts of common agreement. Aristotle writes:

We must . . . set the observed facts before us and, after first discussing the difficulties, go on to prove, if possible, the truth of all the common opinions about these affections of the mind, or, failing this, of the greater number and the most authoritative; for if we both refute the objections and leave the common opinions undisturbed, we shall have proved the case sufficiently.[24]

This account of philosophical justification views "ultimate dis-agreements" as an interim phenomena and supposes that there is ultimately only one set of ontological axioms that avoids all objections and leaves common opinion undisturbed.

The "ultimate disagreement" view is skepticism in ontology. The ontological skeptic first makes the standard skeptical move of setting up the question so that at some point the methods for establishing knowledge fail us, and then exploits the failure to argue that we cannot have basic knowledge in ontology. The other view enables us to avoid such skepticism.[25] To do this, we have to find a construal of ontological doctrines on which their justification is, as it were, a downward process (from the abstract to the concrete) of comparing competing doctrines with the facts in some domain where common agreement can be reached. In this way, the question of choosing between doctrines is no longer set up the way the skeptic wishes and the skeptical argument breaks down.

I take this non-skeptical view of justification in addressing the issue between Platonism, nominalism, and conceptualism. I propose the construal

> *(C)* Ontological doctrines are metatheories about the proper interpretation of theories in the special sciences.

as a way of making ontological doctrines justifiable on the basis of some range of commonly agreed upon fact. But beyond the chance of avoiding skepticism, the view provides us, in principle, with a neutral basis for choosing between different ontological doctrines. This is important because the deeper and more complex philosophical issues become the greater the danger of the partisans of a metaphysical position arguing from their own theory, and accordingly, the greater the need for independent grounds for evaluating the conflicting claims. Our conception of ontological doctrines in *(C)* makes such a neutral basis possible, since it refers such evaluation to the facts and methods representing common opinion in a special science. This is not to suppose that the choice between ontological doctrines can finally be made at any particular point in the history of the special science(s). Like these sciences themselves, such ontological evaluations can only be assumed to yield the correct choice eventually, or as said above, "in principle". Nonetheless, the view we are taking gains for ontological controversies the same degree of independence from partisanship that we suppose in the case of scientific controversies.

On this construal of ontological doctrines as metatheories, Platonism becomes, as indicated above, the existential claim that there is at least one special science in which the proper interpretation of theories takes them to be about abstract objects. Nominalism and conceptualism are, correspondingly, universal claims to the effect that none of the special sciences are about abstract objects. The evaluation of these claims, on our view, is a matter of subjecting the best theories available in these sciences to each of the three ontological interpretations, making the adjustments necessary to ensure a good fit between theory and interpretation, and then assessing the different ontologically interpreted versions of the theories on the basis of the standard factual and methodological criteria for evaluating theories. If it turns out that in just one of the special sciences Platonistically interpreted theories are preferable (relative to these criteria), then the issue is decided in favor of Platonism; if in none of the special sciences are Platonistically interpreted theories preferable, the issue is decided against Platonism. Evaluating ontological doctrines in this way, enables us to provide a resolution of this philosophical issue based on the objective and relatively secure foundation of commonly agreed upon fact and methodology within the special sciences.[26]

Given our construal of Platonism as an existential claim, we have complete freedom in choosing a special science. This freedom enables us to introduce one or another special consideration into the grounds for making the choice of a special science. We can try to choose the special science so as to make the strongest argument for Platonism, or to test the Platonist claim in a special science that has thus far received little attention in this connection. In choosing linguistics as the special science for my argument for Platonism, I have had both these considerations in mind.

This book thus argues, on the basis of grammatical fact and the methodological considerations appropriate to linguistics, that a Platonist interpretation of linguistic theories is preferable to either a nominalist or a conceptualist interpretation. The argument contains the following steps. First, we select a representative set of linguistic theories, theories of natural languages and of language in general, to serve as a way of focusing the issue. This set, as explained above, will be Chomsky's generative, transformational grammars and linguistic theory. Second, we explain how the interpretation of a theory in linguistics is fitted to the theory, how the formal theory and its ontological interpretation are adjusted to one another, and how an ontological interpretation may be detached from formal theories and replaced by another. Third, we vary the ontological interpretation of the theories chosen as our representative over the range of nominalist, conceptualist, and Platonist interpretation and catalogue the differences in the structure of the resulting theories, in their relation to factual evidence in linguistics, and in their standing with respect to methodological criteria. Finally, we employ these differences to argue that Platonistically interpreted theories are preferable to nominalistically or conceptualistically interpreted theories with respect to the evidential and methodological standards that govern the choice of theories in linguistics.

The argument itself takes a number of forms when set out in a detailed and systematic manner. Some of them are straightforward uses of standard methodological considerations and raise few if any questions about the ideas appealed to. Others, which concern matters of explanatory power, will perforce be more controversial. One of the main forms of argument in this category will be a more detailed and systematic version of the argument, described above, showing the inability of psychological views of language to explain grammatically grounded necessary truth. Since this argument rests, in part, on the claim that there are genuine necessary truths in language, and this, of course, is denied by many philosophers, especially Quinians, the argument will be controversial. But it could hardly be otherwise with *any* argument in this area. Arguments against Platonism, such as Quine's,[27] perforce take a stand on whether there are necessary truths in language. The denial of necessity on the part of positivists, Wittgensteinians, and Quinians is just the other side of the anti-Platonist coin, and equally controversial from the viewpoint of the Platonist opposition. The point to keep in mind is that positivism, Wittgensteinianism, Quinianism, and Platonism are, as is clear when they are fully fleshed out, whole philosophies which thus conflict on a variety of issues and have to be judged by how well they do on them all—how satisfying they are as whole philosophies.

There is, then, nothing in the fact that some of my arguments will in this sense be controversial to put off the uncommitted philosopher or linguist as long as these arguments have not neglected any important questions about necessity or about the other more specific topics that arise in the ontological controversy. I have tried not to neglect any important questions, but I have not been able to treat them all. In the case of the questions not treated here, I have given references to treatments of them on which my arguments here can be taken to depend.

The book as a whole is, of course, a further illustration of the approach to the philosophy of language that I have taken over the years, of tackling philosophical problems on the basis of the best theories in linguistics. In this case, however, the argument is as good an illustration of the relevance of philosophy to linguistics as it is an illustration of the relevance of linguistics to philosophy. The principal contribution that the book makes to linguistics is to provide it with a systematically developed alternative to the nominalist and conceptualist interpretations of its theories.

Surveying American linguistics in the twentieth century, we find that nominalism and conceptualism have played a significant role as ontological frameworks for theory construction. The structuralist approach developed by Bloomfield and culminating in the work of Zellig Harris is a clear example of nominalistically-based theory construction. Grammars for this approach are data-cataloguing devices expressing distributional regularities in speech in the form of a segmentation and classification of acoustic signals. The approach that replaced American structuralism, namely, Chomsky's generative, transformational linguistics, is an equally clear example of a conceptualistically-based theory. Chomsky's "psychological realism", as he refers to his theory, holds that a grammar is a theory of the ideal speaker-hearer's knowledge of the language.[28] Chomsky's conceptualism is not the only form of the position found in contemporary linguistics. The most prominent alternative to Chomsky's "competencism" is a position I will call "performancism".[29] This alternative abandons Chomsky's claim that a grammar is a theory of the ideal speaker-hearer's knowledge of the language and claims instead that it is a theory of the grammatical information computed in the on-line processing of speech. Bresnan takes this view in her "realistic model of transformational grammar",[30] and J.D. Fodor, J.A. Fodor, and M.F. Garrett take it in their discussion of semantic representation.[31]

It will not be possible to develop the Platonist framework fully in an essay attempting both to fill the gap in the range of ontological frameworks available to linguistics and to defend a Platonist framework for linguistics against well-articulated, long standing alternatives and against recent philosophical criticism of Platonism in the foundations of mathematics which is easily carried over to the foundations of linguistics.[32] I will develop a Platonist framework for linguistics sufficiently to provide a clear understanding of its position on each of the important issues in the foundations of linguistics, and I will defend it on them, but I make no claim either to have the only possible conception of a Platonist framework or even to have the last word on the exposition of my own conception of Platonism. My claim, insofar as linguistics is concerned, is that the progress of this science over the last two decades in replacing a nominalist theoretical framework with a conceptualist one, notwithstanding its great importance, is insufficient, and that linguistics ought now to replace its conceptualist framework with a Platonist one. My claim, insofar as philosophy is concerned, is that showing linguistics to be about abstract objects establishes Platonic realism.[33]

Notes

1. See Rorty 1967, especially the introductory essay.
2. Fodor and Katz 1962.
3. Katz 1966.
4. Katz 1964: 124–137.

5. Chomsky 1962: 528–550.

6. Chomsky 1966a: Chomsky 1967b.

7. Katz 1966: 188–223.

8. Katz 1972: ch. 4.

9. Cooper 1972: 465–483.

10. Chomsky and Katz 1975: 70–87.

11. For discussion of the distinction between language and theory, see Katz 1977a and Katz 1979c: also Smith and Katz, in preparation.

12. Quine 1960: ix.

13. Quine 1960: ix.

14. See below, ch. 6.

15. Sapir 1921: 4. Note that Sapir uses the words *language* and *speech* interchangeably here.

16. Sapir 1921: 4.

17. Richard Montague and David Lewis have made the suggestion that realism is the appropriate framework for possible worlds semantics, but they have not developed it systematically, and others who share their approach to grammar seem to draw back from the full implications of the position. See, for example, Partee 1979: Montague 1974: Lewis 1969: and Lewis 1975: 3–35.

18. Two remarks. One is that I shall take Chomsky's theory of generative grammar loosely enough to encompass a wide range of different models of grammar and linguistic theory. I thus make no claim that excludes models of formal grammar that depart from this theory in various ways, for example, in having no transformations, as in the case of immediate-constituent grammars, or reduced transformational presence, as in Bresnan 1978. The other remark is that Chomsky's theory is also the most philosophically sophisticated of all versions of conceptualist thinking in linguistics at present.

19. McCawley 1977: 234. Note also Lakoff 1978 for an extreme version of anti-Chomsky psychologism but one that can claim a following in linguistics, psychology, and computer science.

20. Carnap 1952: 208–230.

21. Carnap 1952: 208–230.

22. Hempel 1950: 41–63.

23. Logical empiricists are sometimes prepared to say that even their own philsophizing falls outside the area of cognitively meaningful discourse, but they do not seem to recognize that they thereby advise us to pay as little attention to their philosophy as they advocate we pay to metaphysics.

24. Aristotle, *Nicomachean Ethics,* 1145b–2–7.

25. I am only claiming that the view offers us the chance of avoiding the special skepticism described in the text: I am not making a claim about general skepticism, which calls all knowledge into question.

26. I do not wish to take a position on the precise form for a criterion of ontological commitment. I agree with Quine that "Our acceptance of an ontology is . . . similar in principle to our acceptance of a scientific theory . . . we adopt, at least insofar as we are reasonable, the simplest conceptual scheme into which the disordered fragments of raw experience can be fitted and arranged. Our ontology is determined once we have fixed upon the over-all conceptual scheme which is to accommodate science in the broadest sense". Quine 1961c.: 16–17.

27. Quine 1961c: 1–19.

28. Chomsky 1965: ch. 1.

29. I use these terms in order to be consistent with the terminology of earlier works, see Katz 1977b: 559–584.

30. Bresnan 1978. I will henceforth avoid use of the term *realism* because its traditional ontological use, together with Chomsky's and Bresnan's uses, makes the term misleading here.

31. Fodor, Fodor, and Garrett 1975.

32. Gödel's Platonism in mathematics offers a somewhat different conception of a Platonist framework from mine. Gödel's has features that have drawn serious criticisms from anti-Platonist philosophers and thus there are compelling reasons for departing from what is in many ways a sympathetic position. (See Gödel 1964: 258–273.)

33. The reader who wishes a survey of the philosophical literature on the foundations of mathematics is referred to Parsons 1967.

I

From Harris's Nominalism to Chomsky's Conceptualism

The philosophy of linguistics, like other branches of the philosophy of science, brings us up one level of abstraction from the special sciences. The philosophy of linguistics takes as its subject-matter linguistic knowledge itself and asks what sort of thing this knowledge is.[1] Thus, whereas linguistics tries to construct theories to answer the questions, first, 'What is English, Urdu, and other natural languages?', and second, 'What is language in general?', the philosophy of linguistics tries to construct philosophical theories to answer the questions, first, 'What are theories of English, Urdu, and other natural languages?', and second, 'What is a theory of language in general?'. These latter questions involve a number of further questions about theories in linguistics, their scope, structure, explanatory aims, and methodological constraints. But perhaps the two most important of these questions are (Q_1) and (Q_2):

(Q_1) What is a theory of a natural language a theory of?

(Q_2) What is a theory of language in general a theory of?

The possible answers to a question about the foundations of a discipline—the statements from which one chooses in obtaining the answer—have a dimension of width. A possible answer may be expressed abstractly and concisely or it may be expressed very concretely and elaborately. For example, the possible answers to the question how we acquire knowledge—the answers we call

21

"rationalism" and "empiricism"—can be expressed in the form of succinct slogans, such as "nothing in the mind that has not come through the senses," or in the form of elaborate theories, like Carnap's inductive logic or Chomsky's linguistic theory. More elaborate answers to *(Q₁)* and *(Q₂)* are philosophical explanations of the nature of the objects referred to in talking about natural languages, of the relation that obtains between those objects and true claims about them, and of the way we can come to know that claims about them are true.

To obtain our initial conception of the range of possible answers to *(Q₁)* and *(Q₂)*, we are interested in the concise possible answers. We can determine the concise possible answers to *(Q₁)* and *(Q₂)* on the basis of the relation between the philosophy of linguistics and the other branches of the philosophy of science. We can reasonably expect that the range of possible answers to these questions about the foundations of linguistics will be the same as the range for parallel questions about the foundations of other sciences. Looking at the possible answers to the parallel questions in the foundations of mathematics, logic, physics, psychology, and the other special sciences, we find that the range of answers that have been given derives from, and is limited by, the range of positions on the nature of universals in traditional metaphysics. Thus, we find Platonic realism, conceptualism, and nominalism, together with their various particular forms. Platonic realism holds that universals are real but distinct from physical or mental objects (i.e., non-spatial, non-temporal, and independent of minds). Conceptualism holds that universals are mental, with its particular forms arising from different specifications of the sense of "mental." Nominalism holds that only the sensible signs of language are real; the alledged use of them to name universals is nothing more than reference to space-time particulars with signs that apply generally on the basis of resemblance.

The possible answers to *(Q₁)* and *(Q₂)* are thus applications of these metaphysical doctrines to the special science of linguistics. The Platonist answer to *(Q₁)* is that a theory of a natural language is a theory of an abstract object, something not located in space-time or dependent for its existence on minds that know it; the Platonist answer to *(Q₂)* is that a theory of language in general is a theory of all of the abstract objects that the theories of individual natural languages are theories of. The Platonist philosopher or linguist conceives of sentences in much the same way that Platonist philosophers of mathematics (and many working mathematicians) conceive of numbers and mathematical spaces. G. H. Hardy's description of mathematical reality is typical:

I believe that mathematical reality lies outside us, that our function is to discover or *observe* it, and that the theorems which we prove, and which we describe grandiloquently as our 'creations', are simply our notes of our observations. This view has been held, in one form or another, by many philosophers of high reputation from Plato onwards.[2]

Platonists classify linguistics with the mathematical sciences, rather than with the social, biological, or physical sciences, as also about a reality outside of us and the physical world.

This classification claims that statements about the grammatical structure of sentences are no more *empirical* than statements about numbers on a view like Hardy's. This claim may unnecessarily disturb many linguists who, under Chomsky's influence, have come to think of the term "empirical" as honorific and the term "non-empirical" as pejorative. Such linguists take the meaning of these terms to be, respectively, "what can be settled scientifically" and "what cannot be settled scientifically because it isn't about anything real". But "empirical" only means "about experience or the external world itself". It is just conceptualist or nominalist doctrine that there is nothing real beyond the empirical. The claim in question may be less disturbing and accordingly more fairly treated if it is noted that mathematics seems to settle the truth or falsehood of principles well enough even though it is not about experience: mathematics is not about the kinds of objects that the social, psychological, biological, and physical sciences are about,[3] but nevertheless it is about something real.

The conceptualist answer to (Q_1) is that a theory of a natural language is a theory of the mental faculties, states, or capacities of its speakers. The conceptualist answer to (Q_2) is that a theory of language in general is a theory of deeper aspects of these faculties, states, or capacities. Conceptualists classify linguistics as belonging to psychology (psycholinguistics, cognitive psychology, or perhaps neuropsychology). The nominalist answer to (Q_1) is that a theory of a natural language is a theory of speech-produced physical disturbances in the communication medium. The nominalist answer to (Q_2) is that a theory of language in general is a theory of the common distributional patterns in such physical disturbances.

Given these as the possible answers to (Q_1) and (Q_2), making a case for one ontological position's answers requires showing that those of the other two are less adequate. Thus, we have to demonstrate not only that Platonism is preferable to conceptualism but also that it is preferable to nominalism. In this respect, the choice of Chomsky's theory as our representative of conceptualism is again fortunate. It enables us to obtain, *en passant*, the argument against nominalism that we are obliged to make anyway. It automatically introduces Chomsky's convincing criticism of the nominalism underlying American structuralist linguistics and thus provides us gratis with the argument we require against nominalism in linguistics. Hence, we turn directly to the task of constructing the Platonist case against conceptualism.

The first step in constructing this case is to discern correctly just what the Chomskian revolution was about. The revolution did not, as some popular accounts have it, introduce the transformational approach to grammar. Rather, the revolution changed the ontological framework of linguistics. The Chomskian revolution changed the paradigm of grammatical analysis in one way: the structuralist theory of taxonomic grammar, according to which grammatical analysis consists in segmenting and classifying utterances to obtain a compact catalogue of a corpus, was replaced by Chomsky's theory of generative grammar. But this change was part and parcel of the change from the structuralist's nominalistic interpretation of grammars as theories of acoustic phenomena to the conceptualist interpretation of them as theories of psychological states of speakers. The theory of transformational grammar, which Harris had invented, was neither replaced nor substantially altered.[4] Quite the contrary, Harris's theory was incorporated into the new paradigm of generative grammar, and then refined, extended, and generalized.[5] Chomsky's real innovation was to provide a new way of interpreting the formal apparatus of transformational grammar, which both recast the form of transformational grammar from the taxonomic to the generative and the subject-matter of transformational grammar from the external acoustic effects of speech to its internal psychological causes.

The emergence of Chomsky's conceptualist generative transformational theory out of the revolution in which Harris's nominalist taxonomic transformational theory was overthrown has three noteworthy characteristics: first, the ontological interpretation of a theory in linguistics is stripped away and replaced by a different one, second, the differences between the versions of the theory under the two interpretations are exhibited, and third, an argument for the superiority of the new ontological interpretation is based on these differences. In the present chapter, we will examine Harris's conception of transformational grammar, the way that the nominalist interpretation of transformational grammar was replaced by a psychological interpretation, and Chomsky's argument against Harris's and other nominalist conceptions of grammar, to the effect that they limit the abstractness of grammars so drastically as to rule out the best theories of natural languages. In subsequent chapters, I will use this case as a model of how to separate the ontological interpretation from a theory, fit the theory with a new one, and argue for the superiority of the resulting interpreted theory. I will show how the conceptualist interpretation of transformational grammars can be re-placed with a Platonist interpretation, and I will construct an argument that conceptualist constraints requiring grammars to be psychologi-cally real, like nominalist constraints, so drastically limit the abstract-ness of grammars that the best theories of natural languages are ruled out.

Bloomfield and Harris represent the beginning and the end of Ameri-can structuralist linguistics. Bloomfield created the basic structuralist approach while Harris created its most sophisticated and important theory. Harris's transformational theory of syntactic structure provided, for the first time, a revealing formal theory of the syntactic relations between the sentences of a natural language. But, even though Harris brought structuralist grammatical theory to a level of sophistication and importance that it had not before achieved, his conception of the ontology of transformational theory fell squarely within the struc-turalist tradition. Grammars for Harris were not explanatory theories but compact statements of the distributional regularities in a corpus of utterances.[6] Utterances are the reality of a language. Grammars are theories of the disturbances in the air or deposits of substances on surfaces. As Harris once put the matter:

. . . as part of nature . . . languages can be objectively studied if one considers speech and writing not as expression of the speaker which has particular, introspectively recognized, meanings to the hearer; but rather as a set of events—sound waves or ink marks.[7]

This echoes Bloomfield's earlier proclamations concerning the nominalistic approach to the study of languages,

Non-linguists (unless they happen to be physicalists) constantly forget that a speaker is making noise, and credit him, instead, with the possession of impalpable 'ideas'. It remains for linguists to show, in detail, that the speaker has no 'ideas', and that the noise is sufficient.[8]

Harris's nominalist interpretation of grammars also appears in his attitude toward elicitation. Eliciting grammaticality judgments is not seen as eliciting reports about what a speaker knows on the basis of internalized grammatical rules, but as the prompted production of verbal behavior to compensate for gaps and rarities in a corpus. Harris writes:

In much linguistic work we require for comparison various utterances which occur so infrequently that searching for them in an arbitrary corpus is prohibitively laborious. To get around this we can use various techniques of eliciting, i.e., techniques which favor the appearance of utterances relevant to the feature we are investigating . . . Eliciting is a method of testing whether a certain utterance . . . would occur naturally: in effect we try to provide the speaker with an environment in which he could say that utterance.[9]

How throughgoing Harris's nominalism is may be appreciated by noting that no status whatsoever is accorded internalized rules, enduring dispositions, or habits that might explain why distributional regularities are stable or why certain novel grammatical forms seem to fit into distributional patterns:

. . . even when our structure can predict new utterances, we do not know that it always reflects a previously existing neural association in the speakers (different from the associations which do not, at a given time, produce new utterances). For example, before the word *analyticity* came to be used (in modern logic) our data on English may have contained *analytic, synthetic, periodic, periodicity, simplicity,* etc. On this basis, we would have made some statement about the distributional relation of *-ic* to *-ity,* and the new formation of *analyticity* may have conformed to this statement. But this means only that the pattern or habit existed in the speakers at the time of the new formation, not necessarily before: the 'habit'—the readiness to combine these elements productively—may have developed only when the need arose, by association of words that were partially similar as to composition and environment . . . Aside from this, all we know about any particular language habit is the probability that new formations will be along certain lines rather than others, and this is no more than testing the success of our distributional structure in predicting new data or formulations.[10]

Although Harris's ontological interpretation of grammars was typical of American structuralism, he differed from mainstream American structuralists (e.g., Bloomfield, Block, Trager) in rejecting a scientific conception of linguistics. It was one of the principal aims of Bloomfield and other leaders of the structuralist movement to make linguistics a science. Even though one can easily argue with their strongly positivist conception of science, there is no arguing that they did not have a commitment to remaking linguistics in the image of science as they conceived of it. But Harris, unlike his fellow structuralists, conceived of linguistics as making no claim to strictly scientific truth. He thought of linguistics more in the way that some people think of literary criticism or artistic depiction, as illuminating aspects of their complex subject without involving a claim to be the sole truth. For Harris, the study of languages illuminates its subject matter by means of a variety of alternative treatments, none of which can claim a monopoly on truth. Harris makes no claim to scientific achievement in inventing transformational theory and he criticizes scientific competition among theories—customarily praised as the crucible in which scientific truth is forged—as totalitarian:

Transformational analysis is of particular interest, first, because it can be described and investigated with algebraic tools, and second, because it provides exceptionally subtle analyses and distinctions.

To interrelate these analyses, it is necessary to understand that these are not competing theories, but rather complement each other in the description of sentences.

The pitting of one linguistic tool against another has in it something of the absolutist postwar temper of social institutions, but is not required by the character and range of these tools of analysis.[11]

Moreover, at a time when structuralist phonologists were striving to determine *the* correct phonemic description of natural languages, Harris wrote:

The phonemes resulted from a classification of complementary segmental elements; and this could be carried out in various ways. For a particular language, one phonemic arrangement may be more convenient, in terms of particular criteria, than other arrangements. The linguistic requisite is not that a particular arrangement be presented, but that the criteria which determine the arrangement be explicit.[12]

It is interesting to speculate on the coincidence that it was the structuralist linguist who atypically held that linguists ought not be made into a science that discovered the transformational structure of natural languages. Perhaps other structuralists were too committed to their positivist conception of linguistics as a science to be free to entertain the possibility of all sorts of abstract mathematical structures.[13] Of course, the discovery of transformational theory required intellectual creativity, mathematical sophistication, and an understanding of some of the limits of existing forms of linguistic analysis, but a number of structuralists satisfied these requirements. Their freedom to explore various alternative tools of grammatical analysis may have been restricted, as Harris's was not, by their involvement in scientific competitions in which their tools were pitted against the tools of others.

But perhaps Harris just understood more deeply the descriptive limitation of taxonomic grammars in the treatment of relations between sentences. In pre-Harrisian structuralist syntax, a grammar assigned to a sentence a single phrase marker describing the syntactic relations between its nouns and verbs, modifiers and their heads, articles and nouns, and its other constituents. But these grammars gave no account of the syntactic relations between sentences, such as the relation between an active sentence like "John started the disturbance" and the passive "The disturbance was started by John" or the relation between a sentence like "Jane gave John money" and the sentence "Jane gave money to John". Thus, there was a range of distributional facts about natural languages beyond the power of existing apparatus of taxonomic syntactic description. Harris overcame this failure by providing a revolutionary new mathematical apparatus for handling inter-sentential syntactic relations within the taxonomic conception of grammatical analysis.

To extend the taxonomic description of distributional regularities from intra-sentential structure to inter-sentential structure, Harris created two new levels in the hierarchy of syntactic classes within taxonomic grammars, the level of *kernel sentence-forms* and the level of *transformational structure*. These levels were superimposed on the existing hierarchy of classes of phones, phonemes, morphemes, words, and phrases. The level of kernel sentence-forms contains a well-defined set of structures exhibiting minimal diversity in construction type. These structures serve as the domain for the rules at the transformational level. These "transformational rules" represent the full diversity in construction types in the language. Harris says:

If many different types of construction were exemplified by the various kernel sentences, the kernel would be of no great interest, especially not of any practical interest. But kernels generally contain very few constructions: and applying transformations to these few constructions suffices to yield all the many sentence constructions of the language.[14]

The kernel sentence-forms on which transformational rules operate are, basically, simple declarative structures, including intransitives, transitives, predicate constructions, and so on. Transformational rules are classified into *singulary transformations,* which take a sentence of one construction type, like the active, into a sentence of another, like the passive, and *generalized transformations,* which take two or more sentence structures into one compound sentence structure, like a coordinate construction. Harris's theory contains, among others, transformations that combine "parallel sentences" to produce conjunctions or disjunctions, transformations for "overlapping sentences (word-sharing)" to produce relative clauses, transformations that form nominals from sentences, transformations that create such constructions as interrogatives, and so forth.[15] These transformational rules can be applied to their own output and their application can be iterated any finite number of times.[16] Hence, sentences, including compound sentences, of any degree of complexity and of any construction type can be characterized at the transformational level.

Even if this were the only common ground between Harris's transformational theory and Chomsky's transformational theory in the initial phase of its development,[17] one would naturally think that Chomsky's theory is essentially Harris's theory. The formulation of Harris's new levels was less sophisticated than Chomsky's counterparts of them, and Harris, for reasons that we will come to shortly, didn't formulate them as an account of the base and transformational components of a *generative*, transformational grammar, but there is no mistaking the fact that we have essentially the same theory of intersentential structure.

Some further features of Harris's transformational theory make the sameness of Harris's and Chomsky's theories even clearer. One is that the level of kernel sentence-forms in Harris's theory is, as in Chomsky's, also

. . . the domain of the major restrictions of co-occurrence in the language. The restrictions that determine which member of a class occurs with which member of its neighbor class are contained in the list of actual sentences that satisfy each of the kernel constructions[18]

Another is that transformational rules in Harris's theory are bona fide transformations in Chomsky's sense, namely, structure-dependent mappings of phrase markers onto phrase markers (even though the structure represented in the phrase markers on Harris's theory is highly restricted in comparison to that represented by them in Chomsky's).[19] Harris also originated the idea of transformations as composite entities, built up out of "elementary transformations", and the formal operations out of which Harris's transformations are built includes the standard operations of current theory (*viz.*, deletion, permutation, insertion, copying, substitution for dummy elements, etc.). Harris's notion of a transformational derivation, although unsophisticated by today's standards (in particular, without a theory of generative grammar, he cannot properly constrain these derivations), contains the germ of an important feature of current theory, namely, ordering restrictions on transformational rules:

The successive application of elementary transformations can be called their product. For example, the sentence "May there be mentioned now a certain secret?'' can be derived from ''N may mention now a certain secret'' by the product of transformations $T_p\,T_d\,T_h\,T_q$. . . Some products may not occur or they may occur in one order but not another.[20]

Although more could be said by way of comparing these theories, it is clear already that, essentially, Chomsky's transformational theory is Harris's, with three important differences: first, that Chomsky's is conceptualistically interpreted as a theory about psychological states, second, that Chomsky's is constructed as a theory of generative grammar, and third, that Chomsky's is presented as a scientific theory. Thus, Chomsky's early transformationalism is Harris's transformationalism without nominalism and the ascientific outlook idiosyncratic to Harris's own approach to natural languages.

Harris's other major contribution to linguistics, his theory of discourse analysis,[21] can be seen not only as a new discipline concerned with ''stretches of speech longer than one sentence'',[22] but also as the necessary methodological basis for incorporating transformations into taxonomic grammar. All grammatical rules in taxonomic theory require validation in terms of a substitution test showing them to express a distributional regularity. It must be possible to characterize the categories in the rule as sets of items such that all and only the replacements of one item by another in the same set in a specified diagnostic frame or substitution context preserves some particular distributional property. For example, the category *Article* including the items ''a'' and ''the'' can be characterized on the basis of the substitution test in which replacement of items in the diagnostic frame '____ man' preserves noun-phrasehood. Similarly, to bring transformational rules under taxonomic theory, we must be able to construe their categories as expressions of distributional regularities, in something like the way in which the diagnostic frame '____ man' shows the category *Article* to express a distributional regularity. This is precisely what Harris's theory of discourse analysis promises. The theory seeks to accomodate transformational rules by providing the categories that appear in such rules, such as *Sentence, Passive Sentence, Interrogative, Coordinate Sentences,* etc., with characterizations in terms of diagnostic frames. These frames are sentential positions in discourses (i.e., sequences of sentences). Associated with each frame is a property of discourses that must be preserved when one sentence is substituted for another from the same equivalence class of transformationally related sentences. Discourse analysis thus assigns sentences to distributional sentential classes on the basis of whether the property relevant to such diagnostic frames is preserved on replacements of sentences in these diagnostic frames.

Therefore, Harris's introduction of transformational theory into structuralist grammatical theory did not change the philosophical character of that theory, even though Harris's transformational apparatus extended the descriptive power of taxonomic grammars. The nominalistic interpretation was preserved and imposed on the new apparatus on the basis of an already well-worked out scheme for handling troublesome abstraction at level of immediate constituent analysis. Concepts too abstract to fit comfortably under a nominalist interpretation are dismissed as "convenient fictions". This is the instrumentalism that Mach employed in claiming that molecules are mere *façon de parler*, fictions that may be useful as a means of predicting observable facts but are not to be taken as carrying any implications about the world. Mach writes:

If hypotheses are chosen that their subject can never appeal to the senses and therefore also can never be tested, as in the case of the mechanical molecular theory, the investigator has done more than science, whose aim is facts, required of him—and this work of supererogation is an evil . . . In a complete theory, to all the details of the phenomena details of the hypothesis must correspond, and all rules for these hypothetical things must also be directly transferable to the phenomena. But then molecules are merely a valueless image.[23]

The model in linguistics was provided by Bloomfield's appeal to the device of characterizing abstractions as convenient fictions. As a sophisticated descriptive linguist, Bloomfield found it necessary to use ordering of grammatical rules, but, as a doctrinaire nominalist, he found it embarrassing to have to countenance such abstractions as part of language itself. The solution was to take ordering relations as convenient fictions:

The terms "before, after, first, then," and so on, in such statements tell the *descriptive order*. The actual sequence of constituents, and their structural order . . . are part of the language, but the descriptive order of grammatical features is a fiction and results simply from our method of describing the forms[24]

Harris faced the same problem and took the same solution. Transformations relate sentence-forms, not utterances. Sentence-forms are abstract since they employ general categories like *Noun, Verb, Sentence*, etc. These categories are necessary components of transformations, yet, insofar as they are too abstract to be found *in* the utterances of a corpus, they are as much of an embarrassment as ordering among rules. But this embarrassment can be taken care of in the same way that Bloomfield took care of ordering: abstract categories and sentence-forms can be construed as convenient fictions rather than as concepts that must match reality in a true theory. Furthermore, as we have seen, for Harris, the whole idea of theories in linguistics being put forth as the true representation of reality "has something of the absolutist postwar temper of social institutions . . . [it is] not required by the character and range of these tools of analysis".[25]

Harris construed transformations instrumentally as devices for predicting relative acceptability of sentences on a probabilistic basis. Transformations were taken as formalisms for stating co-occurrence possibilities relative to the distributional regularities in a corpus. Harris wrote:

Given a number of sentences in a kernel form, which have among them a particular acceptability ordering or differentiation . . . all successions of transformations which are permitted, by the definition of their argument will produce sentences to preserve the same acceptability ordering . . . If a sequence or words is not decomposable by transformation into one or more kernel sentences . . . then that sequence is ungrammatical. If it is so decomposable, then it has a certain kind of degree of acceptability as a sentence, which is some kind of reasonable sum of the acceptabilities of the component kernel sentences and the acceptability effects of the transformations which figure in the decomposition.[26]

This provides a strong and a weak notion of ungrammaticality. In the strong sense, if a sequence is so ill-formed as not to be decomposable into a set of kernels, it is "ungrammatical". In the weak sense, decomposable sequences are scaled as relatively acceptable or unacceptable according to values of their kernel basis and mode of decomposition. This account provides no strict, categorical notion of grammaticality. Harris himself observes that his formulation in terms of acceptability

. . . fits into the *fact* that there is no well-defined set of sentences in a language. Rather, some word sequences are clearly sentences, others are odd or even undecidable as to sentencehood in one or another way, and some are entirely impossible.[27]

Because transformations are construed as devices for predicting relative acceptability, the existence of a precise set of transformational rules does not undermine the nominalist's identification of a language with a corpus of utterances. Harris continues the above remarks:

It is thus possible to find a precise set of transformations in a language without having to state a precise set of sentences for the language. Transformations simply tell us that the sense in which an n-tuple satisfies a particular complex sentence is the same as that in which it satisfies some other (and ultimately, some elementary) sentence form. As happens so often in science, in order to describe a particular set of phenomena, we have to start with a class of objects which is different from our initial interest but which is precisely definable and in respect to which we can describe our particular phenomena. In the present case, we set out to describe a relation among sentences, but we have to define a relation among sentence-forms in respect to certain n-tuples which satisfy them.[28]

This was the particular form of structuralist theory that Chomsky encountered when he began linguistics as Harris's student. Chomsky's first major theoretical work reflects the nominalist framework of American structuralist linguistics. Chomsky writes:

There has been some discussion recently as to whether the linguist 'plays mathematical games' or 'describes reality' in linguistic analysis of particular languages, where the phrase 'playing mathematical games' refers, apparently, to the conscious development of a theory of linguistic structure for use in constructing and validating grammars. If by describing 'reality' is meant meeting the anterior conditions of adequacy, then in order to give content and significance to the requirement that the linguist must describe reality, it is necessary to give independent (i.e., outside the particular grammar) characterizations of these conditions, e.g., for sentencehood, by constructing informant response tests to determine the degree of acceptability of evocability of sequences. . . . There seems no reason to consider the constructs established in pursuit of these goals as being in some sense invalid.[29]

One can appreciate the strength of the committment behind Chomsky's initial acceptance of Harris's approach and the Bloomfieldian program underlying it by noting the lengths to which Chomsky goes in defending them. Recognizing the fact that philosophers of science were abandoning the idea that the primitives of a theory must be operationally defined, Rulon Wells questioned the extreme operationalism on which the structuralist position of Bloomfield and Harris rests. Chomsky replies:

Wells has pointed out recently that philosophers have, by and large, rejected as a general criterion of significance, the strong kind of reductionism that we are suggesting as necessary for our particular purposes. He offers this in criticism of Bloomfield's program of avoiding mentalistic foundations for linguistic theory. It is true that many philosophers have given up a certain form of reductionism, of which Bloomfield's program (and our restatement of it) is an instance, as a *general* criterion for significance, . . . However, I do not believe that this is relevant to Bloomfield's anti-mentalism. The fact that a certain general criterion of significance has been abandoned does not mean that the bars are down, and that 'ideas' and 'meanings' become proper terms for linguistics. . . . [any adequate sense of 'significance'] will rule out mentalism for what were essentially Bloomfield's reasons, i.e., its obscurity and general uselessness in linguistic theory.[30]

This quotation not only shows Chomsky's commitment to structuralist theory but also his acceptance of Bloomfield's views on the theory of meaning—an attitude to which, we shall see in Chapter IV, he returns in his recent modifications of grammatical theory.

Chomsky's emancipation from structuralism, together with the subsequent formulation of his own generative version of transformational theory, illustrates how the formal representation of grammatical structure in a linguistic theory can be separated from the interpretation of the theory. We now examine Chomsky's break with Harris to see, first, how a formal theory can be separated from its interpretation, second, how the theory can then receive a completely different interpretation, and third, how to construct an argument for superiority of the new interpretation.

One can distinguish two phases in Chomsky's revolution. The first begins with his disillusionment with American structuralism and ends with his full recognition of the difficulties with the theory of taxonomic grammar and his intention to replace the taxonomic theory of grammar with his newly conceived theory of generative grammar based on an analogy to "category systems" in logic. The second phase begins with the recognition that it is the ontological position of American structuralism that is responsible for most of these difficulties and that the new theory of generative grammar thus requires a new ontological interpretation for grammars. The second phase ends with Harris's transformational theory refitted with a more appropriate psychological interpretation within Chomsky's conceptualist framework.

Chomsky tells us that his disillusionment with Bloomfieldianism had two main sources.[31] One was the difficulties that he encountered in his attempt to construct a grammar of Hebrew on the taxonomic model. In this attempt, Chomsky found it necessary to introduce grammatical concepts that had nothing like the simple classificatory status of the structuralist's notions of phone, phoneme, and so forth. The concepts that he found it necessary to posit in order to write reasonable grammatical rules for Hebrew were ". . . simply abstract elements forming strings that could be mapped into phonetic representation by deeply ordered rules of considerable generality".[32] Chomsky, at first, took this to mean that what he was doing in this attempt was ". . . not real scientific linguistics, but something else, obscure in status".[33]

The other main source of Chomsky's disillusionment with

Bloomfieldianism was the difficulty of specifying the inductive step that, according to structuralist doctrine, takes the linguist from a finite corpus to a syntactic description of the infinitely many sentences of the language. Chomsky tells us that, no matter how hard he tried, the step remained unspecified. He eventually came to suspect the doctrine itself: "The failure of inductive, data-processing procedures at the syntactic level became more obvious the more I worked on the problem".[34]

This inductive step was supposed to be taken on the basis of a *discovery procedure*, i.e., a set of inductive methods for mechanically processing the utterances in a corpus such that, with a sufficiently rich corpus and enough time and energy, these methods grind out a correct taxonomic grammar.[35] The nominalist and empiricist assumptions underlying structuralism dictated that this processing of utterances would work stepwise up from the acoustic signal to higher and higher levels of grammatical classification without circularity. Nominalism fixes the character of the ground level, while empiricism makes sure that higher levels of grammatical classification are built up from the ground without anything entering into the construction above the ground level. These assumptions were the philosophical basis of structuralist requirements on taxonomic grammars, requirements such as strict separation of levels, bi-uniqueness of phonemic transcription, phonemic identifiability of morphemes, and so on. Failure, in principle, to characterize the inductive step is, therefore, a serious blow to the philosophical basis of structuralism.[36]

Chomsky tells us that he tried unsuccessfully for over five years to explain how general classes like 'phoneme', 'morpheme', 'noun-phrase', etc. can be obtained from a corpus by substitution, matching, and the other data-cataloguing operations allowable in discovery procedures.[37] This extensive effort and the circumstances of Chomsky's ultimate decision to abandon structuralism is a perfect example of the philosopher of science's point that a theory, even one with serious, known faults, is not relinquished until scientists have a good conception of the new theory. His conception of the new theory, Chomsky tells us, was suggested by the study of "various category systems":

Two approaches to the specific problem of defining syntactic categories were thus counterposed: a constructive, taxonomic approach and an alternative, no less rigorous or formalizable, that was concerned essentially with the properties of a completed solution.[38]

Therefore, instead of trying to define syntactic categories mechanically on the basis of a discovery procedure that constructs them out of a corpus, the new approach would

> . . . define the notion "grammar" directly in terms of a set of primitive notions applicable to a corpus of data; the phonemes, morphemes, categories, etc. would then be the elements that appear in the highest-valued grammar of the appropriate form meeting the empirical conditions determined by application of the primitive notions to a corpus of data. There would now be no reason to regard phonemes, morphemes, categories, and other elements to be segments, classes of segments, sequences of classes, sets of phenomenal properties (e.g., phonetic distinctive features), and so on. Rather, they would be elements in various abstract systems of representation.[39]

Chomsky further remarks:

> I was particularly struck by the fact that by adopting this non-taxonomic approach I could bring together the two apparently distinct lines of inquiry that I had been pursuing since beginning the study of linguistics: the attempt to define precisely the notions of linguistic theory . . . and the study of generative grammars such as my Hebrew grammar and the grammar of English that I was then working on seriously. The notion "generative grammar" would, in this non-taxonomic approach, be the central notion of linguistic theory, along with the notions of "linguistic level" and "evaluation procedure."[40]

These notions, *generative grammar, linguistic level,* and *evaluation procedure,* constitute Chomsky's major contributions to linguistic theory. Let us look at each in turn. As mentioned above, the idea of a generative grammar emerged from an analogy with categorial systems in logic. The idea was to treat grammaticality like theoremhood in logistic systems and to treat grammatical structure like proof structure in derivations. A generative grammar G of a language L is, thus, a formal system that generates (in the logical sense) the set K_L of all and only the sentences of L, and furthermore, does this in such a way that the derivation of a sentence $s \in K_L$ in G is the basis for marking the grammatical properties and relations of s in L.

The significance of conceiving of grammars as generative is that so conceived grammars could be put forth as scientific theories, in contrast to Harris's ascientific conception of the study of natural languages. Although Harris had the notion of constraints on the application of transformational rules, his theory lacks an overall framework within which to systematically constrain grammatical derivations so that these derivations can be interpreted unequivocally as making explicit predictions about the grammatical properties and relations of sentences. Thus, in the absence of such a framework, there is no way to state the full set of constraints on derivations that uniquely specify the predicted grammatical description of a sentence. Chomsky's conception of generative grammar provides the framework for specifying this notion. Within it, the derivations of a sentence in a grammar G can be automatically converted into the full set of predictions that G makes about the sentence.

Chomsky's notion of linguistic levels bears little resemblance to the notion of levels in structuralist theory. Chomsky's "alternative approach" directly characterizes "the properties of the completed solution" by specifying in linguistic theory's account of generative grammars what grammatical categories and relations can appear at each level in derivations. Indirect specification in terms of procedures for manufacturing grammatical categories and relations out of the acoustic material in a corpus is forsworn. The levels correspond to the stages of derivations in which particular sets of grammatical properties and relations are marked. Since linguistic levels do not have to be constructed stepwise from a corpus, the requirements on the interrelations of levels in structuralist theory are dropped in cases where they do not reflect real divisions in grammatical structure (e.g., separation of allophonics from morphophonemics). Circularities that once appeared as a sign of bad methodology now appear as a sign of good systematic interrelatedness. Thus, instead of expressing distributional relations among occurrences of utterances in a discourse, transformational rules now comprise a distinct syntactic level immediately above the phrase structure level. Discourse analysis no longer needs to be considered together with sentence grammar.

Chomsky's notion of an evaluation procedure replaces the structuralist's notion of a discovery procedure. The goal of an evaluation procedure is weakest that can be set for linguistic theory. An evaluation procedure tells us which member(s) of a set of proposed generative grammars for a language is the preferable theory of the language, i.e., the simplest one that predicts the available evidence about the language. Chomsky's reasons for choosing the weakest goal are that

. . . it is very questionable that [the stronger goal] is attainable in any interesting way . . . I believe that by lowering our sights to the more modest goal of developing an evaluation procedure for grammars we can focus attention more clearly on really crucial problems of linguistic structure and we can arrive at more satisfying answers to them. . . . the weakest of these three requirements is still strong enough to guarantee significance for a theory that meets it. There are few areas of science in which one would seriously consider the possibility of developing a general, practical, mechanical method for choosing among several theories.[41]

These reasons, we note, are matters of what it is reasonable for linguistic research to expect, based on what can be achieved in similar theoretical situations in other sciences. Chomsky argues on this basis that linguistic theory must scale down its expectations.

The second phase of Chomsky's revolution begins at this point. Up to this point, ontological considerations play no role. The contributions concern themselves with the formal structure of theories of natural languages and of language in general. But once Harris's transformational theory was emancipated from its taxonomic formulation and well on the way toward its new formulation in the framework of generative grammar, it became clear that the principal motivation for a taxonomic formulation had been the structuralist's philosophical demand that grammars and theories of grammars be interpreted nominalistically. This demand was the underlying cause of the difficulties Chomsky had in trying to make the abstract categories that he found useful in writing a Hebrew grammar square with the concreteness required of categories in taxonomic theory and in giving general inductive definitions of categories in the form of discovery procedures. It thus became clear that the potential for highly abstract generative grammars could be realized only if a new and far less concrete interpretation for grammars was found.

As we have noted, the rules in taxonomic grammars employed abstract categories like *Noun, Verb, Sentence,* etc. (i.e. constructions that have no realization in a corpus). Such abstract categories are necessary for stating the "sentence-forms" between which transformational relations hold. But, also as we have noted, this use of abstraction was not acknowledged by structuralists as having linguistic reality. Abstract categories, construction-type forms, ordering relations, and such were something to be explained away as not linguistically real on the basis of an instrumentalist philosophy of science. Abstraction is mere *façon de parler:* abstract categories, construction-type forms, ordering relations among rules, etc. are simply computation devices for facilitating the prediction of observables.

But letting abstraction in the backdoor does not remove the difficulties. Even though instrumentalists may, up to a point, explain their embarrassments away in this manner, there is a limit on such attempts to reconcile practice with gospel. Only so much contrary practice can be explained away as *façon de parler*. Once all the interesting constructs in the theory turn out to be *façon de parler,* as was the case with Harris's transformational theory, the game is up. Once too much of the theory is construed as a mere piece of computing machinery with no implications for the subject-matter of the theory, the theory can no longer be taken to be about what it is supposed to be about according to the gospel.

Even if it were arguable whether Harris's theory exceeded the limit, it is clear that Chomsky's use of abstraction in reconstructing Harris's transformational theory went too far to continue to try to save nominalism. Chomsky's commitment to his descriptive work on Hebrew was, moreover, too strong to be abandoned for a doctrine that it was impossible to state with precision, especially when his reconstruction of linguistic theory made full precision possible.

I emphasize these points about the fit between formalized theory and ontological interpretation because they will be important in our examination of Chomsky's psychological interpretation of theories in linguistics. The points have to do with how close an interpretation can be brought to the surface of a theory. Bad fit may show itself in pockets and bulges, in misdirected research, in taking on too much or too little (e.g., taking on discourse analysis within the same theory as sentence grammar, or in trying to characterize syntactic categories constructively out of the utterances in a corpus, etc.). Fictionalist doctrines like instrumentalism naturally arise as means of covering up such pockets and bulges. We shall encounter all of these features of the argument for the transition from Harris's nominalist transformational theory to Chomsky's when we come to the argument for the transition from Chomsky's conceptualist theory to a Platonist one.

Historically, it took a linguist of Chomsky's ability to conceive of the importance of sentence-generating systems for accommodating abstract grammatical categories and further to realize that the underlying problem had to do with the structuralist's nominalist interpretation of grammars as theories about disturbances in the air. Once clearly appreciated, these conclusions are easily recognized as valid. But they demonstrate no more than the need for a conception of grammatical reality that is far more abstract than the structuralist's conception of a particular, concrete, substantival grammatical reality. They do not in themselves determine the choice of a replacement for the structuralist's conception. The choice of conceptualism does not necessarily follow.

Nonetheless, at the time, it seemed the obvious choice. There were a number of factors, beyond the fact that conceptualism is a far more abstract conception of grammatical reality, that made conceptualism seem the right choice. For one thing, conceptualism was, as it were, waiting in the wings. Wundtian conceptualism had been the orthodoxy before Bloomfield's conversion to neopositivist views, and its influence was still strong. In addition to Wundt's, more influential forms of conceptualism were found in Saussurian linguistics, the Prague School, and the work of important American linguists like Sapir and Whorf. Moreover, although Platonism existed as a logical possibility, it did not exist as a real possibility in the *Zeitgeist*.

Another factor was that the climate of philosophical opinion in the social sciences, psychology, and the humanities was changing in the direction of less neopositivist conceptions of scientific theory and practice. Wells, as mentioned above, had sensed that the winds of change. Philosophers, psychologists, and others were beginning to free themselves from the behaviorist, operationalist, and reductionist strictures exposed in neopositivism. In particular, a climate was developing in which researchers were exploring all sorts of abstract cognitive models for the explanation of human and animal behavior.

Still another important factor was the influence of Chomsky's new intellectual contacts in the Cambridge area, to which he came on leaving the University of Pennsylvania. Morris Halle (who was a student of Jakobson's, a prominent member of the Prague school) was especially influential in pressing the case for "psychological realism". Contact with B. F. Skinner was an important influence, too. Skinner at the time was trying to explain human language in terms of reinforcement theory developed in animal psychology. It must have been immediately clear to Chomsky that reinforcement concepts were completely inadequate to explain the enormously complex phenomenon of human language. Skinner's influence took the form of negative conditioning, directing Chomsky to seek better concepts in the theory of generative grammar.[42]

Under these influences, Chomsky adopted a conceptualist framework for linguistic theory in which generative grammars are interpreted as theories of an aspect of the speaker's mind. The reader of the published version of Chomsky's *The Logical Structure of Linguistic Theory* may question this claim when seeing remarks like:

In LSLT the "psychological analogue" to the methodological problem of constructing linguistic theory is not discussed but it lay in the immediate background of my thinking. To raise this issue seemed to me, at the time, too audacious.[43]

Chomsky conveys the impression that psychologism was under active consideration and played an important role in his thinking when he worked out the original statement of his ideas in LSLT, but that timidity prevented him from expressing this feature of his thought. It is hard not to be skeptical about Chomsky's claim that timidity prevented a thought of his from becoming known. And in fact a comparison of the original 1955 mimeograph version of the book with the published, Plenum Press, version strongly suggests that there was no "psychological analogue" in the original statement of his ideas in LSLT. Quotations from the 1955 mimeographed version like the one given above in which Chomsky replies to Wells or like

... I think that there is hope of developing that aspect of linguistic theory being studied here on the basis of a small number of operational primitives, and that introduction of dispositions (or mentalistic terms) is either irrelevant, or trivializes the theory.[44]

make it clear that at the time Chomsky took the same critical attitude as Bloomfield toward mentalistic theories. When these quotations are set beside quotations like

[The Saussurean approach which takes a grammar to represent the speaker's knowledge of the language, "his *langue*"] is the general point of view underlying the work with which we are here concerned. It has sometimes been criticized—even rejected wholesale—as "mentalistic". However, the arguments that have been offered in support of this negative evaluation of the basic Saussurian orientation do not seem impressive. This is not the place to attempt to deal with them specifically but it appears that the "anti-mentalistic" arguments that have been characteristically proposed would, were they correct, apply as well against any attempt to construct explanatory theories. They would, in other words, simply eliminate science as an intellectually significant enterprise. Particular "mentalistic" theories may be useless or uninformative (as also "behavioral" or "mechanistic" theories) but this is not because they deal with "mentalistic" concepts that are associated with no necessary and sufficient operational or "behavioral" criterion.[45]

the extent of the change in Chomsky's thinking about mentalistic theories (since his defense of anti-mentalism against Well's criticism) can be fully appreciated.

The second phase of Chomsky's revolution ends with the adoption of the conceptualist framework within which, over the next more than two decades, constructive work on the theory of generative transformational grammar is to take place. This framework answers (Q_1) by claiming that a grammar is a theory of the internalized rules constituting the idealized speaker-hearer's knowledge of the language, grammatical competence, and (Q_2) by claiming that a linguistic theory is also a theory of competence, the initial competence on the basis of which the idealized language learner acquires a grammatical competence. But, in addition to enabling grammars and linguistic theories to incorporate significantly higher degrees of abstraction, these answers also changed the form of explanation in linguistics. Grammatical phenomena could no longer be explained in terms of probability coefficients expressing distributional patterns, but must be explained in terms of empirical hypotheses about the internalized rules constituting the speaker's grammatical competence. Such hypotheses are intended to fit together with hypotheses about the mechanism for exercising grammatical competence to provide a model of the performance system for speech production and comprehension. Elicitation is now seen as a process of obtaining introspective reports about the properties of the internalized rules. Such reports constitute the main evidential basis for evaluating grammars. Grammatical novelties, for example, the one illustrated in Harris's example of "analyticity," are no longer thought of as theoretically unimportant accidents but are now considered powerful evidence for an enduring grammatical competence capable of significant creativity. At the next higher level of linguistic theory, explanation also takes the form of positing empirical hypotheses about a psychological state. These second level hypotheses, however, postulate innate principles to account for the normal child's ability to learn from linguistic experience. Chomsky's answers to (Q_1) and (Q_2) thus claim that linguistics is a branch of psychology.

Notes

1. First-level, scientific, knowledge does not require having knowledge of this knowledge: mathematicians can produce remarkable facts and theories about numbers without having much of an idea of what numbers are or what it means to say a theorem is true, and linguists, likewise, can produce remarkable facts and theories about sentences without having much of an idea of what sentences are or what it means to say a grammatical description of a sentence is true.

2. Hardy 1940: 123–124.

3. I recognize that some philosophers think that mathematics is about the kinds of objects studied in the empirical sciences. But here I am only sketching the concise possible answers. Adopting any of the available concise answers raises fundamental issues and commits one to a program of spelling out the answer in enough detail to provide a philosophically adequate treatment of such issues. In particular, the reader may wonder how linguistics can appeal to evidence from judgments of speakers about well-formedness, ambiguity, and so forth if linguistics is not empirical. Moreover, it is certainly an empirical fact that speakers of a language form such judgments on the basis of psychological, thus empirical, processes. These are reasonable questions, and I shall try to answer them later in the book where they can be dealt with in the detail they require.

4. See Katz and Bever 1976 for the first statement of this point of view.

5. Harris's transformational theory is significantly more primitive than the highly abstract theories that Chomsky and his followers subsequently developed: this difference was due partly to the fact that transformational theory was so new and partly to the fact that Harris's version was developed within taxonomic theory.

6. For a typical statement, see Harris 1951: 4–24.

7. Harris 1970: 458. ("Linguistic Transformations for Information Retrieval")

8. Bloomfield 1936: 93.

9. Harris 1954.

10. Harris 1954:

11. Harris 1970: 365. ("Transformational Structure")

12. Harris 1951: 72.

13. I wish to thank D. T. Langendoen for this suggestion.

14. Harris 1970: 444–445. ("Co-Occurrence and Transformation in Linguistic Structure")

15. Harris 1970: 443–444.

16. Harris 1970: 444.

17. Compare Chomsky 1964a and Chomsky 1957.

18. Harris 1957: 446.

19. Katz and Bever 1976: 16–18.

20. Harris 1970: 442–443.

21. Harris 1970: 131–348. ("Discourse Analysis")

22. Harris 1970: 346. Harris thought that certain relations among sentences in a discourse did not appear in sentences in isolation.

23. Mach 1893: 57.

24. Bloomfield 1933: 213.

25. Harris 1970: 572.

26. Harris 1970: 555.

27. Harris 1970: 539. (Italics mine).

28. Harris 1970: 540.

29. Chomsky 1975a: 81–82.

30. Chomsky 1975a: 85–86. My references are to pages in the Plenum Press edition because this is the only generally available version of Chomsky's book. But my quotations are taken from the original (1955) mimeographed version because the Plenum Press edition does not faithfully reproduce the original version. For example, in the last line of this passage, the Plenum Press edition says "inherent untestability" instead of "general uselessness in linguistic theory".

31. The account is taken from Chomsky's "intellectual autobiography", appearing as the introduction of the Plenum Press edition of Chomsky 1975a.

32. Chomsky 1975a: 29–30.

33. Chomsky 1975a: 30

34. Chomsky 1975a: 30.

35. Some of the literature on discovery procedures is mentioned in Chomsky's famous discussion of the possible goals of linguistic theory, Chomsky 1957: 49–60. For references, see Chomsky 1957: 52, footnote 3.

36. The philosophical views of the structuralists supported their belief in the reasonableness of discovery procedures as an aim of linguistics. Since they were nominalists, they took a language to consist in co-occurrence patterns in acoustic events, and hence, the learning of a language to consist in acquiring a hierarchical classification of such patterns into phonemic and successively higher level categories. Since they were also empiricists, they believed that the acquisition of such a hierarchical classification presupposes nothing in the way of a priori information about distributional structure in the language; learning a language must consist in inductive extrapolations of co-occurrence patterns observed in a sample of speech, arriving at the linguistic units of the language and their distributional forms. Hence, the fact that children do learn languages constitutes proof, on the structuralists's assumptions, that a discovery procedure exists.

37. Chomsky 1975a: 30.

38. Chomsky 1975a: 31–32.

39. Chomsky 1975a: 32.

40. Chomsky 1975a: 32–33.

41. Chomsky 1957: 52–53.

42. Chomsky 1975a: 39–40.

43. Chomsky 1975a: 35. This appears in the Introduction, newly written for the Plenum Press edition.

44. This remark does not appear in the Plenum Press version but is found on pages 20–21, chapter 1, of the original 1955 version.

45. Chomsky 1963: 327–328.

II

Controversial and Uncontroversial Aspects of Chomsky's Theory

The Alternative

Chomsky's choice of conceptualism to replace nominalism may have been the only reasonable choice under the circumstances, and it conceivably could prove ultimately to be the right one, but there is nothing necessary about the choice, even granting Chomsky's entire case against structuralism. Platonism exists as a real, if undeveloped, alternative. Whatever Platonism's defects, they are surely not those of nominalism. Nominalism's defects stem from the insufficient abstractness of the interpretation of grammars as theories of sound waves and orthographic marks, while Platonism provides interpretations that accommodate the highest degree of abstraction. Since Platonism cannot be rejected for the same reasons as nominalism, new and independent reasons are required to justify conceptualism over this third ontological position.

During the revolution against structuralism and development of the theory of generative grammar, Chomsky appears not to have considered a Platonist alternative. His entire argument for a psychological interpretation of theories in linguistics assumes that a nominalist interpretive scheme is the only alternative and that success in ruling such schemes out is tantamount to success in establishing a psychologistic interpretive scheme. Indeed, during the many years after his successful revolution, and even to the present time, Chomsky has shown no sign of recognizing the logical necessity of providing further support for conceptualism by showing that it is preferable to a scheme that interprets theories in linguistics as theories about abstract objects. Only now has Chomsky, under the stimulus of Montague grammarians who disparage the conception of linguistic theory as being concerned with principles that are "merely psychologically universal",[1] taken note of such an alternative.

In his most recent book, Chomsky claims that a theory of universal grammar in the mathematical sense—one which "attempts to capture those properties of language that are logically or conceptually necessary"—is merely "an inquiry into the concept 'language' " and that such an enterprise is "unlikely to prove more interesting than an inquiry into the concept of 'vision' or 'locomotion' ".[2] Whether or not these considerations, which are all Chomsky has to say on the matter, provide a reason for rejecting the specific approach of Montague grammarians, they surely give no reason for rejecting every approach on which linguistics is a branch of mathematics. In fact, they misrepresent the Platonist approach. The problem is the notion of 'concept of' that Chomsky uses in characterizing Platonism as "an inquiry into the concept of 'language' ". There are, in fact, two notions of 'concept of'. On the one that Chomsky uses, 'concept of' means roughly 'lexical definition of'. Thus, the concept of 'vision' is something like 'the power to form mental images of objects of sight', and the concept of 'locomotion' is something like 'movement from place to place'. On this notion of 'concept of', what Chomsky says about the triviality of the position that linguistics is mathematics is certainly true. It is silly to represent linguistic theory as a lexical investigation of a single word. But, of course, there is no basis for characterizing Platonism in the way Chomsky does, which stacks the deck against it. We can characterize it in terms of the other notion of 'concept of'. On this notion, which is surely the one that gives rise to the more interesting formulation of the Platonist position, 'concept of' means roughly 'conception of the nature of the thing itself'.[3] Here one is referring, not to the meaning of a word, but to the thing the word denotes. Therefore, on this notion, an inquiry into the concept of vision, locomotion, number, language, or natural language is no trivial matter of lexicography, but a highly interesting theoretical enterprise. Granted that, on a Platonist view of the enterprise, such an enterprise isn't empirical, but it surely is not for this reason open to Chomsky's criticism that it is devoid of intellectual interest.

Perhaps Chomsky's failure to consider a Platonist alternative was to some extent a matter of being too conditioned by the particular form his argument took against the only transformational form of taxonomic theory. Chomsky saw the opposition between his transformational approach and Harris's as an "ultimate disagreement" between science, on the one side, and non-science, on the other. As we have noted in the last chapter, Harris saw the different accounts that rival linguists give of a natural language as no more in logical conflict than different literary or pictorial studies of the same subject, while Chomsky, allied on this issue with the mainstream of structuralistic thinking, saw the goal of grammatical research as the discovery of scientific truth. In an obvious reference to Harris's remark about the totalitarian character of the scientific conception of grammatical research (quoted above), Chomsky writes:

There are "competing theories", and "pitting of one . . . against another", in an effort to discover which of several alternatives is valid, . . . [this] is of the very essence of the inquiry.[4]

In the place where he stresses the competition between theories as "the very essence of the inquiry", Chomsky also says that the question is, ultimately, not one that is open to rational determination:

. . . there is no question of "right or wrong". It is merely a question of where one's interests lie. If someone prefers not to adopt a "realist interpretation" of linguistic theory, and thus to make no claim for the empirical validity of the theoretical principles he adopts, I see no argument that could demonstrate to him that his conception must be abandoned. Or conversely.[5]

Chomsky is certainly right in claiming that it is a matter of one's interest which kind of activity one spends one's own time on (questions of moral obligation notwithstanding), and further that no argument can prove that one ought not pursue one's own interests. But the issue here is not a question of personal choice, but a rational question about the proper interpretation for grammars and linguistic theory. This sets Harris's personal choice aside as an irrelevance and focuses on his idiosyncratic claims about how to do linguistics, where we agree with Chomsky and others, against Harris, that the right way is scientific. At this point, Chomsky's mistake emerges clearly: he assumes that the only scientific way of interpreting theories in linguistics is a "realist interpretation" in either the psychological sense of his own approach or the physical sense of the structuralist's approach. But since this is precisely what Platonist realism challenges, the fact that Platonism makes "no claim for the empirical validity of . . . theoretical principles" can no more be a consideration against Platonism than the fact that Chomsky's psychologism makes no claim for the non-empirical, abstract validity of theoretical principles can be a consideration against psychologism. These facts are just features of the issue between the

Platonist view of linguistics as a *mathematical science* and the conceptualist view of linguistics as an *empirical science*. Someone who tried to settle the scientific question about the proper interpretation of theories in linguistics by dismissing approaches that make no claim about empirical validity would be like a Millian philosopher of mathematics who tried to settle the scientific question about the proper interpretation of theories in mathematics by dismissing approaches that make no claim about empirical validity.[6] Chomsky's failure to consider the Platonist alternative may have been due to his viewing the general problem of arguing for conceptualism from the limited viewpoint of his argument (against Harris) in defense of "the empirical validity of the theoretical principles" of linguistics.

It is worth noting at this point that Chomsky's terms "realist" and "realist interpretation" contain an ambiguity which may lend undeserved plausibility to the conceptualist position. On the one hand, the terms are merely labels for Chomsky's conceptualism. As such, they are best thought of as shortened forms of "psychologically realist" and "psychologically realist interpretation". On the other hand, these terms have a definite use in the philosophy of science to refer to an anti-instrumentalist position on which theoretical terms denote real objects in the world. If the ambiguity goes unnoticed, it is easy to slip from one sense to the other, thereby encouraging us to see Chomsky's conceptualism as the bulwark against Machian instrumentalism in linguistics. Thus, it is mistakenly supposed that Chomsky's specific views on the interpretation of theories in linguistics receives support from the general position in the philosophy of science that theoretical terms in empirical science designate actual objects. In fact, this position could support nothing stronger than Chomsky's specifically anti-instrumentalist criticisms of the structuralist's attempt to explain away ordered rules or abstract categories as convenient fictions, where the issue has been antecedently narrowed down to a choice between psychologism and physicalism.[7]

The point becomes clearer when we look at a recent discussion in which Chomsky has criticized some cognitive psychologists for failing to recognize that a theory of competence is to be psychologically real:

I take it that the question at issue is whether it is legitimate to "impute existence" to the "apparatus", the properties of which are characterized by particular grammars or by universal grammar . . . The discussion of "psychological reality" sometimes seems to me to be rather misleading. Perhaps I can explain my misgivings by an analogy.

Suppose that an astronomer presents [a theory about the hidden thermonuclear reactions in the interior of the sun], citing the evidence that supports it. Suppose now that someone were to approach this astronomer with the following contention: True, you have presented a theory that explains the available evidence, but how do you know that the constructions of your theory have physical reality . . .? The astronomer could only respond by repeating what he had already presented . . . it is senseless to ask for some other kind of justification for attributing "physical reality".

Our investigations of the apparatus of the language faculty, whether in its initial or final state, bears some similarity to the investigation of thermonuclear reactions in the solar interior. . . . Challenged to show that the construction postulated in that theory have "psychological reality", we can do no more than repeat the evidence and the proposed explanations that involve these constructions . . . in essence the problems are the same, and the question of "psychological reality" no more and no less sensible in principle than the question of the "physical reality" of the physicist's theoretical constructions.[8]

Chomsky's point is that psychology is concerned with both competence and performance and that it is "senseless" to distinguish them on the grounds that only performance theories are psychologically real or of interest. He is surely right given his supposition about the evidence: theories of linguistic competence must have psychological reality as characterizations of the knowledge that our speech processing mechanism put to use. To suppose otherwise is to abandon the causal explanation of speech in terms of processing models that incorporate representations of linguistic knowledge. Like the astronomy case, the case of competence is an inference to the best causal explanation, with a commitment to accept everything that the inference presupposes. Causal explanations involving theoretical entities account for observable phenomena by showing them to be consequences of such unobservable events. Such explanation becomes nonsense if the causal chain from the observable phenomena leads back to nothing but a convenient fiction.

Note, however, that this argument is relevant only to theories intended to provide causal explanations, and accordingly, it does not help us to draw a conclusion about theories of other kinds. The question whether a grammar is a theory of the speaker's linguistic competence or a theory of abstract objects poses the logically prior question whether grammatical explanation is causal explanation. The anti-instrumentalist arguments that Chomsky brings up against structuralist linguists and cognitive psychologists could apply to the controversy between conceptualism and Platonism only if this prior question has already been settled in favor of grammatical explanation being causal. But, of course, in that case no further argument would be necessary. Therefore, these anti-instrumentalist arguments provide no reason to reject the Platonist framework.

It might be supposed, however, that there are reasons of another kind for rejecting the Platonist framework. Perhaps taking the further step from conceptualism to Platonism would sacrifice some of the significant achievements of the Chomskian revolution. Perhaps some of them are bound up with the conceptualist framework that this revolution introduced. The revolution led to the creation of three new fields of scientific study: formal properties of grammars, semantics as part of sentence-grammar, and a cognitively focused psycholinguistics (in contrast to the earlier behavioristically focused psychology of language). It might be argued that one or the other of these last two fields would have to be sacrificed if conceptualism were abandoned, and that the gains in replacing it with Platonism would not outweigh the immense loss of having to give up these fields.

It is surely true that Chomsky's revolution brought the fields of psycholinguistics and semantics into existence in their present forms and that we ought not give them up. But it is just as surely false that we risk these fields if Platonism replaces conceptualism. Conceptualism is not unique in allowing these scientific developments. Rather, nominalism is unique in precluding them. Recall that, on the structuralist position, higher level grammatical statements must be reducible to statements about the physical aspects of the speech signal. Since semantic structure is not so reducible, meaning cannot be considered a legitimate part of sentence grammar. The change from this position to Chomsky's position that grammars are theories of internalized rules abandons all nominalistic restrictions on grammars and thereby allows meaning a place in sentence grammar. Statements about meaning can be introduced as hypotheses about internalized semantic rules. The development of semantics over the last two decades was made possible simply by dropping the nominalist restrictions on linguistic levels.

Prior to Chomsky, the psychology of language had American structuralism as its only source of scientific ideas about language and both disciplines were strongly under empiricist and behaviorist influence. The psychology of language at the time concerned itself with determining associative connections between linguistic forms and their stimuli and responses. The shift to a conceptualist linguistic theory made it possible to ask far more penetrating questions about the use of language in psychology, principally because this theory provided formal grammars that the psychologist could use as hypotheses about components of the cognitive mechanisms involved in producing and comprehending speech. Furthermore, Chomsky's psychological construal of linguistic theory provided a new approach to the study of language learning. Instead of viewing it empiricistically, Chomsky encouraged psychologists to conceive of it nativistically and himself made explicit proposals about the nature of the innate linguistic schema and about the character of the language acquisition process.

Since Platonism is only a doctrine about the nature of linguistics, it leaves the substantive questions within psychology proper undisturbed. It claims that theories *in* linguistics are not psychological theories, but it says nothing about their use in psychology and it makes no claims for or against the competence/performance distinction, the view that psychological theories of speech production and comprehension are models of internal computation over representations of grammatical knowledge employed in language use or theories of learning acquisition as models of how innately specified possible competences are tested against linguistic experience. Thus, Platonism takes a neutral stance on issues in psychology between empiricists and rationalists or on issues in psychology between behaviorists and mentalists. It thus sacrifices none of the progress in psychology toward theories of speech processing containing rich internal systems for characterizing the grammatical knowledge employed in language use or theories of learning containing rich innate systems for characterizing the knowledge acquired in language learning.

Once the role that Chomsky's proposals played in the progress of semantics and psycholinguistics is thus spelled out, it is clear that we run no risk of reversing the development if we replace conceptualist interpretations of grammars and linguistic theory with Platonist interpretations. The exclusion of semantics from sentence grammar was a consequence of the structuralist requirement of reducibility to the level of physical utterances. Chomsky's conceptualism removes this requirement, but so does Platonism. Platonism, if anything, imposes fewer constraints on the formalization of grammatical structure, and consequently, it, too, removes the nominalism that stood in the way of descriptions of the meaning of sentences being part of their description in the grammar. As for the question of including semantics in sentence grammar, it makes no difference whether the description of the meaning of a sentence is thought of as a hypothesis about the speaker's knowledge of the language or as a hypothesis about abstract objects independent of such knowledge. Furthermore, we run no risk of undermining the progress made in psycholinguistics since, no matter which ontological position we adopt in linguistics, nothing whatever follows about substantive questions in psychology.

Are there, then, reasons not having to do with the Chomskian revolution that would rule out in advance the possibility of a Platonist framework for linguistics? I think not. One can, of course, think of various objections that have been made to Platonist conceptions of the foundations of other disciplines, objections that could be carried over to the foundations of linguistics. These objections include such questions as whether the Platonist's removal of psychological constraints on theories in linguistics leaves them too unconstrained, whether it makes sense to say that we can know the scientific truth about natural languages on a Platonist conception of their nature, and so on. But such objections are the heart of the ontological controversy and thus not objections that would show in advance that the controversy is unnecessary. I shall respond to these objections where they naturally arise.

The Controversial and Uncontroversial in Chomsky's Competencism

This section and the next set the stage for the argument for Platonism. The argument, in a nutshell, is that conceptualism does not go far enough in emancipating linguistics from overly restrictive interpretive constraints on its theories. There is a certain justice in bringing the same charge against conceptualism that it brought against nominalism. Conceptualism does not simply drop all constraints on grammars that go beyond accounting for grammatical facts; it replaces one set of non-grammatical constraints with another. Conceptualism imposes its own psychological constraints, which require grammars, over and above getting the facts about the grammatical structure of the sentences right, to say something about the psychological states of speakers.

The alternative of Platonism enables us to ask whether these constraints, though they replace far more restrictive nominalist ones, might, nonetheless, still be too restrictive. For Platonism represents a genuine freeing of linguistics from all non-grammatical constraints. Platonism represents the ultimate step in the direction of removing constraints that impose a ceiling on the abstractness of grammars by tying them down to one or another particular reality. I shall argue that, in the end, Chomsky's criticism of American structuralism's nominalist constraints—that they stood in the way of theories that are abstract enough to be optimal theories of natural languages—can be brought against conceptualism, too.

In the remainder of this chapter, we shall distinguish systematically between the aspects of Chomsky's theory of generative, transformational grammar that depend on its psychological interpretation, and hence, in the present context, are matters of controversy, and aspects that do not, hence, are neutral and can be preserved in a Platonist framework. In making this separation, we will be doing explicitly what

Chomsky did more implicitly in separating the aspects of Harris's general approach that were consequences of his nominalist framework from the ontologically neutral aspects of transformational theory. This analysis of Chomsky's approach will isolate and highlight the linguistic consequences of imposing psychological constraints.

An ontological interpretation of a formal theory is a set of statements that fix the highest category for the objects in the extensions assigned to referring terms in the theory. Statements of an ontological interpretation can be as succinct as Harris's remark that the objective study of a natural language is about "sound waves or ink marks" or as lengthy as a full theory of the nature of the particular reality in question. Chomsky's statement, though not a full theory is much more detailed than Harris's and has been subject to further development over the years. The basic characterization of Chomsky's position—what I call "competencism"—is the following:

(P1) There is a sharp distinction between *competence* (the ideal speaker-hearer's knowledge of the language) and *performance* (the actual use of language in concrete situations).

(P2) A generative grammar of a language L is a psychological theory about competence in L.

(P3) A linguistic theory (a theory of language in general) is also a psychological theory. It is about the innate knowledge of natural languages that human beings use to learn them. Thus, in an extended sense, a theory of a competence, viz., the initial competence of a human language learner.

(P4) Language use and language learning utilize these respective competences, but it is an empirical question to what extent and how. It is reasonable to think that performance models describing how languages are used and acquisition models describing how they are learned will contain theories of these competences, respectively, but it is not necessary that they do so.

(P5) Linguistic theory has two parts, a recursive enumeration of the humanly possible (though not necessarily actually learnable)[9] grammars and an evaluation procedure. It claims language learning proceeds by a process of hypothesis testing, in which the hypotheses are supplied by the recursive enumeration and the selection is made by primary linguistic data and the evaluation procedure. It selects a preferable grammar from those compatible with the data.

(P₁) and *(P₄)* distinguish competencism from performancism. *(P₂)*, *(P₃)*, and *(P₅)* are the core of Chomsky's conceptualism. Recently, however, a sixth principle has come to loom large in Chomsky's writings, namely:

(P₆) Generative grammars and linguistic theories are ultimately about aspects of the structural organization of the human brain. These psychological theories are reducible to biological theories.[10]

(P₁) expresses the fundamental distinction on which Chomsky's conceptualism rests. Chomsky writes:

We thus make a fundamental distinction between *competence* (the speaker-hearer's knowledge of his language) and *performance* (the actual use of language in concrete situations). Only under the idealization [of an ideal speaker-hearer, in a completely homogeneous speech-community, etc.] . . . is performance a direct reflection of competence.[11]

Then, he uses the distinction to answer *(Q₁)* and *(Q₂)*:

. . . a grammar . . . constitutes a hypothesis concerning the speaker-hearer's knowledge of the language and is to be confirmed or disconfirmed in terms of empirical evidence drawn, ultimately, from investigations of the linguistic intuitions of the language-user . . . The general theory, now regarded as an explanatory theory, is likewise to be understood as a psychological theory that attempts to characterize the innate human "language faculty", and can be tested in terms of its consequences in particular languages.[12]

His unequivocal commitment to competencism is expressed in passages like:

. . . a generative grammar is not a model for a speaker or hearer. It attempts to characterize in the most neutral possible terms the knowledge of the language that provides the basis for actual use of language by a speaker-hearer. When we speak of a grammar as generating a sentence with a certain structural description, we mean simply that the grammar assigns this structural description to the sentence. When we say that a sentence has a certain derivation with respect to a particular generative grammar, we say nothing about how the speaker or hearer might proceed, in some practical of efficient way, to construct such a derivation. These questions belong to the theory of language use—the theory of performance.[13]

On the relation in which the grammar of a language stands to the theory of performance for that language, Chomsky has consistently taken the position that: "A theory of performance (production or perception) will have to incorporate the theory of competence—the generative grammar of a language—as an essential part."[14]

Different forms of conceptualism differ from one another in the degree to which they require the grammar of a language or theories of language in general to reflect the full structure of human cognitive abilities underlying language use and acquisition. Competencism and performancism represent the two principal positions on this dimension. Chomsky's conception of linguistic theory as a theory of the competence of the language learner is the counter-part of competencism for positions concerned with linguistic theories. Accordingly, one of the major internal issues within the conceptualist camp is between those who think grammars should only reflect the knowledge of the language in these cognitive abilities, on the one hand, and those who think grammars should reflect all the cognitive structures that play a role in on-line mechanisms for speech production and comprehension, on the other.[15]

As I mentioned in the introduction to this book, there are a number of reasons for choosing Chomsky's competencism to represent conceptualism generally. Here I wish to emphasize a specific justification for doing so, namely, that in directing my arguments against competencism, the arguments are directed at the most permissive form of conceptualism, that is, the form which allows grammars to reflect the bare minimum of the structure of human cognitive abilities underlying language use. Hence, my arguments will hold against less permissive forms of conceptualism if they hold against competencism. Competencism can be considered the test case.

The principles that characterize a Platonist interpretation for theories in linguistics are *(P7)* and *(P8):*

(P7) A generative grammar for a language L is a theory of the grammatical structure of the sentences of L, and these are abstract objects.

(P8) A linguistic theory is a theory of the grammatical universals of language, that is, a theory of the essential common structure of natural languages.

It should be made clear at the outset that the notion of an *ideal* object appearing in Chomsky's explanation of competence is essentially different from the notion of an *abstract* object appearing in *(P7)*. An ideal object is a construction resulting from the idealization of actual objects and it is used to make statements about them without undue complication. For example, a completely frictionless plane or a perfectly rigid rod are representations of actual physical surfaces and physical bodies which neglect features that would unnecessarily complicate the statement of physical laws. Similarly, Chomsky's notion of the ideal speaker-hearer represents actual speakers and hearers, neglecting performance features that would unnecessarily complicate the statement of grammatical laws. But, in both cases, the laws that employ the construct of an ideal object, are about the empirical objects from which the idealization proceeds, physical surfaces and bodies, in the former case, and actual speakers and hearers, in the latter. In contrast, abstract objects are not idealizations at all. They do not represent anything physical or psychological. They are not a means of simplifying the laws of a discipline. Rather, abstract objects are another ontological kind from the physical and psychological objects that are represented in ideal objects. Like the actual objects of empirical science, they are the things of which the statements in a science are true.

These distinctions should help to remove the temptation to think that, because Chomsky's or another conceptualist's position employs idealizations, it is not really different from the Platonist position. Another version of this confusion is the thought that since Chomsky's grammatical data are about sentence types—which are abstract objects in the first place, rather than sentence tokens, which are datable physical events—his position can't be all that different from Platonism. The thought naturally leads to a too quick refutation of conceptualism on the grounds that it is either just Platonism in disguise or reverts back to nominalism. This is too quick because it overlooks the fact that a circumspect conceptualist will try to reconstruct the notion of sentence type in conceptualistically acceptable terms. Such an attempt would be similar to that of nominalists like Berkeley and Hume to reconstruct the notion of a universal as a particular which is used in reasoning in such a way that nothing which is not true of other similar particulars is inferred. Of course, the conceptualist's attempt may fail,[16] but the quick refutation does not give the conceptualist a chance to try.

Having clarified these points, we can now distinguish between the controversial and uncontroversial aspects of Chomsky's general position. We will use the position he sets out in *Aspects of the Theory of Syntax* updated with *Reflections on Language* and *Rules and Representations*.[17] The first work is the most explicit statement of the position; the latter two add important clarifications and extensions but do not, as I shall show, change the position on fundamental points. My examination of Chomsky's position is organized in terms of the previous classification of his major contributions to the theory of grammar, *the theory of generative grammar, the non-taxonomic conception of linguistic levels,* and *the metatheory of linguistic theory.* I will run through the parts of the position under these headings and tag as controversial anything that depends on the competencist principles *(P₂), (P₃),* and *(P₅).* Others will count as uncontroversial, that is, as belonging to the ontologically neutral core of Chomsky's position (which is not, of course, to say these parts of the position are uncontroversial in other respects).

The theory of generative grammar is squarely within the ontologically neutral core of Chomsky's position. This theory, it will be recalled, was an essential element in the break with Harris's transformational version of structuralist theory. Chomsky's new approach turns the "constructive taxonomic approach" upside down, taking the statement of grammatical notions to be "properties of the completed solution". Chomsky's conception of grammars as sentence generating devices thus reverses Harris's conception of them as devices for decomposing sentences into their various underlying kernel sentence-forms and measuring the degree of their acceptability. Chomsky's *generative* transformational grammars thus provide a well-defined set of sentences. Harris's claim that it is a "fact that there is no well-defined set of sentences of a language" turns out to be an artifact of his conception of grammars. Chomsky's conception of generative grammars shifts the notion of a language from something without clear boundaries to something with sharp boundaries. Since the study of languages in this sense is no longer concerned with predicting degree of acceptability, generative grammar eliminates the apparatus of statistics and probability from the study.[18]

It will also be recalled that Chomsky's theory of generative grammar makes the derivations of sentences in generative grammars the basis for predicting their phonological, syntactic, and semantic properties and relations. Chomsky writes:

We learn nothing about a natural language from the fact that its sentences can be effectively displayed, i.e., . . . constitute a recursively enumerable set. The reason for this is clear. Along with a specification of the class F of grammars, a theory of language must also indicate how, in general, relevant structural information can be obtained for a particular sentence generated by a particular grammar. That is, the theory must specify a class Σ of "structural descriptions" and a function Φ such that given $f \in F$ and x in the range of f, $\Phi(f,x) \in \Sigma$ is a structural description of x (with respect to the grammar f) giving certain information . . . which will indicate whether x is ambiguous, to what other sentences it is structurally similar, etc.[19]

This feature sets transformational grammar on the path of science by providing the notion of system that enables alternative grammatical analyses of a construction to be treated as rival scientific hypotheses, judged on the basis of their predictive success within the system of grammatical rules.

Chomsky's non-taxonomic notion of linguistic levels is also uncontroversial between conceptualists and Platonists. This notion has four aspects. First, there is the elimination of the structuralist conditions on levels of representation in grammars, conditions reflecting a nominalist commitment to allowing only those higher level constructions that are reducible to physical parameters of speech at the lowest level. Second, there is the characterization of levels of grammatical representation in terms of the kind of grammatical properties and relations defined there. Third, there is the extension of the hierarchy to include a highly abstract transformational level, sharply separated from the phrase structure level. Finally, there is an assortment of formal apparatus for grammatical description at the various levels of the hierarchy, e.g., phonological and syntactic features, empty nodes, and so on.

We come now to Chomsky's metatheory of linguistic theory. Here we use Chomsky's own characterization of the components of this theory.[20]

   (i) a universal phonetic theory that defines the notion "possible sentence".

   (ii) a definition of "structural description".

   (iii) a definition of "generative grammar".

   (iv) a method for determining the structural description of a sentence, given a grammar.

   (v) a way of evaluating alternative proposed grammars.

Chomsky supplies the conceptualist interpretation of (i)-(v). Under this interpretation, (i)-(v) become a model of language acquisition with the components

   (I) a technique for representing input signals.

   (II) a way of representing structural information about these signals

   (III) some initial delimitation of a class of possible hypotheses about language structure.

   (IV) a method for determining what each such hypothesis implies with respect to each sentence.

(V) a method for selecting one of the (presumably infinitely many) hypotheses that are allowed by (III) and are compatible with the given primary linguistic data.[21]

Since this interpretation of linguistic theory depends on (P3), it is controversial. But to say this is controversial is not to say that a language acquisition model ought not contain the components (I)-(V). It is only to question that linguistic theory is a theory of the language learner's initial competence. The point is the same as in the case of grammars. The claim that a grammar is a theory of the speaker-hearer's competence is flatly controversial, but this does not make it controversial to claim that competence exists or that there is a competence/performance distinction. Only the further claim that grammars are theories of competence is controversial. Since Platonism rejects only this further claim, it denies only that the theories of competence and performance are contributions to linguistics. Platonism leaves it open whether such theories are contributions to psychology.

Chomsky imposes the conceptualist interpretation (I)-(V) on the requirements (i)-(v) by setting up the conditions of adequacy on theories in linguistics in such a way that only conceptualistically interpreted theories can satisfy them. For example, a psychological interpretation is imposed on linguistic theory by requiring that it satisfy what Chomsky calls the condition of explanatory adequacy:

To the extent that a linguistic theory succeeds in selecting a descriptively adequate grammar on the basis of primary linguistic data, we can say that it meets the condition of *explanatory adequacy*. That is, to this extent, it offers an explanation for the intuition of the native speaker on the basis of an empirical hypothesis concerning the innate predisposition of the child to develop a certain kind of theory to deal with the evidence presented to him.[22]

This condition goes hand in hand with the further two conditions:

A grammar can be regarded as a theory of a language; it is *descriptively adequate* to the extent that it correctly describes the intrinsic competence of the idealized native speaker.

We may . . . say that a *linguistic theory is descriptively adequate* if it makes a descriptively adequate grammar available for each natural language.[23]

Such "conditions of adequacy" can no more be accepted as genuine conditions of adequacy than could Platonistically inspired conditions on which only theories about abstract objects turn out to explanatorily or descriptively adequate. Chomsky's conditions of explanatory and descriptive adequacy must be thought of as internal to the conceptualist framework and cannot be taken to have any legitimacy outside that framework. Accordingly, the conditions together with whatever depends on them are controversial.

The formulation of (I)-(V) expresses Chomsky's "hypothesis testing" conception of a model of language acquisition. (I)-(III) specify the class of available hypotheses about the competence to be acquired, (IV) provides the mechanism for confronting hypotheses with facts gleaned from linguistic experience, and (V) provides a basis for choosing a preferred hypothesis about the competence given the linguistic facts. This conception is not the only one open to conceptualists. There are, on the one hand, the various inductive conceptions proposed by psychologists in the tradition of associative learning theories, which Chomsky opposed in first setting forth the hypothesis testing conception, and there may be, on the other hand, an "organ growth" conception, which he now seems to think of as opposed to the hypothesis testing conception.[24] Conceptualists can, of course, choose any one of these as the basis for a conceptualist interpretation of linguistic theory. Although nothing I have to say about the inadequacy of conceptualist interpretation of linguistic theory depends on which of these conceptions turns out preferable (because what I have to say assumes nothing more than that conceptualism interprets linguistic theory as a model for explaining the competence speakers acquire), something needs to be said about Chomsky's claim that the "organ growth" conception is a new conception of language acquisition. Chomsky presents this conception as if it were different from hypothesis testing. As metaphors, the two notions are different and in a way that makes the organ growth metaphor seem wrongly applied in the case of language acquisition, since the variability between the various possible *normal* final states of organ growth in an individual (relative to the range of possible *normal* environments) is incredibly smaller than the variability between the various possible *normal* final states of language acquisition in an individual (relative to the range of possible *normal* environments), namely, the various linguistic competences for the natural languages that exist or could exist. But when Chomsky explains this metaphor we find that there is no difference between Chomsky's present conception of language acquisition and his earlier hypothesis testing conception.

The appearance of difference is heightened by the fact that Chomsky lumps hypothesis testing together with conditioning and induction as forms of learning[25] in formulating the question of whether language is learned or whether "grammar grows in the mind". But when we come to Chomsky's answer to the question, all but merely verbal differences disappear:

> . . . the question whether language is learned or grows will depend on whether the mind equipped with universal grammar presents a set of grammars as hypotheses to be selected on the basis of data and an evaluation metric, or whether the steady state grammar arises in another way—for example, by virtue of a hierarchy of accessibility (stated, perhaps, in terms of the very same evaluation metric) and a process of selection of the most accessible grammar compatible with the given data.[26]

A "hierarchy of accessibility" is imposed on the set of possible grammars by an evaluation metric (according to *Aspects*,[27] a "specification of a function m such that $m(i)$ is an integer associated with the grammar G_i as its value (with, let us say, lower value indicated by higher number)"). Chomsky says that perhaps the evaluation metric will be the same as set out in *Aspects;* there is nothing for it to be if it isn't. Further, a "process of selection of the most accessible grammar compatible with the given data" is also the same as the hypothesis testing model's process of using a chosen function m to determine a simplest grammar from among those in the set of possible grammars and then using logical function f (according to *Aspects*,[28] a "specification of a function f such that $SD_{f(i, j)}$ is the structural description assigned to sentence s_i by grammar G_j for arbitrary i, j") to determine if the simplest grammar is consistent with the given primary linguistic data. Therefore, the change in metaphor from the 'little linguist' to 'organ growth' represents no fundamental change in Chomsky's conception (insofar as it can be explicitly stated at present) of what the process of acquiring a competence is like. The language organ grows through a process of hypothesis testing in accord with innate specifications of *(I)-(V)*.

In assessing what is controversial in Chomsky's metatheory for linguistic theory, it is quite clear that the interpretation of *(i)-(v)* in terms of *(I)-(V)* is the crux of the issue. But *(i)-(v)*, that is, Chomsky's metatheoretic conditions on the components of linguistic theory, are, in part, determined by the use that will be made of their intended interpretations *(I)-(V)* in a model of language acquisition, and hence, *(i)-(v)* are themselves, in part, controversial. *(iv)* and *(v)* are the principal controversial components, but even *(i)* has a controversial aspect, namely, the claim that a universal definition of "possible sentence" be given in a phonetic theory. This not only ties the notion 'possible sentence' too closely to human linguistic fluency, but, even with respect to human fluency, it is too narrow a restriction on linguistic theory. For the clause would exclude real natural languages like Sign, the natural language of the deaf, which is gestural rather than phonetic.[29] Also, it would too quickly rule out animal communication system like the "dance languages" of the honey bee and science fiction possibilities of various sorts. Such possibilities, while perhaps far-fetched, ought not be excluded by arbitrary fiat. They are part of the question of what a natural language is and we ought to examine the creativity of animal communication systems, their expressive power, and the formal similarities and differences between them and clear cases of natural languages.[30] Furthermore, we also ought to allow for the possibility of natural languages with even more radically different sensible signs (e.g., olfactory ones) since there is no way to preclude such possibilities *a priori*.[31]

With this proviso, Platonists can accept *(i)-(iii)*—independently of *(I)-(III)*—as requirements on a linguistic theory. There is only the problem that Chomsky's statement of the requirement is uneconomical. It seems quite clear that if *(iii)* appears *(i)* and *(ii)* are not needed. How could there be a complete definition of "structural description" that does not contain a universal definition of "possible sentence" or a complete definition of "generative grammar" that does not contain a universal definition of "structural description"? But if the definitions of "possible sentence" and "structural description" are contained in the definition of "generative grammar", only *(iii)* is necessary.

In contrast, *(iv)* and *(v)* are controversial because the only grounds for requiring such components in linguistic theory is a conceptualist construal of the theory as an account of the initial competence of the language learner. In such an account, *(iv)* is needed to derive predictions about linguistic data from a set of candidate grammars and *(v)* to select one grammar from among those not eliminated on the grounds that their predictions conflict with the data.

Apart from such a conceptualist construal of linguistic theory, however, a function satisfying *(iv)* can no more be considered a component of a theory about language in general, and hence a statement about natural languages, than a computation function that computes the logical consequences of, say, thermodynamical theory can be considered to be about atoms, molecules, and thermodynamical phenomena. Such computation functions are merely pieces of logical or mathematical apparatus for deducing the implications of any statements whatever. Such functions are not specific to a particular discipline like grammar or thermodynamics, but provide a general way of extracting the content of any theories in science including logic and mathematics themselves. *Modus ponens* will surely appear in the function that computes the predictions a grammar makes about sentences, but this cannot be taken to be grounds for saying that *modus ponens* states something about natural languages *per se*. If such functions are about anything, they are about implication, and their use in linguistics or physics is mere application.

The metric that satisfies *(v)* orders the possible grammars so that, given a function *f*, we can select a preferable grammar from those whose implications squares with the available evidence about the grammatical structure of the sentences in the primary linguistic data. The ordering is based on the simplicity with which candidate grammars systematize the statements they make about the grammatical structure of sentences. Now, just as the computation function is, apart from conceptualism, better viewed as outside linguistics (as a part of logic and mathematics), so such a simplicity metric is, apart from conceptualism, better viewed as outside linguistics. Here, too, there is no relevant difference between the metric for determining the simplest systematization of a set of facts from one special science to another. Thus, it seems wrong to claim that a general metric for choosing the simplest systematization of a body of scientific facts is a statement about the phenomena in one specific science.

An important corollary of counting *(iv)* and *(v)* as controversial is that Chomsky's construction of linguistic theory as an evaluation procedure also counts as controversial. This is not to claim that Chomsky's arguments against the structuralist's conception of linguistic theory as a discovery procedure are not telling against that conception, but only to claim, again, that Chomsky's argument is limited to a choice between that conception and his. In the broad context including the choice of a Platonist conception of linguistic theory, there is no reason for insisting that a linguistic theory has to tell us, for any suitable corpus C and pair of grammars G_1 and G_2, which of G_1 and G_2 is the better grammar of the language from which C is drawn.

From a Platonist standpoint, it is natural to regard the application of such a computation function and simplicity metric to be part of the general methodology of the sciences, a subject concerned with explicating the logico-mathematical apparatus used to make methodological choices in the special sciences and belonging to the theory of knowledge. If the clauses *(iv)* and *(v)* are, as it were, kicked upstairs, to be requirements on an account of general methodology in the sciences, then linguistic theory itself becomes a theory of the set of abstract objects whose subsets are the sets of sentences that particular grammars are theories of. As a theory about the sentences of natural languages collectively, linguistic theory seeks to achieve the traditional aim of universal grammar, namely, to state the invariances in the grammatical structure of sentences over the full range of natural languages. Accordingly, the interpretive principles *(I)-(V)* and the particular clauses *(iv)* and *(v)* are the principal matters of controversy between conceptualism and Platonism at the level of linguistic theory.

A Neutral Basis for Settling the Controversy

The basis on which we try to settle a controversy between two opposed policies for assigning ontological interpretations to theories must not itself employ criteria that favor one policy. The controversy between Harris's nominalistically interpreted transformational theory and Chomsky's conceptualistically interpreted one could not have been settled on a basis partisan to one or the other theory. Thus, I will set out neutral criteria that conform closely to our ordinary, pretheoretical conception of what we want a theory of language to be. These criteria reflect the standards implicitly assumed in the controversy between Chomsky's conceptualism and Harris's nominalism, rely on customary notions of scientific methodology, and imply nothing about the interpretation of theories within linguistics or other sciences that is relevant to the conceptualism/Platonism issue.

In rejecting Chomsky's notion of descriptive adequacy for grammars for identifying grammars with theories of "the intrinsic competence of the idealized native speaker", I do not reject everything Chomsky includes under this notion. The passage quoted above in which Chomsky defines "descriptively adequate grammar" goes on to say that

The structural descriptions assigned to sentences by the grammar, the distinctions that it makes between well-formed and deviant, and so on, must for descriptive adequacy, correspond to the linguistic intuition of the native speaker[32]

Platonism agrees that a necessary condition on grammars is that they correctly predict grammatical properties and relations such as well-formedness. Linguistic theory, on both Platonist and conceptualist approaches, has to contain definitions of the grammatical properties and relations of sentences that relate formal structures in derivations to native speaker's linguistic intuitions. These definitions connect a vocabulary of terms, those the native speaker uses to express intuitions about sentences, with formal structures in grammatical derivations. Hence, besides *(i)-(iii)*, linguistic theory must contain definitions like

(D₁) A sentence *s is grammatical in the language L* if, and only if, the optimal grammar of L represents *s* as a sentence at the syntactic level, i.e., a derivation of *s* exists at the syntactic level.

(D₂) A sentence *s is ambiguous in a language L* if, and only if, the optimal grammar of L assigns *s* two or more representations at the semantic level.

(D₃) A sentence s_i *and a sentence* s_j *are synonymous in a language L* if, and only if, the optimal grammar of L assigns s_i and s_j the same representation(s) at the semantic level.

(D₄) A constituent c_i *and a constituent* c_j *are homonymous in a language L* if, and only if, the optimal grammar of L assigns c_i and c_j the same representation at the phonological level but different representations at the semantic level.

that exhaust the range of grammatical properties and relations of sentences in natural languages.[33]

Another requirement that ought to be mutually agreeable is that grammars provide a rich enough account of grammatical structure for us to *explain* the grammatical facts of the language that call for explanation. Predictions make a brute claim that something is the case.[34] In contrast, explanations supply an account of the conditions that show how or why what is the case is the case. This difference makes it desirable for us to treat explanation as a further standard.

The fact that Chomsky reintroduced explanation into linguistics after American structuralism had banished it in favor of their pure descriptivism may encourage some to associate explanation in linguistics uniquely with Chomsky's approach and to conceive of it solely in psychological or causal terms.[35] But such a conception of explanation is too restrictive. Psychological and causal explanations are not the only kinds of explanation. The conditions cited in showing how or why something is the case do not have to be psychological or causal in order to explain the how or why of phenomena. In other kinds, the conditions can be structural, the reasons mathematical or logical.[36] Consider the following typical grammatical example. Many people are puzzled by the fact that the words "flammable" and "inflammable" are used synonymously, for instance, to express a warning on tank trucks. The explanation is, roughly, that the "in" in "inflammable" is not a negative prefix, as it first seems, because "inflammable" is derived from the verb "inflame" and that "flammable" is derived from the noun "flame" by addition of the adjective forming suffix "able". The full explanation requires an account of the derivations of these adjectives that exhibits the syntactic conditions determining their synonymy and an account of the structural reasons why the adjectives are apparently but not really antonymous forms.[37]

If a grammar can predict each grammatical property and relation of every sentence in the language, then *ipso facto* it is conceivable that it also provides a basis for explaining all grammatical phenomena in the language that merit explanation. I know of no way to prove this one way or the other. Thus, for safety's sake, it seems prudent to assume that complete prediction does not entail complete explanation, and thereby impose the further requirement of explanatory completeness on grammars. This way, at most, we risk redundancy. Hence, we include *(D₅)*.

> *(D5)* A grammar G is an optimal grammar for the language L only if G implies every true evidence statement about L and G provides the grammatical basis for explaining every grammatical phenomena in L that merits explanation.

Corresponding to *(D5)*, we have the requirement

> *(D6)* A linguistic theory T is correct only if T defines the notion 'generative grammar' (i.e., recursively enumerates the class of generative grammars containing the optimal generative grammar(s) for each natural language) in such a way that all and only the universals of language appear as clauses specifying the form and content of generative grammars, and only if T provides a basis for explaining every grammatical fact about natural language in general that merits explanation.

for linguistic theory. There are two points to note about *(D6)*. First, it is neutral in the controversy between conceptualism and Platonism, whereas Chomsky's notion of explanatory adequacy is not. Second, although *(D6)* conforms to the Chomskian format of stating universals of language as clauses of the definition of 'generative grammar', there is nothing in Platonism that requires conformity to this format. Moreover, the question whether this way of stating the universals of language is desirable has recently been raised and the issue has yet to be debated in the literature.[38] Nonetheless, I have retained Chomsky's format because in this discussion I wish to eliminate all issues not directly involved in the controversy between conceptualism and Platonism.

(D5) and *(D6)* as they stand are only necessary conditions for optimality of grammars and correctness of linguistic theories. What makes *(D5)* and *(D6)* fall short of sufficiency is that predictive and explanatory completeness underdetermine the choice of theories. This, however, is a familiar situation in science. Normally, when faced with

equally successful predictive and explanatory theories, scientists prefer the one(s) that systematize the facts most efficiently. The most efficient systematizations are the ones that require the least in the way of independent entities (states, etc.) in order to predict and explain the same phenomena. Thus, insofar as the evidence from successful prediction and explanation supports less theoretical weight in the case of simpler theories, they are preferred because they are more likely to be true on the avialable evidence. Since these are general considerations, this preference holds not only in the case of incomplete evidence but also in the case where the evidence is complete but still various possible theories survive confrontation with it. Therefore, we may obtain necessary and sufficient conditions by reformulating (D_5) and (D_6) in the manner of (D_5') and (D_6').

(D_5') A grammar G is an optimal grammar for the language L if, and only if, G satisfies (D_5) and there is no grammar simpler than G that also satisfies (D_5).

(D_6') A linguistic theory T is correct if, and only if, T satisfies (D_6) and there is no linguistic theory simpler than T that also satisfies (D_6).

It might be supposed that a Chomskian would object to introducing simplicity in the sense of Occam's razor into the criteria for deciding between theories in linguistics, since on occasion he has questioned this notion; but he has appealed to it in constructing some of his arguments.[39] We shall consider the principal questions raised by Chomsky's references to simplicity in the last chapter. Here let us consider only whether there is an objection to the use of simplicity in these criteria.

The objection would run like this. Chomsky claims that the relevant notion of simplicity for linguistics is that of an empirical hypothesis expressing the innate metric. The metric determines the human language learner's preferences concerning the ways that facts about a language are systematized. Such a metric could turn out to be the same as the simplicity principle that governs the choice of hypotheses in science, but it could also turn out different. In the latter case, so the objection goes, the linguist should use the metric that reflects the child's preferences since the rules that the linguist is trying to state in constructing a grammar are the ones that are selected by the metric that children use in language learning.

The objection begs the question. The reason it offers for the linguist to use the metric that reflects the child's preferences assumes the conceptualist position in taking the rules that the linguist is trying to construct to be the competence acquired by the child. But the objections is undercut in two other ways. First, any account of the innate metric that we might entertain is an empiricial hypothesis which is an inductive extrapolation based on the use of simplicity in the sense of general methodology. Our confidence in the account thus depends in part on our confidence in the basis for its extrapolation, for choosing it over other hypotheses compatible with the evidence. But then if we overrule the simplicity principle in general methodology in favor of the empirical hypotheses about the innate metric in choosing theories in linguistics, we provide a counter-example to the methodology that the empirical hypothesis itself rests on.

Second, since the linguist, like other scientists, ought to do everything possible to select the theories that are most likely to be true, the linguist ought to follow the canon of simplicity in general methodology in cases where it conflicts with the innate metric. To claim that the linguist ought to do otherwise is to recommend choosing theories whose greater theoretical weight puts a greater strain on the supporting evidence, and hence, to recommend choosing theories that are less likely to be true.

Similar reasons show that the notion of logical implication that appears in (D_5') and (D_6') is also to be obtained outside linguistics, from the general methodology of science (as part of its account of how a prediction about an object in the domain of a science is obtained from a theory about the domain). Thus, simplicity and logical implication can be taken as neutral in the controversy between conceptualism and Platonism in linguistics.

The critical question is whether the notion of an evidence statement appearing in (D_5') and (D_6') can also be taken as neutral. This seems at first problematic because Chomsky rests his conception of the kinds of evidence which are relevant to grammars on his conceptualist view of the nature of grammars. Recently, he described the range of evidence that he takes to bear on the construction of grammars:

. . . it is possible to imagine discoveries in neurophysiology or in the study of behavior and learning that might lead us to revise or abandon a given theory of language or particular grammar, with its hypotheses about the components of the system and their interaction. The abstract nature of these theories permits some latitude in interpretation of particular results, especially insofar as we do not have a clear picture of how cognitive structures are embedded within the theory of performance. Latitude is not total license, however. The theoretical psychologist (in this case the linguist), the experimental psychologist, and the neurophysiologist are engaged in a common enterprise, and each should exploit as fully as possible the insights derived from all approaches that seek to determine the initial state of the organism, the cognitive structures attained, and the manner in which these structures are employed.[40]

More recently, Chomsky has carried this view to the extreme of denying that any alternative to it makes sense. He writes:

... The evidence available in principle falls into two epistemological categories: some is labelled "evidence for psychological reality," and some merely counts as evidence for a good theory. Surely this position makes absolutely no sense[41]

The very idea of "psychological reality" is bogus:

What is commonly said is that theories of grammar or universal grammar, whatever their merits, have not been shown to have a mysterious property called "psychological reality". What is this property? Presumably, it is to be understood on the model of "physical reality". But in the natural sciences, one is not accustomed to ask whether the best theory we can devise in some idealized domain has the property of "physical reality"[42]

Finally, Chomsky strengthens the statement of his view on evidence:

What the best evidence is depends on the state of the field. The best evidence may be provided by as yet unexplained facts drawn from the language being studied, or from similar facts about other languages, or from psycholinguistic experiment, or from clinical studies of language disability, or from neurology, or from innumerable other sources. We should always be on the lookout for new kinds of evidence, and cannot know in advance what they will be.[43]

On Chomsky's view of evidence, no restriction is placed on the notion of an evidence statement, and hence, the references to evidence statements in (D_5') and (D_6') can be construed so broadly as to cover statements in linguistics, experimental psycholinguistics, clinical psychology, neurology, and "innumerable other sources". As a consequence, theories in linguistics could be evaluated on the basis of judgments concerning the grammatical properties and relations of sentences and on the basis of findings about "the initial state of the organism, the cognitive structures attained, and the manner in which these structures are employed". It would then be possible for conceptualistically interpreted grammars to be optimal relative to the latter while Platonistically interpreted grammars are optimal relative to the former. Since each ontological position could have its own conception of evidence, there would be no common criteria for evaluating theories in linguistics and hence no neutral basis for judging between conceptualist and Platonist views of the subject.

If a view as to what linguistics is about can determine whether one or another kind of fact is relevant to evaluating theories in linguistics, then any view about the nature of linguistics can be self-verifying. In particular, the view of the American structuralists that linguistics is about noise and deposits of ink and graphite becomes as defensible as any other view about the nature of linguistics. Given the licence to decide the relevance of different kinds of facts to the evaluation of theories of natural languages, structuralists could insist that the kind relevant to such evaluation are facts about the probability of occurrence of utterance tokens in a corpus. Thus, American structuralism could easily defend its nominalistically interpreted taxonomic grammars (with minimally abstract categories and a graded conception of acceptability) as preferable to conceptualistically interpreted generative grammars on the grounds that taxonomic grammars provide the best account of the relevant grammatical evidence about natural languages. Allowing ontological positions to make their own decisions about the relevance of evidence makes as much sense as allowing each side in a civil suit to decide what evidence will be admitted in court.

The question of what evidence is relevant to choosing between theories of a natural language thus has to be decided in an ontologically non-partisan manner. The question is an *a priori* one. The competing claims about the subject-matter of linguistics on the part of nominalism, conceptualism, and Platonism are *a priori* theses about what kinds of things, and hence what kinds of facts, are in the domain of linguistics. It would be absurd to construe these claims as *a posteriori* insofar as, until they are settled, there is no determination of the kind of things to try to obtain experience of. There would be no idea of where to look for relevant evidence if nothing had been settled about the domain of theories in linguistics. To put a point on it, empirical evidence can not decide between the view that linguistics is an empirical discipline and the view that it is not.

Chomsky's claim that a distinction between evidence of a purely grammatical nature and evidence of psychological reality ''makes absolutely no sense'' is based on assuming that the linguist's question ''Does my theory have psychological reality?'' is parallel to the physicist's question ''Does my theory have physical reality?'' Chomsky is right about there being something senseless in a physicist asking this question about the best theory he or she can devise. It has been devised as a theory of physical reality. Thus, Chomsky's assumption that the linguist's question is parallel begs the question. For the linguist's question to be parallel we have to suppose that linguistics bears the same relation to psychological reality that physics bears to physical reality, but this is to have already settled the question in favor of the view that the linguist is a psychologist whose theories are constructed as theories of psychological reality. If one faces the question squarely instead of begging it, it makes perfectly good sense to ask whether the best theory we can devise about a language is also a theory of some psychological reality.

Chomsky says that evidence for theories in linguistics can come not only from languages but from "psycholinguistic experiment", "clinical studies of language disability", and "innumerable other sources". What other sources? Can evidence for theories in linguistics come from experiments with glowworms or clinical studies of dandruff? Even if we "cannot know in advance what they will be", there must at least be a criterion to apply at the time to rule out sources with no relevance to theories in linguistics. It is, moreover, easy to see what it is. It is no accident that, when Chomsky turns from facts about the structure languages to additional sources, he mentions psycho*linguistic* experiments and clinical studies of *language* disability. Relevant sources, not surprisingly, concern themselves with language. Experiments with glowworms and clinical studies of dandruff are irrelevant sources just because they have nothing to do with language. The criterion we apply to determine the relevance of a factual source to theories in linguistics is whether the source concerns the subject-matter of linguistics, language.[44]

But a source can concern a subject-matter in either of two ways. It can be about the subject-matter directly (in the case of linguistics, it can be about the grammatical structure of the sentences in the language) or indirectly (in the case of linguistics, it can be about some variable correlated with a feature of the grammatical structure of sentences). Hence, in linguistics, as in other sciences, there are two kinds of evidence, *direct evidence,* which is evidence about the grammatical structure of sentences obtained from native speakers's intuitive judgments about their structure, and *indirect evidence,* which is evidence operationally obtained about the use of language or about psychological or neurophysiological correlates of linguistic processing. The latter includes such things as reaction time and errors in production or comprehension. Indirect evidence can bear on questions about grammatical structure in sentences by means of a chain of inferences from assumptions about the connection between sentence structure and aspects of use, psychological or neurophysiological correlate, and so forth. Thus, indirect evidence depends on direct evidence for its legitimization as a relevant source of facts, and direct evidence has a prior claim over indirect evidence.

When Chomsky took a less extreme position of these matters, he himself stressed the priority of direct evidence over indirect evidence. He wrote:

It is important to bear in mind that when an operational procedure is proposed, it must be tested for adequacy (exactly as a theory of linguistic intuition—a grammar—must be tested for adequacy) by measuring it against the standard provided by the tacit knowledge that it attempt to specify and describe. Thus a proposed operational test for, say, segmentation into words, must meet the empirical condition of conforming, in a mass of crucial and clear cases, to the linguistic intuition of the native speaker concerning such elements. Otherwise, it is without value.[45]

And further

... there is no way to avoid the traditional assumption that the speaker-hearer's linguistic intuition is the ultimate standard that determines the accuracy of any proposed grammar, linguistic theory, or operational test[46]

The priority of direct evidence—its status as the ultimate standard on what is a matter of grammar—derives from the fact that direct evidence reflects the state of grammatical structure without intermediate agency or influence. The dependency of indirect evidence derives from the fact that it reflects the state of grammatical structure through a causal chain that terminates in behavioral or neurphysiological phenomena. Insufficient correlation to insure that grammatical structure is reflected through such intervening factors without distortion is what makes some behavioral or neurophysiological phenomena grammatically misleading; absence of grammatical structure to be reflected in behavior of glowworms or the biology of dandruff is what makes them grammatically irrelevant.

It should be noted that I am not denying Chomsky's claim that "it is possible to imagine discoveries in neurophysiology or in the study of behavior and learning that might lead us to revise or abandon a given theory of language or particular grammar". The relation between direct and indirect evidence does not rule out arguments in linguistics from evidence obtained from experiment or observation. It only rules out arguments based solely on such evidence, that is, ones not backed up with validating direct evidence.

We thus obtain a neutral basis for settling the controversy between conceptualism and Platonism. The basis is the one implicitly assumed in settling the controversy between nominalism and conceptualism in the Chomskian revolution. It derives from the fundamental concern of linguistics with languages and from the general distinction between direct and indirect evidence within science. Since, as we have seen, indirect evidence in the study of grammar is also evidence about the grammatical structure of sentences, indirectly arrived at, this basis can be explicitly formulated by taking the term "evidence statement" appearing in (D_5') and (D_6') to refer to statements asserting that a sentence or set of sentences either has or does not have a particular grammatical property or relation (for example, one of those defined in definitions like (D_1)-(D_4)). Thus typically, evidence statements for a language will mention particular sentences of a language and will make metalinguistic predications about the mentioned sentence's having a grammatical property or relation, for example,

(1) "Revolutionary new ideas appear infrequently" is grammatical in English.

(2) "Visiting relatives can be annoying" is ambiguous in English.

(3) "John loves Mary" and "Mary is loved by John" are synonymous with each other but not with "John is Mary's lover".

(4) "charge" in the expression "charge with larceny" and "charge" in the expression "charge a stiff price" are homonymous in English.[47]

Notes

1. Chomsky 1980a: 29.
2. Chomsky 1980a: 28–30.
3. This is the distinction I make in Katz 1972: 450–452.
4. Chomsky 1975a: 39. Recall that the theory of grammars as generative systems allows us to impose constraints on grammatical derivations so that divergent claims about a natural language can be compared on the basis of competing predictions the rules are forced to make.
5. Chomsky 1975a: 39.
6. It is worth emphasizing here the importance of being clear on the various uses of the key term "empirical" in attempting to determine what grammars are theories of. The term "empirical" has the unfortunate use in current linguists of referring to claims for which there could exist evidence to decide their truth: "non-empirical claims" on this use are claims for which no evidence could be relevant, claims that are metaphysical in the worst sense. There is also the standard use of "empirical" on which it refers to claims for evidence from sense experience, and equivocation between these two uses encourages some linguists to think that claims to which empirical evidence in the sense of evidence from experience is irrelevant are *ipso facto* metaphysical in the worst sense.
7. For a general discussion of the realist/instrumentalist controversy in the philosophy of science, see Maxwell 1962: 3–27.
8. Chomsky 1976: 1–24.
9. As I read Chomsky, he would not accept the learnability criterion proposed in Wexler, Culicover, and Hamburger, 1976, basically, because it is performancism at the level of linguistic theory. There is no more reason for linguistic theory to be under this learnability constraint than there is for a grammar to be under the constraint that it characterizes sentences in such a manner that each and every one can be uttered by a speaker who has internalized the grammar.
10. Chomsky 1975b: 36–37; also Chomsky 1976.
11. Chomsky 1965: 4.

12. Chomsky 1965: 8.

13. Chomsky 1965: 9.

14. Chomsky 1967a: 435–436.

15. Valian 1979: 1–26.

16. I would argue that it does fail, and for the same reasons that the nominalist's attempt at reconstruction fails. The problem is how the particular chosen to replace the universal can have only the required generality. The alleged answer is that it functions as a standard, and we can say that any other particular belongs to the class that the universal determines if, and only if, it bears the proper resemblance to the standard particular. How, then, does the notion of resemblance get acceptably reconstructed? If it does not get reconstructed, we are still left with a universal, and no way of reconstructing it. The conceptualist attempts at the reconstruction of universals in terms of psychological particulars will, I think, fare no better, but I cannot pursue the point here.

17. Chomsky 1965, 1975b, 1980a.

18. It is thus no surprise to find Chomsky choosing the very terms "acceptable" and "unacceptable" to name the performance contrast that he is at pains to distinguish from the competence contrast of grammatical vs. ungrammatical: ". . . let us use the term 'acceptable' to refer to utterances that are perfectly natural and immediately comprehensible without paper and pencil analysis, and in no way bizzarre or outlandish. Obviously, acceptability will be a matter of degree, along various dimensions." Chomsky 1965: 10. See also Chomsky 1964b: 35–39.

19. Chomsky 1959a: 138.

20. Chomsky 1965: 31.

21. Chomsky 1965: 30.

22. Chomsky 1965: 25–26.

23. Chomsky 1965: 24.

24. Chomsky 1980a: 134–140: Chomsky 1980b: 52–58.

25. Chomsky 1980a: 52–53.

26. Chomsky 1980a: 54.

27. Chomsky 1965: 31.

28. Chomsky 1965: 31.

29. Bellugi and Klima 1979.

30. The best study to date of the "dance language" of honey bees suggests that these systems are not, in fact, natural languages. See Janda 1978.

31. The controversial clause of *(i)* probably entered Chomsky's conception of linguistic theory from the psychologism underlying the phonological work of Jakobson and the Prague School and from the Sapir tradition in American linguistics. A more circumspect examination of the issue along the lines I have suggested in the text will show that a far more abstract notion of the sensible signs of the language is needed, a notion leading to a universal definition of *possible sentence* that makes no reference to features of any particular sensory mode.

32. Chomsky 1965: 24.

33. For an account of exhaustiveness, see chapter 4.

34. A grammar G predicts the fact that a sentence S has a property or relation R just in case linguistic theory defines R and the structural description of S in G, together with the definition of R, implies that S has R.

35. Criticizing Trubetzkoy's attempts at phonological explanation, Martin Joos, a leading structuralist, wrote, "Children want explanations, and there is a child in each of us; descriptivism makes a virtue of not pampering that child". Joos 1958: 96.

36. For example, consider the request for explanation in the question, why is it that when a two-place predicate is added to a monadic first-order language, the decision problem for theoremhood becomes undecidable.

37. The synonym of "flammable" and "inflammable" can be predicated merely by noting that they receive the same semantic representation, and their non-antonymy can

be predicted merely by noting that "in-" in "inflammable" is not semantically interpreted on the basis of negation rules in the manner of "in-" in cases like "insincere" or "insatiable". But such predictions would not constitute an explanation, but only a precise statement of what it is about these adjectives that calls for explanation.

38. Johnson and Postal 1980, especially ch. 14.

39. For example, Chomsky questions it in Chomsky 1966b, and he makes explicit use of it in the arguments in Chomsky 1957, for example on p. 43.

40. Chomsky 1975b: 37.

41. Chomsky 1980a: 108.

42. Chomsky 1980a: 106–107.

43. Chomsky 1980a: 109.

44. Chomsky is right that we cannot know in advance what factual sources will be relevant to theories in linguistics, but this is not because we have no *a priori* criterion of relevance: it is only because application of the criterion depends on our state of knowledge of the putative source.

45. Chomsky 1965: 19.

46. Chomsky 1965: 21.

47. I am aware that, in the above discussion, I have adopted a philosophical position with which some philosophers of science will quarrel. I have taken it for granted that ontological positions cannot in a partisan way determine the kind of evidence on which they will be evaluated. This, of course, runs counter to the view of the so-called "new philosophers of science". Feyerabend writes, "Each theory will possess its own experience, and there will be no overlap between those experiences". (Feyerabend 1965: 202.) My own answer to this view is found in Katz 1979c: See also Shapere 1966: 41–85.

III

Introductory Platonism: Grammatical Knowledge and Its Object

Fundamental Distinctions

Platonism in linguistics makes two separable claims. The first, and weaker one, is that linguistics is not a psychological science, that its theories are not about states of mind, mental events, or their neurological realizations, but about sentences and languages directly in the way that we ordinarily take linguistics to be about sentences and languages.[1] The second, and stronger claim, is that sentences and language are abstract objects and thus linguistics is about abstract objects. The argument we shall make for Platonism has two parts, one to support each of these claims. Together, they show that only a Platonist framework enables linguistics to have optimal grammars and a correct linguistic theory in the sense of (D_5') and (D_6').

The argument as a whole is directed at the features indentified in the last chapter as controversial aspects of Chomsky's conceptualism and their counterparts in other forms of conceptualism. Its main criticism is the same as Chomsky's criticism of nominalism, namely, that the constraints imposed put too low a ceiling on the abstractness of grammars for them to be optimal. The present chapter provides the main argument supporting the claim that linguistics is not psychology while chapter V provides the main argument supporting the claim that linguistics is about abstract objects.

These claims are separable to the extent that the first can be maintained independently of the second. This might suggest to some that the shortcomings of conceptualism could be avoided without at the same time having to defend Platonism. The idea would be to defend the first claim but not the second. This approach, while surely the easier one to follow, has the defect of all negative definitions. It tells us what a grammar is *not* a theory of (*viz.,* psychological states, events, etc.) but not what it *is* a theory of.[2] Moreover, the approach is "theoretically unsatisfying" in another way. If, as we may assume, the alternatives of nominalism and conceptualism have been ruled out, then, insofar as the only other ontological position is Platonism, the approach of defending only the first claim must either make it a matter of principle to take no ontological stand or the approach must be counted as simply shirking the harder but admittedly necessary job of constructing a defense of Platonism. The former alternative makes it a matter of principle to ignore the only genuine philosophical question a philosopher can ask in this connection while the latter tries to make laziness a virtue. Because of the unsatisfactoriness of this approach, I have treated the two separable claims as theoretically connected parts of the same position.

The claim that linguistic theories are not about psychological phenomena but straightforwardly about sentences and languages rests on the general epistemological distinction between knowledge that we have of something and the thing(s) that we have knowledge of. There are special cases of this distinction in a wide range of disciplines. In mathematics, we distinguish between the numbers themselves and the knowledge of them that humans have and use in distinguishing quantities and calculating. We take Fermat's statement that no whole numbers or fractions exist such that $x^n + y^n = a^n$ (where n is a whole number greater than 2) to be about *numbers*. Would anyone for a moment think of claiming the Wolfskehl prize for a demonstration about human mathematical competence or performance?[3] The empirical sciences provide, if anything, even clearer examples.

In mathematics and other sciences, then, we find special cases of the general epistemological distinction which are parallel in all relevant respects to the Platonist's distinction between sentences and natural languages, on the one hand, and the knowledge that speakers have about their structure, on the other. The parallel may be illustrated in the partial comparison:

Mathematics	Logic	Language
Ideal calculator's knowledge of the natural numbers	Ideal reasoner's knowledge of implication	Ideal speaker's knowledge of the sentences (language)
The natural numbers	The implication relations	The sentences (language)

This parallel is itself suggestive. The application of the general epistemological distinction in the special sciences of mathematics and logic seems entirely unproblematic. There is no temptation to conflate the psychological study of the ideal calculator's knowledge of number with the mathematical study of numbers, or to conflate the psychological study of the ideal reasoner's knowledge of implication relations with the logical study of implication relations. But, if there is a clear distinction in these disciplines, why conflate psychological study of the ideal speaker's knowledge of a language with the grammatical study of the language? Since the parallel holds perfectly with respect to the relevant aspects of these cases,[4] it is hard to see how there could be a genuine distinction in mathematics and logic while there is none in linguistics. The fact that there is no reason to explain why these parallel cases ought not sort out the same way puts the conceptualist in the awkward position of having to make the farfetched claim that a theory of numbers in mathematics *is* a psychological theory of human knowledge of number and a theory of implication in logic *is* a psychological theory of human knowledge of implication.

The Platonist has the more plausible position. In distinguishing between linguistic reality—as a realm of sentences and languages outside us—and our human knowledge, however idealized, of that reality, the Platonist is applying the general epistemological distinction in linguistics, too. Thus, the Platonist's position can take the more plausible view of mathematical and logical theories without having to produce a justification for treating linguistics differently—a justification that seems not to be available.

Chomsky's claim that grammars are theories of a special kind of human knowledge suggests that he sees no distinction between knowledge of a language and the language itself. Passages like

The set of rules and principles that determine the normal use of language I will refer to as . . . the 'grammar' of the language. There is an ambiguity in the usage of this term that should be noted; that is, the term 'grammar' is also used for the explicit theory, constructed by the linguist, which purports to be a theory of the rules and principles, the grammar in the first sense, that has been mastered by the person who knows the language. No confusion should arise if the distinction is kept in mind. The linguist's grammar is a theory, true or false, partial or complete, of the grammar of the speaker-hearer, the person who knows the language. The latter is the object of the linguist's study.[5]

taken together with passages like

A grammar of the language L is essentially a theory of L. Any scientific theory is based on a finite number of observations, and it seeks to relate the observed phenomena and to predict new phenomena by constructing general laws in terms of hypothetical constructs. . . . Similarly, a grammar of English is based on a finite corpus of utterances (observations), and it will contain certain grammatical rules (laws) stated in terms of the particular phonemes, phrases, etc. of English (hypothetical constructs).[6]

—which abound in Chomsky's writings—make it seem clear that he thinks that a language like English is some kind of rational reconstruction out of notions that enter into the explanation of the speaker's normal use of language. But our sense of having a hold on Chomsky's view disappears when we consider also his explicit answers to the question what natural languages like English are. In one place, he writes that: ". . . such notions as 'the English language' are not linguistically definable, but are rather socio-political in nature."[7] In another he supports this sentiment:

. . . consider the concept of 'language' itself. The term is hardly clear: 'language' is no well defined concept of linguistic science. In colloquial usage, we say that German is one language and Dutch another, but some dialects of German are more similar to Dutch dialects than to other, more remote, dialects of German.[8]

There are three possible positions available in the light of such statements, none of them attractive. One position stresses these last two quotations, claiming that notions like 'English', 'French', etc. and 'natural language' are not proper concepts of linguistics. This is like claiming that the concept of number is not a concept of mathematics but a socio-political one (or that the concept of implication is not a logical concept but a socio-political one). One can appreciate that, in connection with these notions as with many others, adjustments of the ordinary notion may be required in their scientific, formal explication.

But nothing warants the astounding claim that 'English,' 'French,' etc. and 'natural language' are not concepts of *linguistic* science.

When Bloomfield saw that his use of ordering relations constituted an embarrassing use of abstraction, he denied that the use of such relations has implications for linguistic reality by invoking an instrumentalist philosophy on which these relations are mere *façons de parler*. Chomsky is here doing something similar. Acknowledging the legitimacy of notions like 'English', 'French', etc., and 'natural language', independently of the psychological notions of 'the ideal speaker's knowledge of English', 'the ideal speaker's knowledge of French', and so on, constitutes an embarrassment for Chomsky's conceptualism at least as bad as the embarrassment that ordering constituted for Bloomfield's nominalism. For if 'English', 'French', etc. are proper concepts for linguistics, it is hardly plausible that linguistics is about psychological states rather than about English, French, etc. and language. Thus, Chomsky seems to take a way out, as Bloomfield did, by denying that linguistic reality contains objects of study of the kind that linguistics traditionally takes to fall under the concepts 'English', etc. and 'language'. Chomsky, of course, makes no appeal to instrumentalism. Rather, he authoritatively asserts that it is a mistake to believe that we will find principles that distinguish languages and dialects.[9] On the other hand, he is relatively sanguine about the application of science to the problem of studying competence. To the outside observer, however, the reasons for optimism or pessimism in the one case will seem as weak or as strong as the reasons in the other. The difference Chomsky sees between the two cases must be taken to reflect his commitment to conceptualism.

Stressing the second of the above quotations from Chomsky avoids these difficulties in a natural way but the position is no more attractive than the previous position because it concedes the Platonist's distinction between the language and the speaker's knowledge of it. The term "grammar" is now three-ways ambiguous: $grammar_1$ refers to the speaker-hearer's implicit or tacit "rules and principles that determine the normal use of language"; $grammar_2$ refers to the linguist's theory (on the conceptualist's view) "true or false, partial or complete, of the grammar of the speaker-hearer"; $grammar_3$ refers to the scientific theory of the language itself "based on a finite number of observations, and . . . seek [ing] to relate the observed phenomena and to predict new phenomena by constructing general laws". The fact that it might empirically turn out that the $grammar_2$ of English and the $grammar_3$ of English are the same theory is besides the point. This possibility is of no more significance than the possibility that an $arithmetic_2$ might turn out the same as an $arithmetic_3$ or a $logic_2$ might turn out the same as a logic₃. Such an outcome would be an astonishing coincidence of research programs guided by different theoretical aims.

The last of the positions available refuses to make the Platonist distinction but does not relegate the notions of 'English', 'French', etc. and 'natural language' to the socio-political vocabulary (with notions like 'Fatherland', 'national will', etc.). But, in order for this position to escape the objection that there is some distinction to be drawn between a language and the ideal speaker-hearer's knowledge of it, the conceptualist has to provide an explanation of how talk of natural languages can be conceived of as logical construction out of talk about their speakers.

Not only is there not the slightest suggestion of how such a logical construction might be carried out, there is, moreover, good reason to think it cannot. Such a construction would identify the language that a speaker has knowledge of with a part or aspect of that knowledge. The construction takes the ideal speaker's knowledge to be basic and the language to be constructed out of it, but the ideal speaker's knowledge, with which the construction starts, is identified as knowledge of a natural language. Thus, we have to know at the outset what "English" refers to in the characterization "the ideal speaker-hearer's knowledge of English". The characterization employs the term "English" to specify the knowledge in question, just as the characterization "the ideal reasoner's knowledge of propositional logic" employs the term "propositional logic" to specify the knowledge in question. Since, at the very beginning of the construction, it is necessary to determine the result of the construction in order to get the construction off the ground, there is an uneliminatable prior reference to the notion of English. The fact that there is no independent explanation constitutes a vicious circularity: the basic notion of the ideal speaker-hearer's knowledge of English cannot be made sense of without first making sense of a component notion which, *ex hypothesi*, cannot be made sense of independently of making sense of the entire basic notion.

With respect to the criticisms just made of the three possible positions, the first is the least unattractive, the second concedes Platonism its claim, and the third does not get off the ground. The conceptualist thus seems stuck with saying that English, French, etc. and natural language are not really proper concerns of linguistics. Grammars are theories of the grammatical competence of the language user and linguistic theory is a theory of the initial competence of the language learner. Linguistics is a branch of psychology. That's it; there's no more to it. Our response will, of course, be that the conceptualist position is exactly like claiming that number is not a proper concern of mathematics or that logic does not study implication.

The distinction between the language that a speaker knows and the knowledge the speaker has of the language clarifies the Platonist claim that discoveries in psychology and neurophysiology cannot, of themselves (i.e., without sufficient direct evidence), justify revising or abandoning a theory of language in general or a theory of a particular language. Given the distinction, even if such a discovery were to demonstrate that the cognitive structures underlying our knowledge of English cannot contain a certain grammatical rule, that rule can nonetheless be part of what the knowledge is knowledge of, namely, English. English, on this distinction, is a distinct thing from the cognitive structures constituting our knowledge of English.

Of course, such cognitive structures would not be knowledge of English unless they stood in the proper knowledge-of relation to English. The point is that the knowledge-of relation, by virtue of which a set of internalized principles standing in that relation to a language counts as knowledge of the language, is loose enough to accomodate situations in which rules of the grammar of the language do not appear in the set. Knowledge of something—a language, arithmetic, New York, etc.—does not require that absolutely every fact about the object known be reflected in the knower's internal representation. Absolutely complete, perfect knowledge requires this, but we do not withhold credit for knowledge from everyone lacking absolutely complete, perfect knowledge. We would not for a moment think of denying that someone had knowledge of a subject because there is *some* fact he or she did not know. There would be no actual speakers of any natural language if such denials were legitimate.

It is, of course, not possible at present to explicitly define either the actually used knowledge-of relation or the idealized knowledge-of relation. But this doesn't matter as long as the points about them that we have just made are valid. If so, then it makes no more sense to rely solely on psychological or neurophysiological experiments to settle claims about the grammatical structure of English than it does to rely on Mill's "pebble experiments" to settle claims about numbers. No matter what the outcome of such experiments, such indirect evidence itself affords no grounds for an inference from facts about the cognitive states of speakers to facts about the language. To show that such an inference is valid, it would be necessary to adduce direct evidence to show that the cognitive system is knowledge-of the language and the cognitive states in question are among those in the system that veridically reflect the grammatical structure of the language known.

Thus, as we observed in agreeing with Chomsky's claim that ". . . it is possible to imagine discoveries in neurophysiology or in the study of behavior and learning that might lead us to revise or abandon a given theory of language or a particular grammar'',[10] the Platonist does not deny that it is possible to argue from the behavior of speakers to the properties of language. But such argumentation presupposes that the knowledge exercised in the behavior bears the appropriate relation to the language that it is knowledge of.

This having been said, it will be clear how Platonism can both concede the truth of Chomsky's claim and yet itself claim that empirical evidence can never on its own compel us to revise or abandon a grammar that is justified on the basis of unchallenged direct evidence: the conflict between the grammar and the cognitive states for which the empirical evidence is evidence *ipso facto* undermines the presumption that these cognitive states veridically reflect the structure of the language. Empirical evidence shows no more than that speakers have internalized *some* principles, but for the internalized principles to be counted as knowledge of the language they must be related in the proper way to the language. Hence, arguments from empirical evidence always contain the premiss that the internalized principles satisfy the criterion for saying that their possessors have knowledge of the language in question. Since that criterion must judge internalized principles by their account of the structure of sentences in the language, an inconsistency between the results of experiments and sound direct evidence about the structure of sentences is sufficient to show that the internalized principles are *not* knowledge of the language.

The Excesses of Psychological Constraints in Linguistics

Given the distinctions made in the previous section, we begin to understand why it is that conceptualistically interpreted theories in linguistics are too severely restricted in their level of abstractness to be optimal grammars and correct linguistic theories: because conceptualism construes such theories as representing cognitive structures on one side of the knowledge-of relation while optimal grammars and correct linguistic theories are representations of the objects on the other side. The difference is that representations of cognitive structures have to reflect the characteristics of the mental or neural medium in which the speaker's knowledge is realized to the extent that and in the way that these characteristics do shape the form of this knowledge.[11] If the knowledge-of relation is loose enough and if these characteristics shape linguistic knowledge in important enough ways, then representations of the conceptualist's cognitive structures will not be the best representations of the languages they are knowledge of, nor of language in general.

Platonism is thus a liberalization in the sense that, in construing grammars and linguistic theories as theories of the objects known, it drops the constraints that force these theories to be faithful to grammatically extraneous characteristics of the mental or neural medium. If a grammar is required to represent only the structures necessary to predict and explain all the grammatical facts about the sentences of a language, it can be abstract enough to be among the simplest systematizations of such facts.

I will now present a number of arguments against conceptualism suggested by this perspective. We begin with what is in this connection the most salient feature of conceptualism, namely, its *a priori* commitment to tolerating in grammatical representations *any* features that may turn out on empirical investigation to be features of the speaker's knowledge of a language.

Chomsky's argument for conceptualism, as we recall, contains no reasons to show that psychological constraints are adequate but only reasons to show that they are more adequate than nominalist ones. Hence, the emergence of Platonism—which places neither physicalist nor psychological constraints on theories in linguistics—makes it necessary for the justification of conceptualism go beyond Chomsky's argument. The onus of proof is on the conceptualist to demonstrate why psychological constraints ought not to be considered an ad hoc and unnecessary imposition.

Not just any reason will do. The reason for imposing psychological constraints will have to dispel the at least *prima facie* oddity of claiming that a grammar is a better theory of the grammatical structure of sentences if it is also a psychological theory. (This is the same sort of oddity that attends the claim that a logic is a better theory of implicational structure if it is also a psychological theory.) It will not be enough to ridicule the traditional boundary separating linguistics and psychology as being of no serious scientific concern but of only bureaucratic interest:

. . . a line separating the two disciplines, linguistics and psychology, in terms of the kinds of evidence they prefer to use and the specific focus of their attention . . . has always seemed quite senseless. Delineation of disciplines may be useful for administrating universities or organizing professional societies, but apart from that it is an undertaking of limiting merit.[12]

Poking fun at academic administrators and organizers of professional societies is not an unenjoyable or completely unworthwhile pastime, but its enjoyment and value ought not distract us from recognizing that, for the most part, the delineations administrators and organizers use are reflections of the boundaries of the sciences themselves, not bureaucratic inventions. These delineations are sometimes wrong, but even then there are usually substantive considerations behind them that cannot be lightly dismissed. Implementing the general demarcational nihilism Chomsky expresses would turn the spectrum of well-focused academic disciplines into chaos. One wonders what Chomsky has in mind in implying that it is "an undertaking of limited merit" to continue treating, say, mathematics, botany, history, psychology, and astronomy as separate disciplines.

One hears it said that a theory of a natural language which is not psychologically real would have no intellectual interest. The remark cannot mean simply that such a theory would be of no interest to conceptualists. It has to mean that the theory would be of no interest to anyone. If, however, there were a theory that had no psychological reality but that satisfied (Ds') or just correctly predicted the grammatical properties and relations of the examples which have up to now appeared in *Language* and *Linguistic Inquiry*, linguists, to say the least, would be quite interested.

Furthermore, psychological constraints cannot be justified on the grounds that they would help to reduce to manageable proportions the currect proliferation of English grammars and linguistic theories. Although we hear this sentiment often enough nowadays, reduction, *per se* cannot be a reason for introducing psychological constraints into linguistics. If it were, we would also have reason to introduce aesthetic or numerological constraints. The sentiment unwarrantedly assumes that psychological constraints are appropriate, which is just what is at issue.

It also assumes, and this point is less noticed in discussions of psychological constraints in linguistics, that a multiplicity of grammars or linguistic theories is in itself a bad thing. Why? Think of how many different (equivalent) theories of propositional calculus there are. Does this fact cause logicians sleepless nights? Why should the parallel case in linguistics cause the linguist sleepless nights? What is wrong with taking such equivalent theories, whether notational variants like a Polish notation formulation and a *Principia Mathematica* formulation of the same system, or equivalents like two axiomatizations of propositional logic with different but expressively equal sets of connectives, to be equally acceptable for linguistics?

We can sharpen this line of argument by specifying more precisely the appropriate sense of equivalence between theories:

(EQ)   Two grammars G_i and G_j of the same language L are equivalent theories of L if, and only if, G_i and G_j imply the same sets of evidence statements about the grammatical properties and relations of sentences in L, G_i and G_j provide equally good bases for explaining grammatical phenomena in L, and G_i and G_j are indistinguishable in terms of simplicity and other relevant canons of methodology.[13]

Grammars that are equivalent in the sense of *(EQ)* cannot be distinguished in terms of anything they say about the language they are theories of, nor is one distinguishable from the other on grounds of methodology. Neither can have any better claim to being the truth about the language than the other, so what sense does it make to say one is objectively correct as a theory of the language and the other not? It seems highly unreasonable to say that the one which meets psychological constraints is preferable *as a theory of the language.* Would the fact that a version of propositional calculus, say, in Polish notation, meets psychological constraints, while another version, say, in *Principia* notation, fails be a reason for the former's being preferable *as a theory of logical implication?*

Conceptualists have to say that there is a substantive *linguistic* choice between grammars that are variants in the sense of *(EQ)* even though the variants that are not psychologically real say exactly the same thing about the language as those that are. Since it would seem that what is relevant to judging a theory of a language like English is what the theory says about the language, the choice between equivalent theories ought not, contrary to what conceptualists claim, be a substantive choice for linguists. No one would suppose for a moment that a propositional logic expressed with just implication and negation is a better theory of truth-functional structure simply because it turns out to be psychologically real while equivalent logics expressed with other connectives are not. But if a preference for psychologically real theories over equivalent ones is wrongheaded in logic and mathematics why isn't the preference equally wrongheaded in linguistics? And if, as conceptualists say, the preference for psychologically real theories is rightheaded in linguistics, what makes it wrongheaded in logic and mathematics?

Let us extend this line of argument. Suppose the set of grammars $\{G_1, \ldots, G_n, \ldots\}$ contains all of the simplest grammars that predict and explain every grammatical fact about each sentence of English. It could happen that no grammar in the set satisfies the psychological constraints imposed by even the weakest version of conceptualism, none is realizable in the information processing system underlying human linguistic ability. Let us suppose further, as is clearly possible, that some grammar G^* which is outside $\{G_1, \ldots, G_n, \ldots\}$ is best as an empirical theory of the relevant aspects of this information processing system (either competence or performance). This could happen in three ways. First, G^* could be more complex than the grammars in $\{G_1, \ldots, G_n, \ldots\}$ but equivalent to them in predictive and explanatory power. There are two cases here. One is for the grammars $\{G_1, \ldots, G_n, \ldots\}$ to be expressed in a notation different from that in which G^* expressed, in the manner of the difference between Polish notation and *Principia Mathematica* notation, but where the notational complexity in the case of G^* far exceeds that of its logical counterpart in the comparison. The other is for G^* to use more complex rules, rules with more symbols, or more rules. For example, the basic operations out of which transformational rules in $\{G_1, \ldots, G_n, \ldots\}$ are composed might be deletion, copying, and insertion while those for the transformational rules in the case of G^* might be these plus the independent movement operation. In this example, G^* is more complex because copying and deletion together can reproduce the effect of a movement operation.

Now, *ex hypothesi* the psychological evidence shows that the tacit rules constituting the speaker-hearer's competence are best described by G^*,[14] even though the grammars in $\{G_1, \ldots, G_n, \ldots\}$ are simpler extrapolations from the facts about grammatical structure, that is, use the minimum necessary apparatus. Thus, the scientific choice between the grammar G^* and some grammar in $\{G_1, \ldots, G_n, \ldots\}$ thus reflects the higher conflict between the simplicity canon that figures standardly in linguistic practice and the native simplicity metric that conceptualists advocate. What do we say to resolve the conflict: that linguistic practice is not good enough for the discipline of psychology, or that the discipline of psychology is not the discipline of linguistics? Since the practice of linguists here is nothing more than a special case of good scientific practice generally, we have to reject the less parsimonious extrapolation G^* and resolve the higher conflict in favor of the canon that chooses the more parsimonious extrapolations. The stronger, psychological constraints that conceptualists impose on grammars are excessive in asking us to pass over the best scientific theories in favor of lesser ones.

Second, a grammar G^* can be as simple as the grammars in $\{G_1, \ldots, G_n, \ldots\}$ but differ from them in predictive and explanatory power; third, G^* can be both more complex and different in predictive and explanatory power. Since *ex hypothesi* $\{G_1, \ldots, G_n, \ldots\}$ contain the optimal grammars of the language, the cases in which G^*'s predictions diverge from theirs are cases in which G^* makes false predictions about the structure of sentences. These cases are especially interesting because they show that the grammatical component in the speaker-hearer's information processing mechanism can be a false theory of the grammatical structure of the language. Let us consider how this might happen. We are all familiar with the fact that computer and calculator companies sometimes construct these devices with functions that incorrectly determine values of arithmetic operations for cases of computations that will never arise in use. The companies do this because the incorrect functions are otherwise equivalent to the correct functions but more economical to build in or to operate with in on-line computations. The incorrect functions expedite construction or computation, posing no risk of error because the erroneous values can never be calculated within the operating range of the device. Now, since what Texas Instruments or Hewitt-Packard do as a matter of course God or Nature ought to be able to do in principle, it can happen that the grammatical component of our information processing mechanism makes false, though in performance underivable, predictions about the grammatical structure of sentences.[15]

Now, there can be no question in a case of this kind but that G^* has to be rejected as a theory of the language. It is false. Conceptualists, however, are forced to accept such false theories even though there are theories available that make no false predictions, since they have imposed their psychological constraints as a matter of philosophical principle. If conceptualists are serious about their philosophical commitments, they have to prefer G^* insofar as the psychological evidence has shown it to represent the cognitive structures underlying the speaker-hearer's use of language. Yet, in forcing them to prefer G^*, the conceptualists' philosophical commitment forces them to accept a false theory needlessly. This is surely a *reductio ad absurdum* of the philosophical commitment to conceptualism.

A conceptualist might respond that this type of counterexample is besides the point because such cases are only logical possibilities while conceptualism makes an empirical claim that theories in linguistics are about the mind or brain. Not at all. The conceptualist's claim is a claim about the scope of the empirical but is not itself an empirical claim. As we observed above, the issue between the conceptualist and Platonist is an *a priori* issue about whether linguistics is an empirical science or not, and hence, the conceptualist claim is an *a priori* claim. The decision to impose psychological constraints on theories in linguistics is made independently of empirical knowledge of the character of the cognitive states in question, and their imposition, being a consequence of *a priori* considerations to adopt a particular ontological position, must take the consequences with respect to logical possibilities. Since the imposition of these constraints is a decision to treat linguistics as empirical no matter what the character of these cognitive states turn out to be empirically, conceptualism has to stand behind its ontological position even if it turns out that such cognitive states falsely characterize the grammatical structure of some sentences.[16]

Hence, the decision to impose psychological constraints allows any features to count as grammatical aspects of the language so long as it is empirically shown that they reflect the appropriate mental or neural properties of the cognition of speakers. The various counterexamples that I have brought up show that it is possible for the speaker's cognitive states to contain a system of tacit linguistic principles outside the class of systems that correctly account for the structure of the language. Being *a priori* committed to claiming that, were things as they are hypothesized in these examples, it would be right to prefer G* over the grammars in $\{G_1, \ldots, G_n, \ldots\}$, conceptualism is shown inadequate even if by empirical coincidence G* is actually in $\{G_1, \ldots, G_n, \ldots\}$.

The reason for this excessiveness of psychological constraints on theories in linguistics is that, in making knowledge of a language—rather than the language it is knowledge of—the subject-matter of theories in linguistics, conceptualism commits such theories to having to reflect features of the particular psychological character of the medium in which the knowledge is realized. In the above counterexamples, I exploited the fact that, logically, the psychological character of the medium in which human knowledge of a language is realized might be any of a vast spectrum of logical possibilities. In the arguments below, I will exploit the closely related fact that, logically, there is a vast range of different possible mediums within which knowledge, albeit not human knowledge, of a language might be realized. No one, I take it, would be so chauvinistic as to insist that the particular mental or neural medium with which we as humans are endowed is the only one that could exist in intelligent creatures that communicate in English, French, and other natural languages. It is, then, clearly a possibility that the grammatical systems that can be realized in the mental or neural makeup of the different forms of intelligent life throughout the universe may differ radically.

Let us thus suppose we are visited by intelligent aliens from outer space, who can communicate with us in English just as well as we do with one another. Imagine that the aliens are indistinguishable from us in any Turing imitation game.[17] By ordinary standards, these creatures speak English. Now, suppose further that psychological and/or neurological examination shows that these creatures have minds or brains so radically different from human minds or brains that the grammatical systems realizable in theirs as knowledge of a natural language are nothing like the systems realizable in our minds or brains. Hence, their internal grammar of English is nothing like ours. Do the aliens speak English?

It is clear that conceptualists, since they take the possible grammars to be those that, in principle, are realizable within the human mind or brain, would have to answer that the aliens do not speak English. The extent of the differences between their grammatical system and ours can be as great as one likes, as long as the implications of the two systems coincide over a sufficiently large range of performance to make their utterances linguistically indistinguishable from ours. Hence, even though, judging by ordinary standards, everyone else would say the aliens speak English, the staunch conceptualist would have to make the counter-intuitive claim that they do not.

Conceptualists might try to minimize the counter-intuitiveness of their position by saying that these creatures speak a language closely related to English, one whose divergence from English is in relevant respects so slight that mutual intelligibility with speakers of English is not lost. This, however, concedes the Platonist's criticism by admitting criteria for distinguishing the genuinely grammatical aspects of internalized grammars (which differ so slightly as to be undiscoverable in any form of the Turing imitation game) from the merely psychological aspects (which *ex hypothesi* differ so greatly).[18] Moreover, the criteria on which we count ourselves as speakers of the same or a different natural language, say, as speakers of French but not Chinese, automatically counts these aliens as speakers of English, too. Our criterion for determining who speaks a natural language is simply a standard of mutual intelligibility something like

(MI) X and Y speak the same language L if X and Y can, in principle, pronounce any sentence of L (i.e., the sentences they stumble on or fail to pronounce are isolated cases or beyond their performance limits and can be explained away) and the best hypothesis about the verbal exchanges between X and Y is that they associate the same meanings with sentences (i.e., cases of comprehension failure can be explained away as due to extra-grammatical factors or normal departures from ideal knowledge of L).

The conceptualist cannot get around the conclusion that the aliens speak English by appealing to a theoretically concocted criterion for speaking the same language. Theories depend on evidence and evidence on native informants. The standard of mutual intelligibility also determines who can legitimately count as a native informant in the first place. Indeed, there is no reason why the creatures from outer space cannot serve just as well as any of us for the grammarian of English. If, by accident, a comprehensive grammar of English were based only on evidence from these aliens, there would be no grounds for denying its status as a correct grammar of English once we learn that no human happened to serve as a native informant. Would anyone say that it was not Sanskrit but some other language by the same name if historians were to find out that the native speakers of Sanskrit were not really humans but aliens from outer space who came to India in the 3d century?

A grammar written for the language the aliens speak, assuming they speak intelligibly with us and we with them in the sense of *(MI)*, is as much a grammar of English as a grammar written for the language we speak in speaking intelligibly with one another. This point can be sharpened. Surely it is possible that, unbeknownst to us, some of us undergo severe brain changes (due to, say, special prenatal conditions, radiation, or pesticides in the environment). These changes affect the structures that realize linguistic competence and make a small number of us, you, I, Chomsky, and a few others, as different linguistically from the rest of English speaking humanity as the alien creatures. Nobody knows about our alienization because the changes are unobservable. So we go our merry way. I read Chomsky *in English* and write criticisms *in English* of his views about what grammars are theories of; and you read me *in English* and criticize my claims *in English*. Or, at least this is what we take ourselves to be doing. When the truth about our brain changes comes to light, the staunch conceptualist will say that neither you, nor I, nor Chomsky really spoke and wrote English. This is, of course, outlandish. We do not just think we are speaking and writing in English, we are and know it.[19]

The claim that the grammar of English is the theory of the cognitive structures which underlie the *human* English speaker's fluency is thus too arbitrarily chauvinistic to be accepted. No single system of cognitive structures from among the enormous range underlying the communicative abilities of humans, aliens, mutated humans, etc. can be relevantly and non-self-defeatingly distinguished from the others. On the other hand, an ecumenical conceptualist claim that the psychological theories of all such cognitive structures are equally the grammar of English won't do either. Collectively, these theories contain all sorts of inconsistencies. Recall, for example, the earlier point about G^* making false predictions or having rules constructed out of different sets of primitives. There are also incompatibilities between aspects of the mental or neural structures in these various groups of creatures. We cannot abstract away from them without abstracting away from the psychological medium in which competences are realized and paying attention only to invariances across the range of cognitive systems that reflect the grammatical properties and relations of English sentences. Such abstraction would collapse conceptualism into Platonism.

The conceptualist's psychological constraints on grammars are excessive, then, because they require that a grammar represent a language only in the particular form that knowledge of the language takes when such knowledge is realized in the human mind or brain. The constraints impose a ceiling on the level of abstractness grammars can attain by requiring their representations to reflect the specific psychology of one class of creatures capable of having knowledge of a natural language. Though not nearly as excessive as the nominalist's constraints, the conceptualist's are still excessive. There is no reason why linguistics has to settle for less than the best theories, even if less is not nearly so bad as what came before.[20]

Notes

1. This claim is perhaps what Hjelmslev had in mind in writing, "As phonemes are linguistic elements, it follows that no phoneme can be correctly defined except by linguistic criteria, i.e., by means of its function in the language. No extra-linguistic criteria can be relevant, i. e., neither physical nor physiological nor psychological". See Hjelmslev 1936: 49.

2. Quine, in a different context, makes what I take it is the same point when he says that scientists who can describe the behavior of the objects they study but do not know what kinds of things those objects are are in a "theoretically unsatisfactory situation". Quine 1961f: 47. ("The Problem of Meaning in Linguistics")

3. In 1908 the German professor Paul Wolfshehl created a prize of 100,000 marks for the first person to prove Fermat's last theorem. See Bell 1937: 72.

4. There seems to be no real account of human arithmetical competence or human logical competence in psychology. But this is surely just a matter of the direction that psychology has taken, a historical accident, as it were. There could be such theories, and even theories of the initial competence underlying the acquisition or arithmetic and logical competence. Piaget's research is easily seen as a contribution to their development. See Piaget 1965 and also Osherson, 1974; Osherson 1975; Osherson 1976.

5. Chomsky 1975c: 299–320.

6. Chomsky 1957: 49.

7. Chomsky 1980c.

8. Chomsky 1980a: 217.

9. Chomsky 1980a: 217–220.

10. Chomsky 1975b: 37.

11. Statements like Chomsky's that "A theory of performance (production or perception) will have to incorporate the theory of competence—the generative grammar of a language—as an essential part" (Chomsky 1967a: 435–436) make the acceptability of a formal theory of psychologically realized knowledge explicitly depend on the theory's being a faithful model of the relevant cognitive or neural structures in the same sense in which, say, Crick's and Watson's double helix model is a faithful model of the structure of DNA.

12. Chomsky 1976: 12–13.

13. Examples of equivalent quantification theories arising from different choices of connectives and quantifiers for their primitive bases suggest examples of equivalent grammars arising from different choices of phonological, syntactic, and/or semantic primitives. A somewhat different example of equivalent grammars would arise if the transformations of a language neither decrease nor increase syntactic information relevant to semantic interpretation. Then, we could construct variants that are exactly

the same except that the semantic rules of one grammar apply exclusively at the level of deep syntactic structure while the other's apply exclusively at the level of surface syntactic structure. There is clearly a wide variety of ways in which equivalent theories can differ.

14. For illustration of how psychological data can bear on this question see Mayer, Erreich, and Valian 1978.

15. Empirical science can in principal establish that the syntactic rules constituting the speaker-hearer's competence conflict with the theory that is the simplest and predictively best account of the language, even though those rules and that theory may predict the same facts in all observable cases. We can in principle check the circuitry.

16. Indeed, if by some miracle the true theory of the cognitive states underlying the speaker's use of language were to coincide perfectly in all its predictions with the grammars in $\{G_1, \ldots, G_n, \ldots\}$ this would no more support the *a priori* claim of conceptualists than would the coextensionality of "creature with a heart" and "creature with a kidney" support the claim that these expressions are synonymous.

17. Turing 1950.

18. It would also give away the show if the conceptualist were to reply that such unlimited differences in the psychology of these races do not count because sameness of language is really a matter of the grammatical properties and relations being predicted in the same way by the internalized systems. This, too, abandons the heart of the conceptualistic claim that linguistics is psychology.

19. Some variations on this example: If such a change took place in your brain last night, then you spoke English up to last night, but you no longer do. If such a change were to occur, then disappear, and then recur, cyclically, you would be switching languages regularly. Further, if such a change were to take place in one part of your brain while the grammatical structures in another (functionally autonomous) part remained like those of ordinary terrestrial speakers of English, the conceptualist would have to say that you have become bilingual.

20. It might be thought that this argument proves too much because, if sound, it shows that neither the theory of the alien's cognitive system nor the theory of ours can be correct to the exclusion of the other, and therefore no theory can be *the* correct grammar of English. But, although there will be no unique correct grammar of English, there is nothing here to preclude a number of grammars from being correct grammars of English. All of them can be optimal in the sense of *(D5')* and equivalent in the sense of *(EQ)*. Why is this not enough for the view that linguistics is a branch of mathematics?

IV

Conceptualist Skepticism about Meaning

Introduction

This chapter prepares the way for the argument in the next by showing that conceptualist criticisms of meaning and analyticity are untenable. Such preparation is necessary because in the present climate of opinion skepticism about meaning is taken quite seriously. In this introduction, I will explain why I have in part rested my case for Platonism on notions about which there is antecedent skepticism.

The argument set out in the next chapter assumes that grammars have a level of semantic representation at which the analyticity of sentences is marked and linguistic theory has a component semantic theory that defines analyticity. Given these assumptions, the argument shows that conceptualism's ceiling on the abstractness of theories in linguistics limits their explanation of analyticity to accounts that fail to do justice to the most important facts about the logical structure of natural language. The argument is a full development of the argument presented in the introduction that conceptualism offers us nothing stronger than a nativistic account of how human beings might be genetically programmed to think that some class of propositions true no matter what, but offers us no account of what it is for propositions to be true no matter what. Real necessary truth is not relativized to what is humanly conceivable, even as genetically determined. Nor is it relativized to what may be thinkable in terms of what our genetic endowment might become under nomologically possible evolution. Real necessity sets absolute limits for all thought, and hence, conceptualism falls short of what is required to explain the necessary truths expressed by the analytic sentences of natural languages.

Now, since this argument concerns itself exclusively with analytic truth, one might well wonder about the prudence of relying on it in the present climate of skepticism about meaning. One might think it would be better to make the anti-conceptualist argument in connection with logical truth or some other species of necessary truth about which there is less antecedent doubt. But the trouble with such an alternative argument—which indeed is already available in Frege's criticisms of psychologism[1]—is that it shows nothing about the failure of conceptualism *as an interpretive policy for theories of natural languages*. Arguments about logical and mathematical truths may show that conceptualism is inadequate for logic and mathematics, but they would not establish its inadequacy for linguistics. The reason is that logical truths like Peirce's law or DeMorgan's theorem and mathematical principles like induction or Fermat's theorem are not matters of language but matters of theory.[2] Their truth does not rest on the grammatical structure of natural language, but on logical or mathematical fact. Accordingly, if we are trying to establish the failure of conceptualism in linguistics, we have to construct an argument in connection with the kind of necessary truths that owe their apoditic character to language alone, and this means that the argument has to be based on analytic truth even though there is less antecedent doubt about other species of necessary truth. The only reasonable strategy is to try to remove the grounds for the skepticism about analyticity.

The approach I will take is to examine such skepticism as it is expressed in performancist and competencist positions in the philosophy of linguistics. This expression, as it turns out, introduces the philosophically more familiar skepticism of Quine and others. Thus, our examination will not neglect any of the grounds on which semantic skepticism rests.

Performancist Skepticism

I have chosen Fodor, Fodor, and Garrett's (henceforth "FFG") version of performancist skepticism as representative of this form of skepticism.[3] One reason for this choice is that their version is the most clearly and systematically developed version of performancist criticism that I am aware of. Another reason is that FFG's version is philosophically, and in certain respects psychologically, more sophisticated than other versions. Still another reason is that FFG set out their version as an attack on the existence of a level of semantic representation in grammars. Replying to their position from a competencist standpoint, we can both eliminate this performancist objection to semantic representation and show that competencism is the stronger version of conceptualism. Finally, in the course of their attack, FFG raise the issue of whether analytic truth is different from other forms of necessary truth. This enables us to further explain the language/theory distinction.

FFG state their performancism as a psychological reality requirement on the semantic level of representation in grammars.[4] The requirement is that such a level ought, *inter alia,* to satisfy *(A)*. The

(A)   Semantic representations are psychologically real in the sense that, given appropriate idealizations, understanding a sentence requires the recovery of its semantic representation.[5]

requirement is a special case of a general requirement on the psychological reality of all levels of grammatical representation:[6]

The sort of psychological reality claim that *A* expresses is presumably not specific to the semantic level. In fact, those who hold that the semantic level ought to satisfy *A* usually do so because they endorse the psychological reality of structural descriptions at all the levels that the grammar postulates.[7]

There are a number of defects in the generalization of *(A)* as a performancist requirement on grammars. A major one is that it fails to mention sentence production, language acquisition, or grammatical operations in speech recognition.[8] It singles out speech recognition for a special position as touchstone of psychological reality without there being a relevant difference between this area of performance and any other to base the distinction in position on. A non-arbitrary performancism would treat all performance areas alike.

Another defect in FFG's formulation of the performancist position is its insistence on recovery of a representation for it to count as psychologically real. Why is actual recovery necessary? Suppose there is a feature of, say, semantic representation that is neither encoded in speech production or recovered in comprehension, but which, nonetheless, has to be referred to in an explanation of what is encoded or recovered. It seems implausible, on the generally anti-instrumentalist line, that such a feature should *ipso facto* be treated as not having psychological reality. Hence *(A)* ought to be reformulated as *(A')*.

(A')   A grammar of a language *L* must be psychologically real in the sense that the distinctions it makes figure in the explanation of on-line computations (as linguistic determinates) in the speech production and comprehension of sentences of *L*.

Having reformulated *(A)* as *(A')*, consistency dictates *(A")*

(A") A linguistic theory must be psychologically real in the sense that the distinctions it makes must figure in the explanation of the on-line computations in the process by which the language learner selects a grammar (in the sense of *(A')*) based on an exposure to the sentences of a language.

Semantic representations are psychologically real if and only if they appear in a psychologically real grammar in the sense of (A') or in a psychologically real linguistic theory in the sense of (A").

But it is the psychological reality constraint *(A)* rather than *(A')* that is assumed in FFG's argument against a level of semantic representation: the argument is that there is no evidence for and evidence against the claim that understanding involves recovery of semantic representations. Hence, the defects which make it necessary to replace *(A)* with *(A')* and *(A")* refute the argument at the outset. Assuming for the sake of argument that semantic representations are not recovered in understanding sentences, they might, nevertheless, be psychologically real *in the performancist's sense* without actually being recovered by virtue of being encoded in production or playing a role in language acquisition or figuring in the explanation of the understanding of sentences. Therefore, FFG's argument is too narrowly conceived, even on strictly performancist grounds, to support its sweeping conclusion about the unreality of semantic representations.

Let us now drop the issue between *(A)* and *(A')* and turn to a different set of objections to FFG's position. *(A)* is an essential link in FFG's argument. It enables them to argue from *psychological data* about how people behave in their use of language to the conclusion that there is *linguistic evidence* against the level of semantic representation in grammars. Without this link, psychological evidence of this sort need have no more bearing on the existence of a semantic level than hiccups, belches, wheezes, and snorts have on the existence of a phonological level. FFG's argument, logically speaking, requires an explanation of why a position that rejects *(A)* as a criterion of what is relevant to the existence of a grammatical level is unacceptable. Since FFG fail to provide such an explanation, the argument is unconvincing.

The ordinary linguist's view of a grammar is that a grammar is a theory of a natural language, and nothing more. It seeks to predict every grammatical property and relation of every sentence, explain puzzling facts about linguistic structure, and to do these things as a good scientific theory ought to do them. On such a view, the grammar generates semantic representations and pairs them with meaningful sentences as its basis for predicting semantic properties like the ambiguity of "bank" and relations like the synonymy of "halatosis" and "bad breath". Questions of the role of grammatical representations in speech production or comprehension do not enter the picture. The correctness of the predictions of such semantic properties and relations are judged on the basis of the intuitions of fluent speakers about the structure of sentences, in abstraction from the influence of performance variables.

This "ordinary linguist's view" precludes (A) as a criterion for the adequacy of a grammar; those who accept the view will find FFG's argument unconvincing because it fails to allow for this abstraction. FFG consider this view of grammars in their "overview",[9] but the only reason they offer for their claim that it is unsatisfactory is its Platonistic character. In particular, they pose the issue as a choice between their position, which they claim is methodologically respectable, and a Platonized version of the "ordinary linguist's view", which they claim is methodological mysticism. But FFG's identification of this ordinary view with Platonism is surely mistaken. Non-Platonists can take this view just as well. Indeed, J. A. Fodor and M. F. Garrett once took the view themselves without adopting Platonism. They wrote:

It should be emphasized that, in showing a predicted complexity order fails to obtain, one has not shown that the grammar is disconfirmed. A grammar is simply an axiomatic representation of an infinite set of structural descriptions, and the internal evidence in favor of the structural descriptions modern grammars generate is so strong that it is difficult to imagine their succumbing to any purely experimental disconfirmation. Rather, one would best interpret negative data as showing that an acceptable theory of the relation between competence and performance models will have to represent that relation as abstract, the degree of abstractness being proportional to the failure of formal features of derivations to correspond to performance variables.[10]

Given a form of the ordinary view distinct from the Platonist form, the fact that FFG argue only against a Platonist form means that the essential step in their argument from psychological data about performance to linguistic evidence about the grammar is not valid. Even assuming that FFG are right about Platonism, there are still grounds for concluding that performance data of the kind they rest their argument on are not relevant to matters of grammar.

Consequently, FFG are in no position to claim, as they do, that they have exclusive rights to a criterion of psychological reality. FFG say that their constraint *(A)* ". . . assigns semantic representations a role in the comprehension of sentences", and that this role, together with their role in "other psychological states or computations", constitutes their sole claim to existence in the grammar.[11] But Chomsky's competencist criterion of psychological reality provides another basis for such claims. This criterion rests on a conception of the grammar, not as a theory of the language user, but as a theory of the speaker's idealized knowledge of the language. FFG's narrow on-line notion of reality is thus irrelevant. The competencist's idealization goes beyond the idealizations involved in constructing a performance model. Chomsky makes clear that a grammar in his sense idealizes away also from the aspects of idealized performance necessary to a performance model. Chomsky's notion of "an ideal speaker-listener . . . who knows the language perfectly" involves abstractions from "such grammatically irrelevant conditions as memory limitations, distractions, shifts of attention and interest", and "errors (random and characteristic) in applying his knowledge of the language in actual performance".[12]

Thus, on-line type constraints are replaced by constraints that follow from the competencist's conception of the abstract cognitive representation of grammatical structure. *(A)* is replaced by *(R)*:

(R) A grammar of a language must be psychologically real as an abstract representation of the knowledge an ideal speaker-hearer has of the grammatical properties and relations of the sentences of the language.

Therefore, the following general criticisms can be made of FFG's arguments. Since *(A)* cannot be justified as the only alternative to a Platonist interpretation of grammars, or even as the only psychologically oriented alternative, there is no support for FFG's premiss that psychological data about performance is linguistic evidence against a level of semantic representation. Indeed, on the competencist alternative, psychological data of the kind that FFG's arguments appeal to, namely, data concerning on-line events involving high speed speech operations—error and reaction scores—is just the kind that ought not count as linguistic evidence about representation in grammars. For competencists, such data reflect only aspects of the way language users employ their knowledge in on-line tasks rather than aspects of what an ideal speaker-listener knows about the grammatical structure of the language. Accordingly, the competencist can give *a priori* grounds for idealizing away from just the data on which FFG base their arguments. The grounds are a principle like *(M)* relating idealized conditions to actual ones:

(M) As actual conditions more closely approximate to ideal ones, the predictions of the laws formulated over ideal objects to actual observations more closely approximate.

Now the actual conditions in the experiments that FFG cite, and even in normal language use, involve high speed calculation of responses to complex situations, and hence such conditions do not approximate very closely to the ideal ones employed in the formulation of the ideal speaker-hearer construct. Quite the contrary. Thus, it is natural to expect that, under such extreme divergence, grammatical information available to the language user will assume a heuristically abbreviated, and in many respects incomplete, form. This is the crux of the idea underlying heuristic programming models: such information could hardly serve the purpose of expediting on-line processing if it didn't take forms that are poor reflections of the too rich information in a full grammar. Error scores, reaction time differences, and similar measures reflect the heuristically abbreviated form of the language user's information and the exigencies of actual performance and are, therefore, no grounds in themselves for inferences about the proper form of a grammar for a language.[13]

We turn now to the particular arguments FFG make against semantic representation. They term the position that endorses semantic representation "the analytic approach". This approach, which has been traditionally been called "intensionalism", holds the following principles. First, meaning is not reducible to something else. Meaning itself is the proper object of study in linguistic semantics. Second, linguistic semantics is as much a part of grammar as syntax. Third, the aim of linguistic semantics is to deepen our pretheoretic understanding of meaning by developing a formal, theoretical account of the semantic structure of sentences, like that which grammar gives of their phonological and syntactic structure. Fourth, meaning is the aspect of sentence structure responsible for synonymy relations, meaningfulness, meaninglessness, ambiguity, redundancy, and other semantic properties and relations in natural languages. Fifth, the meaning of a sentence and its logical form are identical; linguistics thus describes the level of the grammatical structure that determines the application of laws of logic to sentences. Together, linguistics and logic provide, on the intensionalist view, an explanation of the basis for logical inference in natural language.

FFG characterize the analytic approach as having the aim of constructing a semantic level in grammars at which the representations assigned to sentences meet the conditions (B) and (C).[14]

(B) Semantic properties and relations of sentences, in particular, their entailment relations, must be definable over semantic representations.

(C) Some syntactically simple lexical items are explicated in semantic representations as having the same semantic structure as syntactically complex phrases of the language.

They claim that the analytic approach is "inherently unable to account for a variety of pertinent facts about the way people understand sentences".[15] These "pertinent facts" are supposed to provide two kinds of evidence, "intuitive evidence" and "experimental evidence", against the analytic approach. The argument from this evidence is intended to establish the desirability, first, of grammars without a semantic level, that is, without a level at which the *meanings* of sentences are represented, and second, of a theory of the comprehension of sentences which states the speaker's knowledge of reference not in terms of semantically determined extensions but in terms of so-called "meaning postulates" that directly connect linguistic objects with their extensions.[16] I will present their claims regarding intuitive and experimental evidence in turn, following each with specific criticisms. Then I will develop criticisms that apply equally to the arguments from both kinds of evidence.

FFG claim that, although the analytic approach predicts an asymmetry in the complexity of sentences like (1) and (2),

(1) Cats chase mice

(2) Cats catch mice

because of the greater decompositional richness of "chase" compared to "catch", people do not in fact intuitively detect this asymmetry. Judgments based on intuition, FFG claim, disconfirm the predicted complexity order, relative to a criterion like:

(D) All other things equal, the relative complexity of a pair of sentences should be a function of the relative complexity of the definitions of the words that the sentences contain.[17]

One trouble with this claim is that it is unclear what FFG are referring to under the term "intuition". On the one hand, they might mean people's awareness of the underlying grammatical structure of sentences. If this is what FFG mean, then their mere claim that intuitions about cases like *(1)* and *(2)* or "bachelor" and "unmarried" "do not appear to support the asymmetries of semantic complexity that definitional theories predict" is hardly credible.[18] The examples in question are standard cases in the literature. Therefore, if a sizable number of people had not had exactly the intuition that definitional theories predict, the hue and cry would surely have gone up long ago.

When FFG switch to the examples *(1')* and *(2')*

(1') The man hit the ball

(2') A man hit a ball

and claim that although the analytic approach predicts that sentences with definite articles ought to be more complex than corresponding ones with indefinite articles, "Patently, intuition does not support any such differences in complexity", their account of what people's intuitions are is credible.[19] However, now the dubious part of their claim is why they should think that the analytic approach, which is intensionalist, is committed to Russell's extensionalist definitions of the definite and indefinite article, on which the counter-intuitive complexity predictions depend. Russell's definitions give, not an analysis of the senses of a sentence like *(1')* or *(2')* but only an extensional account, another sentence that will be true and false under the same conditions.[20] Such definitions are a truly bizarre account to foist on an approach that seeks to represent senses and takes synonymy as the condition for identity of sense.

On the other hand, FFG might be using "intuition" to refer to people's estimate of the difficulty in understanding sentences. On this construal, however, intuitive judgments are irrelevant to the point at issue: the issue is about the structure of sentences in the language while the judgments are about subjective states, the informant's sense of the difficulty in comprehension.[21] The judgment that a sentence like *(1)* is as easy to understand as a sentence like *(2)* is essentially different from a genuinely grammatical judgment like the judgment that the noun phrase "the ball" is a syntactic component of the verb phrase in *(1')* or the judgment that the sense of "try to catch" is a semantic component of the sense of "chase". Judgments about relative difficulty in comprehension are introspective reports, like judgments about thoughts, feelings, and imaginings. They report about subjective experience, while a judgment that *(1)* does not semantically entail *(2)* states an objective fact of English. If today I make one judgment about the relative difficulty of understanding two sentences and tomorrow or a year from now I make the opposite judgment, both judgments can be correct. But if today I make one judgment about a grammatical relation between two sentences and tomorrow or a year later I make the opposite judgement, only one judgment can be correct. The compatibility of the former judgments is due to the possibility that I may change and this reveals that the judgments are about my subjective states. The incompatibility of the latter judgments shows that they are not about something subjective but about an objective fact of English. Since the analytic approach concerns the facts of English whereas the "intuitive evidence" concerns subjective experience, FFG's claim, on this sense of "intuition", is irrelevant to the truth of the analytic approach.

FFG also claim to have experimental evidence that words like "bachelor" and "kill" cannot be handled by the analytic approach.[22] FFG call such words "purely definitional negatives" ("PDN" for short) because, according to the analytic approach, they contain morphologically unrealized negative elements. On the one hand, PDN's contrast with "explicitly negative free morphemes" such as "not" and with "morphological negatives" such as "unhappy" or "impossible". On the other hand, PDN's contrast with "implicit negatives" such as verbs like "doubt", "deny", and "fail". The distinguishing feature of implicit negatives is that their "scope exhibits such typical reflexes of negation as *any, much, give a damn*, etc.". A special syntactic relation governs the co-occurrence of these negatives with other constituents.

On the assumption that "bachelor" is synonymous with "unmarried adult human male" and "Brutus killed Caesar" semantically entails "Brutus caused Caesar not to be alive", the analytic approach holds that the semantic representations of "bachelor" and "kill" contain negative elements.[23] FFG do not present experimental data to support their claim that PDN's do not contain a negative element. Their findings consist of reaction times to correct evaluations of the validity of arguments like *(3)* and *(4)* involving PDN's and explicit negative constructions.

(3) If practically all of the men in the room are not married, then few of the men in the room have wives.

(4) If practically all of the men in the room are bachelors, then few of the men in the room have wives.

Comparing reaction times of subjects, it was found that reaction times were faster for sentences like *(4)* with PDN's in them. FFG put their results as follows:

Arguments containing PDN's . . . were significantly easier than the paired arguments containing explicit negatives. Moreoever, and most important, the differences between PDN's and explicit negatives was significantly greater than the differences between explicit negatives and either implicit or morphological negatives.[24]

FFG take these results to constitute evidence against the analytic approach.

Even granting all their background assumptions, this is not so. These results can be explained *consistently with* everything that the analytic approach says about words like "bachelor" and "kill". For such results would be expected just from the fact that it takes longer to perform more syntactic operations than less. Since in the case of *(3)* subjects are required to look up three morphemes, namely, "not", "marry", and "-ed", while in the case of *(4)* they are required to look up only two, namely, "bachelor" and 'Plural', *(4)* ought to be the easier of the two arguments to evaluate. Similarly, we would also expect the morphological negatives and the implicit negatives to line up with the explicit negatives in this contrast, since they, too, require subjects to perform extra syntactic computations. Such computations are required because of the special syntactic restrictions imposed by implicit negatives on appropriate constituents in their scope.[25]

Now we turn to the general criticisms of FFG's arguments. We note again that these arguments are intended to establish the superiority of their extensionalist approach using meaning postulates over the intensionalist analytic approach. The arguments make no sense unless they are designed to show that the meaning postulate approach is a better account of the evidence. But, as comparative, these arguments are logically incoherent because the evidence in question, if sound, would count equally against both approaches—and for the same reason. Both approaches assume that, for any item, there are a fixed number of independent properties that constitute the minimum required to determine the implications depending on the item's logical structure. The analytic approach represents the item in the form of a semantic representation containing a semantic marker for each such property. The meaning postulate approach represents the item with a meaning postulate for each such property, (for example, a statement of the form $'(x)(I_x \supset E_x)'$, where "I" is the item and "E" an expression in the language coextensive with one of the properties). Thus, on both approaches, whenever there is an implication relation between an item and some expression, if the relation is not explainable on the semantic specifications already given, a further semantic specification must be provided. Otherwise, the account of implication is incomplete. Assuming completeness, the formalization in both approaches will contain the same number of semantic specifications. Since, moreover, there is no reason why the computation of n meaning postulates should take less time than the computation of n semantic markers,[26] FFG also have to predict that the reaction time of subjects to *(4)* is no faster than to *(3)*. Hence, their experimental evidence cannot in principle establish the superiority of their approach to lexical structure.[27]

My second general criticism is that FFG's arguments mistakenly assume that relative complexity is a semantic relation under *(B)*. Since it is this assumption that enables them to say that semantic representations are obligated to predict differences in relative complexity of senses, if the assumption is false, intuitive and experimental evidence showing that semantic representations do not predict relative complexity as well as do meaning postulates cannot establish the inferiority of the analytic approach. If I am right that complexity is not a semantic relation, then the analytic approach can no more be considered deficient for not predicting differences in relative complexity than it can for not predicting differences in I.Q. scores or hair color.

FFG's mistake is due to their failure to draw the distinction between what can be *predicted* from a formal representation (at a grammatical level) and what may be *calculated* from the representation. The distinction can be illustrated in connection with the familiar tree representation of phrase structure. The representations of two sentences S_1 and S_2 may enable us to calculate that S_1 contains exactly 17,375,031 morphemes more than S_2, or that the ratio of phrases to clauses in S_1 is the same as the ratio of occurrences of "fudge" in S_1 to occurrences of "jellybeans" in S_2, but these facts about S_1 and S_2 are not predicted by the grammar. The point is that what a formalism for a grammatical level predicts depends on what grammatical properties and relations are defined at that level. Syntactic notions like 'well-formed', 'subject-of', 'interrogative', and 'imperative' are defined at the syntactic level, and hence, syntactic representations of S_1 and S_2 can be expected to predict whether they are well-formed, whether they have the same subject, whether they are interrogatives or imperatives, and so on. The features of a formalism that can be said to *predict* are the configurations of symbols that enter into the definitions of the appropriate grammatical properties and relations. Such features are only a small proper subset of those appearing in the formalism. A great many relations in grammatical representations make no direct contribution to the predictive power of a grammar.

Relative complexity of sense is one such relation. Suppose that we have semantic representations of "chase" and "catch", say R_1 and R_2, that are the simplest formalisms that explicate the contributions of the senses of these words to the meanings of sentences. Suppose also that R_1 represents a more complex sense than R_2. If the relation of relative complexity of sense is not in the set of semantic properties and relations, then what can be calculated about relative complexity on the basis of R_1 and R_2 is *per se* irrelevant to confirming or disconfirming what R_1 and R_2 claim about the meaning of "chase" and "catch". Even though we can calculate complexity differences from such semantic representations and compare the results with data about the complexity of sentences like *(1)* and *(2)*, we obtain no evidence (pro or con) about the semantic hypotheses R_1 and R_2.

To determine that a relation like relative complexity is outside the set of semantic properties and relations, we have to show that the class of pretheoretically clear cases of semantic properties and relations does not contain the relation in question and that no legitimate extension of the class does either. We can assume that the pretheoretically clear cases of semantic properties and relations include synonymy, ambiguity, meaningfulness, semantic anomaly, and such. We can also assume that the controversial case of relative complexity is not a pretheoretically clear case. The issue, then, comes down to whether there is a legitimate extension of these clear cases that includes the relation of relative complexity.

Before demonstrating that there is no such extension, it should be noted that what we have said so far already reveals a gap in FFG's argument. What we have said shows that their argument has to supply a reason for thinking that relative complexity is a semantic relation. Since they fail to provide a reason for believing it to be a relation for which semantic representations must account, they have failed to provide grounds for taking their data to be evidence against the analytic approach.

To show, on our side, that there is no legitimate extension of the pretheoretically clear cases that includes 'x is a more complex sense than y' among the semantic properties and relations, we require a principle to determine when the addition of a new property or relation further articulates the domain picked out by the pretheoretically clear cases and when the addition causes it to overstep its boundaries. J. A. Fodor himself suggests the right principle. He writes:

> . . . a science has to discover what it is about; it does so by discovering that the laws and concepts it produced in order to explain one set of phenomena can be fruitfully applied to phenomena of other sorts as well.[28]

Sciences, Fodor is saying, ultimately learn what they have to explain by determining what further phenomena fit the pattern of what they have thus far successfully explained.

But what about the things a science does not have to explain? It is clear that we cannot conclude that a new phenomenon is outside the domain of a science from the fact that the phenomenon does not fit the pattern of what has thus far been successfully explained. We don't *know* whether explanation has as yet gone far enough. But, this being so, we can surely use the very reasons we have for thinking that we have gone far enough to argue that a new phenomenon that fails to fit the explanatory pattern to which the clear cases have been shown to conform is outside the domain of the science. We thus arrive at the principle *Z:*

(*Z*) A property or relation *K* not belonging to the set of clear cases of semantic properties and relations is semantic if, and only if, the clear cases and those established as extensions of them are representative and their definitions enable us to define *K*.

We may illustrate the application of *(Z)*. Since synonymy, ambiguity, meaningfulness, meaninglessness, and analyticity are a representative set of clear cases of semantic properties and relations, we can show that the property of redundancy is semantic but the relation of rhyme is not. Redundancy is the property exhibited by *(5)* but not *(6)*.

(*5*) naked nude

(*6*) naked nudist

Given *(Z)* and the definition of synonymy,[29] *(7)* shows that redundancy

(*7*) A modifier-head construction *E* is redundant if, and only if, *E* is synonymous with the head of the construction.

is semantic. No such definition will be possible for rhyme because rhyme is a correspondence of terminal sounds, but the definitions of synonymy, ambiguity, meaningfulness, and so on do not refer to representations of sound at all. Since such definitions do not enable us to define rhyme, by *(Z)*, rhyme is a non-semantic relation.

Now to show that relative complexity, like rhyme, is non-semantic. If the definitions of synonymy, ambiguity, meaningfulness, and so on do not permit us to formulate a condition that determines exactly the set of ordered pairs of senses for which '*x* is a more complex sense than *y*' holds, then that relation is non-semantic. First of all, note that it will be possible to formulate a sufficient condition for the one proper subset containing pairs of senses like that of ''bachelor'' and ''male''. In such cases, the condition for one sense to be as complex as another is identity, and the condition for one to be more complex than another is that the former includes but is not included in the latter. But the extension of $'x$ is a more complex sense than y' contains indefinitely many pairs of senses outside this proper subset. In such cases, neither sense is identical to a component of the other, and the apparatus for determining sense inclusion and instances of the same sense does not enable us to formulate the required condition. To determine the extension of $'x$ is a more complex sense than y' for these cases, it is necessary to go beyond this apparatus by introducing a device to count the components in the formal representation of each sense and then compute their complexity ordering. The fact that such a counter is necessary means that the definitions of the semantic properties and relations do not suffice to define the relation of relative complexity of senses. Thus, (Z) permits us to infer that on present evidence the relation is non-semantic.

This last phase of the argument is parallel to Chomsky's argument that the complexity of center-embedding in sentences is a performance rather than a competence phenomenon.[30] Chomsky points out that the aspects of structural descriptions that define syntactic properties and relations do not suffice to determine differences in the amount of center-embedding (correlating with differences in degree of intelligibility). He argues that in order to make such determinations it would be necessary to go beyond standard syntactic apparatus by introducing a counter to compute the number of center-embeddings in a sentence (comparing the result of such a computation with the results of others or with some constant—like the upper bound on storage in immediate memory—in order to determine the point of unintelligibility absolutely).[31] Chomsky resists the introduction of such novel apparatus into syntactic theory, choosing instead to treat these unintelligible sentences as a matter of extra-grammatical factors. His rationale is that to handle such unintelligibility as a case of ungrammaticality would require a radical and ad hoc change in syntactic theory, but by treating the unintelligibility as unacceptability rather than as ungrammaticality it is possible to avoid such a change and to provide a natural explanation of the phenomenon in terms of the procedures language users employ in syntactic recognition. Needless to say, we likewise recommend a performance account of phenomena that are effects of semantic complexity.

FFG end their discussion with some considerations that they think support their approach over the analytic approach. The first such consideration is that ". . . no a priori reason exists for drawing the line between comprehension and inference at the point that A-C specify rather than at some other point".[32] As a claim about performance, this is hardly exciting. It is difficult to imagine how there could be an a *priori* way of separating aspects of the on-line processing of sentences in speech into those that are a matter of comprehension and those that are a matter of inference. But, as a claim about grammar, FFG's claim is more interesting but false.

This issue is this. If, as FFG claim, there is no distinction between analytic entailments like *(8)* and logical implications like *(9)*, then

(8)   John is a bachelor
      Therefore, John is unmarried

(9)   John is a bachelor
      Therefore, John is a bachelor or a bartender

meaning postulates are the proper apparatus for the linguist and logician. This is because meaning postulates treat such cases uniformly (i.e., it was Carnap's idea to extend the treatment of logical relations to meaning relations by modeling postulates for the latter on logical postulates). On the other hand, if there is a distinction between analytic entailments like *(8)* and logical implications like *(9)*, such that the former hold solely by virtue of meaning while the latter hold also by virtue of the existence of a law of logic (e.g., $p \supset (p \vee q)$ in the case of (9)), then semantic representations are the proper apparatus, since they treat such cases as fundamentally different.

FFG offer neither an argument to support their claim nor an explanation of why they fail to count the arguments for the distinction on the part of various philosophers, such as Wittgenstein,[33] as at least providing *prima facie* reason for separating cases like (8) and (9). The explanation is perhaps that the influential Fregean dogma that analyticity is only a species of logical truth, which is widely believed nowadays, makes it seem unnecessary to do so.[34]

There are three criticisms of the Fregean dogma. First, Frege's assimilation of analyticity to logical truth was entirely gratuitous, and the same is true of the same assimilation by those, like Quine, who follow him.[35] Second, a proof-theoretic distinction can be made between implications like *(8)* and like *(9)*.[36] Third, a model-theoretic distinction can also be made between implications like *(8)* and *(9)*.[37] The first criticism needs no elaboration here. The third is too extensive to be set out here. I will sketch the second to give an idea of the distinction.

The proof-theoretic distinction between *(8)* and *(9)* exhibits their difference as one of whether the logical form of the premiss suffices by itself to warrant the conclusion or whether the implication depends also on a law of logic to justify the step to the conclusion. The notion of a premiss "sufficing by itself" to warrant a conclusion is a simple extension of the notion of an analytic truth: just as *(8')* is necessary

(8') Bachelors are unmarried

because the senses of its terms make the predicate's applicability a condition of the application of the subject, so *(8)* is valid because these definitions make the truth of the conclusion a condition of the truth of the premiss. There is inclusion of one logical form in another in both cases *(8)* and *(8')*. There is no such inclusion in *(9)* or in the inference from *(10)* to *(11)*.

(10) Sue is smarter than Moe and Moe is smarter than Lem

(11) Sue is smarter than Lem

(12) (x) (y) (z) ((smarter than$_{x,y}$ & smarter than $_{y,z}$) $\supset$ smarter than$_{x,z}$)

Even if we take the meaning postulate to be a semantic specification about the logical form of the comparative construction in sentences like *(10)* and *(11)*, the implication exhibited in *(10)* and *(11)* is not fully warranted by a relation between their logical forms (i.e., by itself showing the implication to hold). On inspection, one can see that the logical form of the premiss *(10)* does not contain the conclusion *(11)*. *(10)* is a conjuction whose first conjunct compares the intelligence of Sue and Moe and whose second and only other conjunct compares the intelligence of Moe and Lem. *No part of the logical form of (10) compares the intelligence of Sue and Lem:* the individual constants "Sue" and "Lem" do not appear as co-arguments of a predicate in *(10)*. Similarly, the antecedent of *(9)* does not have a logical form in which "John" is an argument of the predicate "is a bartender". These logical implications contrast with analytic entailments like *(8)*, where the logical form of the premiss contains a proposition in which "John" is an argument of "is unmarried". Furthermore, even after we take the inferential step of instantiating *(12)* with "Sue" for "x", "Moe" for "y", and "Lem" for "z", the conclusion "Sue is smarter than Lem" does not follow without an application of *modus ponens*. The implication therefore, holds partly in virtue of laws of logic, and hence, unlike analytic entailments, not solely by virtue of the logical form or meaning of the premiss and conclusion.

Given such a distinction between analytic entailments and logical implications—drawn precisely at the point that *B* and *C* specify—the alleged virtue of the meaning postulate approach, that it treats implications arising from the meanings of words as continuous with implications arising from the necessary connections between propositions expressed by laws of logic, becomes its chief vice. We can now argue that semantic representations are the proper apparatus for grammar, since this apparatus treats implications arising from meaning alone as discontinuous with implications that depend on subsumption under logical laws.

The meaning postulate approach to linguistic semantics not only opts for a less constraining notation for semantics but, in fact, rejects the enterprise of described meanings. The term "meaning postulates" is a misnomer. Meaning postulates do not postulate anything about meaning. They say nothing about meaning. Instead they merely add clauses to the definition of 'admissible model' for the language. That is, meaning postulates put further conditions on what can count as an extensional interpretation. Moreover, the extensional conditions imposed by meaning postulates are not even restricted to conditions that reflect meaning. Meaning postulates can reflect any relations that hold in all possible worlds. They are indiscriminate between meaning relations, logical relations, mathematical relations, and any other necessary relations. Accordingly, a meaning postulate, in saying nothing about one kind of necessary connection that it does not say about the others, says nothing about meaning.[38]

FFG's next consideration in favor of meaning postulates is that the assumption that meaning postulates are computed in understanding speech might help solve the puzzle of how people understand sentences so fast.[39] FFG hypothesize that what has to be recovered in speech comprehension are meaning postulates expressed in a primitive vocabulary where there is a predicate for each surface content word. On this hypothesis, they propose to explain the speed of human sentence comprehension in terms of the light computational load "on processes that must be assumed to be on-line".[40]

This explanation of the speed with which people understand sentences provides no support for meaning postulates because it depends entirely on the assumption that the information recovered in understanding sentences is very close in form to the content words of their surface structure. Hence, the explanation does not require the assumption that lexical information is stated in the form of meaning postulates. The explanation can also be given with lexical information stated in the form of semantic representations. The dictionary can be set up in accord with FFG's assumption about the relation between the formalism for predicates and the surface structure of content words. Then, the representations that are accessed in speech comprehension will contain few semantic markers, each corresponding fairly directly to surface structure constituents, and we thereby obtain the same "light computational load" explanation of the speed with which people understand sentences.[41]

Even assuming that meaning postulates were essential to this explanation, there would still be no grounds for claiming that the explanation supports an argument against a level of semantic representation *in grammars*. Their explanation can be accepted while preserving the level of semantic representations by employing an explanatory device for semantic processing similar to what Bever has already proposed in the parallel case of explaining the speed with which humans process syntactic structure.[42] Bever imagines coupling a grammar that generates standard syntactic representations with a performance model having *perceptual strategies* for expediting the recognition of constituent structure. The system as a whole functions as a heuristic programming device: syntactic representations serve as parsing criteria in the fail-proof procedures and perceptual strategies play the role of the heuristics. Similarly, we can imagine coupling a grammar that generates standard semantic representations with a performance model having *semantic strategies* in the form of meaning postulates for expediting the recognition of logical structure. Not only can the same explanation of the speed of comprehension be given with meaning postulates in the role of strategies at the semantic stage of speech processing, but the explanation makes the special *raison d'être* for semantic representations clear.

FFG's last consideration supporting their approach is that ". . . it seems clear that even if we do have definitions in our grammar, meaning postulates are still indispensible".[43] One argument for this claim is that

> For, as has been widely recognized, there will almost certainly be residual inferences that turn on 'content words' even after the process of definitional decomposition has gone through.[44]

It *is* widely recognized that present attempts to describe the semantic structure of even the most ordinary words leave a residue of inferences unaccounted for. This, however, means very little because the residue might, as is only to be expected in so young a science as semantics, exist simply because such attempts have not as yet had a chance to achieve success, and the residue might be progressively eliminated as the science of semantics matures.

There is another construal of FFG's claim, namely, that the residue will resist all attempts of semanticists to achieve success. Even if such attempts have gone as far as they can go, so that the descriptions are complete from the semantic point of view, there is still a residue of unexplained inferences. But this construal, too, offers no grounds for their claim. There is no reason why we shouldn't explain this un-eliminatable residue as not semantically explainable because the inferences are logical in the sense discussed above of depending on the laws of logic in addition to meaning. The fact that some inferences are left unexplained by a complete semantic description is itself a sufficient reason to count the inferences as logical as opposed to semantic. The issue here is again whether there is a distinction between implications analytic and logical implications.

The final consideration FFG propose for the indispensibility of meaning postulates is that

. . . all theories which embrace A-C that have so far been proposed do employ meaning postulates under one guise or other. . . . In Katz's work, for example, they appear as 'redundancy rules'.[45]

The latter claim is false. A comparison of meaning postulates and redundancy rules shows that they are quite different. Meaning postulates, it will be recalled are clauses in the definition of 'admissible model' for the language. Carnap introduced them to fill the gap in his extensional account of intensions: two expressions have the same Carnapian intension just in case they are assigned the same extension in each state-description.[46] Carnap realized that a full treatment of sameness of intension requires a treatment of meaning and synonymy to fill the gap in the analysis of the logical structure of a language created by the distinction between so-called logical vocabulary and extra-logical vocabulary. Consequently, he introduced meaning postulates so that the notion of same intension could be defined as sameness of extension in those state-descriptions under which all postulates, including meaning postulates, are true. Meaning postulates thus handle sentences like (8) in a fashion parallel to logical truths like (9): they all come out to be L-truths in an appropriately formulated artificial language.

Redundancy rules have no such use. While meaning postulates function to state meaning relations, not as such, but as necessary connections between extensions relative to an artificial language, redundancy rules are part of the apparatus for describing meanings as such. They function, relative to a dictionary containing semantic representations, to abbreviate the entries. Such abbreviatory conventions are written in the form (13), where the arrow is the instruction for

(13) $(M_1), \ldots, (\text{Artifact}), \ldots, (M_n) \longrightarrow (M_1), \ldots, (\text{Artifact}),$
$(\text{Physical Object}), \ldots, (M_n)$

re-writing symbol sequences having the form displayed on the left of the arrow as symbol sequences having the form displayed on the right. The connective in a meaning postulate like *(12)* is material implication. The symbols in redundancy rules refer to semantic markers, elements of semantic representations; the symbols in meaning postulates refer, *inter alia,* to objects in the world. Redundancy rules state invariances over lexical semantic representations: *(13)* expresses the invariance that every lexical representation that contains the semantic marker '(Artifact)' also contains the semantic marker '(Physical Object)'. The redundancy rule thus makes it unnecessary for the semantic marker '(Physical Object)' to appear in lexical semantic representations having the semantic marker '(Artifact)'. In capitalizing on invariances in this way, redundancy rules effect an enormous economy over the dictionary as a whole.

Clearly, then, redundancy rules are not meaning postulates. The latter make claims about the extensions of expressions in the language. Redundancy rules make no such claims. A meaning postulate like *(14)*

$(14) (x)(A_x \supset PO_x)$

claims that the extension of "artifact" is included in the extension of "physical object", whereas the redundancy rule *(13)* refers not to artifacts and physical objects but to the elements of semantic representations in semantic derivations. Redundancy rules only make claims about semantic derivations of sentences in a grammar.[47] Moreover, as abbreviatory devices, the redundancy rules are wholly eliminable from the grammar of a language without any loss in its descriptive power. The grammar of the language would become much less economical, but no less true. In contrast, meaning postulates are not eliminable without loss in descriptive power since theories using meaning postulates rely on them to state implications running off of expressions in the extra-logical vocabulary of the language. Therefore, FFG's claim that meaning postulates are indispensible in all theories of semantics is false.

Competencist Skepticism

The leaders of the competencist and performancist wings of the movement that overthrew the behaviorist and empiricist structuralist approach in linguistics—a movement that explicitly presents itself as mentalist and rationalist—have not been steadfast defenders of meaning. To the contrary, the more the leaders of both wings of this movement have become staunch conceptualists, the more they have become critics of meaning, siding with its behaviorist and empiricist critics. Why?

Many of the reasons vary from individual to individual, but one does not and thus warrants special mention at the outset. It is that meaning poses a similar problem for both the conceptualist and the behaviorist-empiricist position. The problem for the latter position is that meaning and analyticity cannot be defined in terms of behavior or explained as inductively generalized, experiential concepts. If meaning is part of the grammatical structure of natural language, then there will be sentences in natural languages whose grammatical structure characterizes them as necessary truths. As a conception of how we come by our knowledge of a natural language, empiricism can be asked to account for how we know such necessary truths insofar as knowledge of them is part of our knowledge of our native language. Strict forms of empiricism like Bloomfield's or Quine's have no chance meeting this demand.[48] Inductive procedures can only provide an account of knowledge of contingent connections (of varying degrees of strength comparable to degrees of confirmation); they cannot account for knowledge of connections with the "superstrength" of necessity (connections that hold in all possible worlds). The problem for conceptualism is similar. As I argued in the introduction, necessary truth itself cannot be accounted for on the conceptualist position because conceptualism allows nothing stronger than a notion of necessity relative to the laws of human cognitive processing. Such a psychological or biological notion can explain what, by virtue of their native linguistic capacities, human beings have to conceive of as true no matter what, but it cannot explain what, in absolute terms, is true no matter what. Thus, because meaning introduces a species of necessary truth into natural languages, it poses for conceptualism much the same problem it posed for behaviorism and empiricism. Desire to escape this problem may underlie the antipathy that conceptualists with otherwise strong mentalist and rationalist sympathies have had to meaning.

From this perspective it is easier to understand why Chomsky, who has strongly opposed behaviorism and empiricism in linguistics, psychology, and philosophy,[49] has never found the notion of meaning congenial and, at both the beginning of his career[50] and at present, has held a skepticism comparable to that of many empiricists and behaviorists. I have already given examples of Chomsky's early skepticism about meaning, a skepticism which essentially echos Bloomfield's criticism of meaning. Here is an illustration of his recent skepticism:

Why then raise the question of the possibility of a universal semantics which would provide a complete and accurate representation of every sense of each lexical item, and the rules which determine the meaning of expressions in which these expressions appear? There are, I think, good reasons to be skeptical about such a program. It seems that other cognitive systems—in particular our system of beliefs concerning things of the world and their behavior—intervene in our judgments of sense and reference, in an extremely intricate manner, and it is far from clear that it would make sense, even in principle, to try to separate these different elements of what in informal usage or even in technical discussions we call the "sense of a linguistic expression". I believe that *one cannot separate semantic representation from knowledge of the world.*[51]

and

... with Wittgenstein, I do not think that one can characterize the word "chair" in isolation from beliefs about the world: in the semantic representation, everything interacts.[52]

Even during Chomsky's least skeptical period, he has the same misgivings, e.g.,

... That nonlinguistic beliefs, intentions of the speaker, and other factors enter into the interpretation of utterances in so intimate . . . a fashion that it is hopeless and misguided to attempt to represent independently the 'purely grammatical' component of meaning, the various 'readings' of expressions in the sense of the standard theory, and the relation between such readings and a syntactic structure[53]

The doubts raised about semantic representation at this period are the very same doubts on which Chomsky bases his ultimate decision to explicitly exclude meaning from grammar.

Methodological parallelisms. What are Chomsky's arguments for semantic skepticism? In his autobiographical introduction to the published edition of *The Logical Structure of Linguistic Theory,* Chomsky directs the reader to an alleged argument in earlier works for his skepticism on the issue of whether linguistic theory defines a semantic level of representation:

Katz has perhaps been the clearest advocate of the view that linguistic theory provides a system for the representation of meaning. . . . My own view is more skeptical. In ATS it is argued that the line of demarcation (if there is one) between syntax and semantics is most unclear, and that it is also questionable whether the theory of meaning can be divorced from the study of other cognitive structures (ATS, p. 159). I suspect that Katz's approach is legitimate over an interesting range, but that much of what is often regarded as central to the study of meaning cannot be dissociated from systems of belief in any natural way.[54]

But on turning to *Aspects*, we find no argument. Instead, we find the following significantly weaker attitude:

. . . one should not expect to be able to delimit a large and complex domain before it has been thoroughly explored. A decision as to the boundary separating syntax and semantics (if there is one) is not a prerequisite for theoretical and descriptive study of syntactic and semantic rules. On the contrary, the problem of delimitation will clearly remain open until these fields are much better understood than they are today. Exactly the same can be said about the boundary separating semantic systems from systems of knowledge and belief. That these seem to interpenetrate in obscure ways has long been noted. One can hardly achieve significant understanding of this matter in advance of a deep analysis of systems of semantic rule, on the one hand, and systems of belief, on the other.[55]

Although it is clear that these remarks contain no argument for skepticism about meaning, it might seem as if they nonetheless reveal some special obscurity about semantics whose recognition alone would make one properly sympathetic to it. To see that these remarks do not provide such support, let us look closely at the notion of delimitation that plays so large a role in the discussion. The appearance that Chomsky's remarks convey of there being something specially obscure and problematic about the boundaries of semantics comes, I think, entirely from an equivocation in Chomsky's use of the term "delimitation". When the two senses of "delimitation" are distinguished, and Chomsky's remarks are then construed on each sense separately, it is clear that neither construal provides a reason for his skepticism.

The fixing of limits expressed in the term "delimitation" can be *either* a matter of extensionally separating the phenomena in a field, one by one, into those belonging to a particular domain of the field and those not belonging to the domain *or* a matter of intensionally characterizing the nature of the boundaries that mark one domain off from others in the field. If we construe Chomsky's remarks with respect to the former concrete sense of "delimitation", it is obviously true that one should not expect to delimit a domain before thoroughly exploring it. Nor, on this sense, should one expect a delimitation of the domain of syntax in the near future. Delimitation in this sense is a feature of extremely advanced scientific fields.

If instead we construe Chomsky's remarks with respect to the latter, abstract sense of "delimitation", one not only can but *must* delimit a large and complex domain before exploring it. In science, this delimitation is a theoretical specification both of the kinds of objects in a domain and of the properties and relations that make the domain distinctive. It is thus false on this sense that one should not expect a delimitation of semantics in advance of exploring it because delimitation in this sense is a precondition of a serious attempt to explore a domain. Without some reasonably accurate, even if only partial, theoretical specification, the attempt to investigate the domain would lack guidelines to insure that scientific investigation is being conducted in the right part of the field. The danger of proceeding without such guidelines is that investigations can blindly wander over a number of distinct domains, accumulating a heterogeneous set of phenomena that cannot be systematized.

Distinguishing the two ways of understanding "delimitation" and construing Chomsky's remarks on each, it is clear that the first construal makes them true but not at all damaging to the theory of meaning while the second makes them false. Thus, on neither construal do Chomsky's remarks provide grounds for semantic skepticism.

A methodological parallelism between phonology, syntax, and semantics is suggested by these considerations about delimitation. All three domains require initial theoretical specification, and have received them along similar lines. Further, students of all three face the same potential problem of interpenetration of their phenomena with the extragrammatical. Since the initial theoretical specifications of syntax and phonology do not draw a sharp line between the phenomena of these domains and extragrammatical phenomena, the parallel difficulty of distinguishing semantic from extragrammatical phenomena cannot be good methodological grounds for skepticism about the domain of meaning.

Such a parallelism is clear in the case of phonology. The problem of interpenetration for the phonological component, the other interpretive component of the grammar, is the same as that for the semantic component. The pronunciation of sentences is permeated with articulatory noises of all kinds, such as burps, pause fillers, language mixtures, artificial pronunciations like foreign accents, voice and sound imitation, drunken slurrings, and so on. Phonological interpenetration is no different in principle from semantic interpenetration, but it is not taken by Chomsky to raise parallel serious questions about whether phonology can be regarded as a legitimate part of grammar. Phonological interpenetration is considered an expected feature of natural speech—a matter of performance. Pronunciation in natural speech is considered the product of inputs of various kinds, of which phonological competence is only one. The problem of grammatical representation at the phonological level is thus defined on the basis of a prior abstraction from all inputs to phonological performance but phonological competence.

There is no reason not to treat semantic interpenetration in the same way. Chomsky's characterization of linguistic theory encourages us to do so:

Linguistic theory is concerned primarily with an ideal speaker-listener, in a completely homogeneous speech community, who knows the language perfectly and is unaffected by such grammatically irrelevant conditions as memory limitations, distractions, shifts of attention, and interest, and errors . . . in applying his knowledge of the language.[56]

We thus ought to be able to say also that the interpenetration of extragrammatical beliefs, intentions, etc. with semantic competence is an expected feature of natural speech. The meanings of uses of sentences can be considered the products of inputs of various kinds, of which semantic competence is only one, and the problem of grammatical representation at the semantic level can similarly be defined on the basis of a prior abstraction from all inputs to semantic performance but semantic competence.

Hence, there seems to be unequal treatment of cases that are perfectly parallel. Chomsky never considers the problem of semantic interpenetration as simply another instance of the need for a competence/performance distinction, though, given his conception of linguistic theory, one would think this the most natural thing for him to do. Is there any justification for his not treating the interpenetration of meaning and extragrammatical belief, intentions, etc. in the same way as the interpenetration of pronounciation with burps, pause fillers, and other articulatory noises are treated?

One possible reason for applying a double standard in the treatment of phonology and semantics might be that theoretical specification of the domain of meaning is somehow different from theoretical specification of the domain of phonology or syntax. But this does not seem so. Semantics does not lack an initial theoretical specification. It is specified as the domain whose objects are senses of sentences, compositionally determined from the senses of their constituents, and whose distinctive properties and relations include synonymy, meaningfulness, semantic anomaly, ambiguity, redundancy, analyticity, and contradiction. Such an initial specification of semantics seems no different in kind or less adequate than an initial specification of phonology as the domain whose objects are the pronunciations of sentences and whose distinctive properties and relations include simple rhyme, alternation of sound, rhythm, and stress, or of syntax as the domain whose objects are sentences and whose distinctive properties and relations include well-formedness, sentence type (e.g., interrogative, declarative, imperative, and hortatory), ellipsis, and agreement.

Semantics seems to be on a par with phonology and syntax: in each case, there is considerable pretheoretic plausibility in the choice of objects and the properties and relations seem to be the ones that are determined by the objects in question.

The initial theoretical specification of semantics does not, of course, provide an exhaustive enumeration of the properties and relations in the domain. But this is also true of the specifications of phonology and syntax. It is hard to see how all the properties and relations for any domain could be known in advance. Moreover, nonexhaustiveness in the case of semantics causes no special problem insofar as the criterion for recognizing valid new properties and relations, and distinguishing them from ones belonging outside the domain, is the same in all three domains of grammar. The criterion is simply a generalization of the principle *(Z)*, roughly, a new candidate property or relation for a grammatical level belongs to the domain represented at that level just in case the principles that define the initially specified clear cases of properties and relations define the new property or relation, too. Thus, there is no reason that justifies different treatment having to do with the initial specifications of phonology and syntax, on the one hand, and semantics, on the other.

Perhaps there is some special problem in the case of semantics in developing its initial specification into a comprehensive theory that defines the properties and relations in the domain and provides principles to predict and explain phenomena. One often hears the claim that semantics is especially troubled by an overabundance of theories—the use theory, the referential theory, the possible worlds theory, the mental image theory, stimulus-response theories of various kinds, Fregean theories, and so on. The claim seems to be that there are too many different ways of systematizing the domain of meaning for us to ever select a best theory. But this claim runs counter to the scientific attitude that a proper application of scientific method will, in the long run, settle the question as to which of the competing theories is best, and Chomsky does not offer a reason to think that the application of the scientific method to semantics is less effective than its application in other areas. Moreover, this claim is not one that syntacticians like Chomsky can make to support skepticism about meaning. There is now a similar proliferation of theories in syntax. For example, the 1979 conference on current approaches to syntax (the Eighth Annual University of Wisconsin Milwaukee Linguistics Symposium) had speakers representing thirteen different approaches to syntax: Relational Grammar, Role and Reference Grammar, Functional Grammar, Epiphenomenal Syntax, Cognitive Grammar, Equational Grammar, Trace Theory, Functionally Interpreted Base Generated Grammar,

Corepresentational Grammar, Daughter-dependency Grammar, Montague Grammar, Tagmemics, and Stratificational Grammar. Even these do not exhaust the major approaches to syntax now being pursued. For example, Postal's Arc-pair Grammar and Bresnan's Realistic Grammar were not represented.

Some people seem to think that semantics has a special problem in connection with evidence, in particular, that judgments about semantic properties and relations are intuitively problematic in ways that judgments about syntactic or phonological properties and relations are not. This, however, is an impression that comes from too superficial a comparison: the impression comes from comparing prominent semantic examples like "Bachelors are unmarried men" with prominent syntactic examples like "Flying planes can be dangerous" or "Revolutionary new ideas appear infrequently". The mistake in such comparisons is that the semantic examples are prominent because they are the center of philosophical controversy about analyticity while the syntactic examples are extremely uncontroversial, clear cases of syntactic properties that played an influential role in the development of generative grammar. For a fair evaluation of the question of whether semantics faces a special problem about evidence, we have to make some effort to find comparable cases.

If the effort is made, it turns out that there is no clear reason to suppose that semantic judgments are especially troubled. Equating examples is difficult, but it is easy to produce cases in semantics that are as clear as the clearest in syntax. For example, it is clear that "crowd" and "mob" are semantically similar in having senses that express a group action, that both are antonymous with "solo" in this respect, that "naked nude" is redundant, and that "Jones murdered Smith" analytically entails "Jones killed Smith".

Even if we assume that semantic judgments are overall more difficult than syntactic ones, this does not in itself count as a reason for skepticism about meaning. (We might similarly conclude that syntactic judgments are overall more difficult than phonological ones.) What needs to be shown, but hasn't been, is that the problem with semantic judgments is not just an accident, depending on such things as insufficient training in judging semantic properties and relations, too little theoretical guidance, and so on. The notion of a judgment is a three-term relation. Hence, not only must cases be equated, so must judges and insofar as possible the properties and relations. When we equate highly skilled judges in semantics and syntax—for instance, J. L. Austin and Jespersen—it is hard to think that the difficulties which less skilled people have with semantic judgments represent more than differences in ability, training, etc. If so, the differences do not reflect any question of objective fact or the possibility in principle of evidence, and hence, there is no basis here for thinking that semantic judgment warrants skepticism.

The only thing left about the process of developing the initial specification of semantics into a comprehensive theory that might show that semantics is especially troubled is the character of the process itself. Perhaps the process of theory construction in semantics is somehow more troubled than in syntax or phonology because unclear cases constitute a special stumbling block in semantics.

But this cannot be the case since the parallelism also extends to the way in which disagreements about the status of unclear cases are resolved. The explanation that Chomsky offers for unclear cases in syntax is open to us in semantics. Chomsky claims that a sentence like "The man who the boy who the students recognized pointed out is a friend of mine", although an unclear case because of disagreement about whether its unintelligibility is a matter of ill-formedness or not, is well-formed. He argues that its unintelligibility is better seen as due to performance factors.[57] Chomsky uses the competence/performance distinction to argue that the unintelligibility turns on factors involved in the use of language and not on factors involved in grammar, that is to say, not on formal features of rules. Now, there is nothing here that restricts this line of argument to syntax and phonology. Hence, it can serve as a model for the handling of unclear cases in semantics.

Let us consider an example. Some who adopt the verificationist theory of meaning claim that a sentence like "Everything is decreasing by half its length at every moment" is meaningless because the world would look the same whether it is true or false and hence no observations would verify it.[58] Most of us would disagree, saying that the sentence has a meaning despite the fact that we can't determine its truth value (that's how we know that we can't). So the sentence is an unclear case in semantics. But using Chomsky's line of argument as a model it is easy to show how to handle the case. We have to show two things. First, that the principles that describe the clear cases—here the distinction between meaningful and meaningless sentences like "An itchy scalp can become painful" and "An itchy shadow can become truthful"—imply a classification of the unclear case, and second, the peculiarity of the unclear case can be attributed to a performance factor. It seems reasonable that we might show that the principles that describe the clear cases of the distinction between meaningfulness and meaninglessness, viz. those involved in semantic selection restrictions, imply that the sentence "Everything is decreasing by half its length at every moment" violates no selection restriction and hence is meaningful. Further, it seems reasonable that we might show that the sentence's peculiarity can be accounted for on the basis of extra-grammatical factors such as knowledge that universal, constant length changes produce no observable effect. Thus, testability, which is a matter of language use, is distinguished from meaningfulness, which is a matter of grammatical structure. Since the knowledge of how it is possible to prove or refute, which is assumed in supposing that the sentence in question is peculiar, is extragrammatical, the peculiarity itself can be regarded as a performance matter. Just as we try to explain the problems a speaker has in understanding utterances of multiply-center-embedded sentences in terms of how these sentences overload on-line computation space, so we can try to explain the problems a speaker has in understanding utterances of untestable sentences in terms of how these sentences run counter to our expectations that people will try to say what they have evidence to think is true.[59]

Conflict between methodology and skepticism: explication. Given this methodological parallelism and the fact that Chomsky's skepticism thus treats similar cases dissimilarly, it follows that his skepticism conflicts with his general methodological position and his practice in phonology and syntax. In this and the next section, I exhibit two cases of such conflict. I wish to show that Chomsky's skepticism is under-mined by conflict with what is otherwise a consistent theory and practice.

Chomsky calls the process of developing a theoretical specification into a theory that separates the phenomena into those within and those outside a domain "explication".[60] He writes:

. . . in order to set the aims of grammar significantly it is sufficient to assume a partial knowledge of sentences and nonsentences. . . . In many intermediate cases we shall be prepared to let the grammar itself decide, when the grammar is set up in the simplest way so that it includes the clear sentences and excludes the clear non-sentences. This is a familiar feature of explication.[61]

Explication in semantics differs from explication in syntax or phonol-ogy only in regard to the properties and relations involved. For example, in syntax, one assumes "a partial knowledge of sentences and non-sentences", whereas, in semantics, one assumes a partial knowledge of which sentences are meaningful and which not.

Explication in semantics, as in syntax and phonology, takes place both at the level of linguistic theory and of grammar. At the level of linguistic theory, our partial knowledge of the set of semantic proper-ties and relations is used to construct hypotheses about their definitions and the definition of further properties and relations. At the level of grammar, our partial knowledge of the extensions of particular semantic properties and relations with respect to the language in question is used to construct semantic representations of sentences that predict the full extensions of these semantic properties and relations.[62]

Given that the construction of semantic rules is a process of explication, interpenetration should never, in principle, be relevant to the question of whether meaning is within grammar. Explication commits linguistics to handling "intermediate" or unclear cases by letting "the grammar itself decide, when the grammar is set up in the simplest way" to handle the clear cases. Since interpenetration is responsible for unclear cases and for unclarity in large enough amounts to produce poorly demarcated portions of the boundary separating semantics from systems of extragrammatical knowledge and belief, both these problems ought to resolve themselves with continued explication for larger and larger samples of clear cases. Given appropriate revisions when necessary, explication must eventually provide semantic representations that sort unclear cases in accord with generalizations from the clear cases. Thus, there can be no fundamental problem of dissociating meaning from other cognitive structures. Either the semantic representations set up so far for the clear cases of semantic properties and relations determine the extension of some semantic property or relation in an unclear case or not. If they leave open the question of whether certain sentences are in the extension, we can continue the explication. As long as, at each point, the semantic system set up for the clear cases decides the unclear ones, and incorrect decisions are eventually revised in subsequent extensions of the semantic system, then automatically the simplest semantic system that ultimately predicts the clear cases of semantic properties and relations will correctly decide the unclear cases and thereby the boundary questions for the domain of semantics. Hence, Chomsky's own methodology of explication undermines his skepticism.

Conflict between methodology and skepticism: relativization. At one point in the development of generative semantics, Lakoff took essentially the same position concerning the interpenetration of syntactic structure and extragrammatical belief, etc. that Chomsky takes on the interpenetration of semantic structure and extragrammatical belief, etc.[63] Lakoff argued that the syntactic property of well-formedness is determined by the beliefs speakers have in the speech context, and consequently, that well-formedness cannot be an absolute property. Chomsky argued against this attempt to relativize syntax to facts about the speaker's beliefs, intentions, etc. on the basis of his methodological position. Thus, insofar as Chomsky's attempt to relativize semantics is, except for the syntax semantics difference, exactly the same thing as Lakoff's, we can turn Chomsky's argument against relativization in syntax on his own relativization in semantics.

Chomsky's argument in reply to Lakoff begins by observing that the facts that Lakoff cites can be handled without resorting to the extreme of blurring the boundary between systems of syntax and systems of extragrammatical belief, intention, etc. Well-formedness, Chomsky suggested, can be defined independently of the speaker if the presupposition of a sentence (in a special sense to be made clear shortly) is distinguished from the question of its satisfaction. The grammar can assume the task of stipulating that a sentence like *(15)* expresses the

(15) John called Mary a Republican and then *she* insulted *him*

presupposition that for John to call Mary a Republican is for him to insult her.[64] Chomsky goes on to explain:

The relation between [(15)] and the presupposition . . . holds independently of anyone's factual beliefs; it is part of the knowledge of the speaker of English, quite apart from his beliefs, or John's, or Mary's. In general, . . . that grammar generates sentences and expresses the fact that these sentences carry certain presuppositions. *It makes no reference to specific beliefs.*[65]

The stand that Chomsky takes against Lakoff's attempt to relativize the notion of well-formedness can be taken with respect to Chomsky's own attempt to relativize semantic notions to systems of knowledge and belief. Specifically Chomsky's point is this:

"Well-formedness is a theoretical term. We are free to define it so that it takes its place within a sensible theory. One terminological proposal—the one I would advocate as the most natural—would be this:

(I) define "well-formed" so that [*(15)*] is well-formed independently of the beliefs of John, Mary, or the speaker;

(II) assign to the semantic component of the grammar the task of stipulating that [*(15)*] expresses the presupposition that for John to call Mary a Republican is for him to insult her.[66]

Adopting Chomsky's format *(I)* and *(II)*, we can avoid the relativization of notions like meaningfulness and anomaly to extragrammatical factors and keep semantic distinctions (like that between meaningfulness and anomaly) separate from performance distinctions (like that between the normal and the bizarre). Applied to semantics, the format is something like:

(I') define "meaningful" and "anomalous" so that the sentences in question are meaningful or semantically anomalous independently of the beliefs of the people in the speech context, etc.

(II') assign to the theory of performance the task of stipulating what possible significance a use of a sentence might have in speech contexts of various sorts.

Thus, there is no problem in taking a contextually bizarre sentence like "No human ever has used or ever will use any sentence" to be semantically non-deviant because a theory of performance explains why speakers judge the sentence to be bizarre in most contexts.

This comparison clearly brings out the rigid double standard underlying Chomsky's skepticism about meaning: although there is the same potential problem for syntax and semantics that much of what grammarians regard as central to the study cannot be dissociated from systems of belief,[67] syntactic theory enjoys the protection of Chomsky's methodology but semantic theory apparently does not. The conclusion is clear, too. Since there is no fundamental difference between the relativization of syntax and the relativization of semantics, if syntactic relativization can be dismissed once questions of grammar are separated from questions of context in the manner of (I) and (II), then semantic relativization can be dismissed once questions of grammar are separated from questions of context in the manner of (I') and (II').

Chomsky and the semantic competence/performance distinction. The two conflicts discussed in the previous sections suggest that Chomsky's doubts about the dissociability of meaning from extra-grammatical belief, etc. rest on a confusion between competence and performance in matters of semantics. I recognize that this is a rather surprising thing to suggest about the originator of the competence/ performance distinction in linguistics, but in light of the things Chomsky says about meaning we are left with no other explanation. Take the following remarks of Chomsky's:

. . . consider such a sentence as *I am not against MY FATHER, only against THE LABOR MINISTER,* spoken recently by a radical Brazilian student. Knowing further that the speaker is the son of the labor minister, we would assign to this utterance a reading in which the emphasized phrases are coreferential. On one reading, the sentence is contradictory, but knowing the facts just cited a more natural interpretation would be that the speaker is opposed to what his father does in his capacity as labor minister, and would be accurately paraphrased in this more elaborate way. It is hardly obvious that what we "read into" sentences in such ways as these . . . can either be sharply dissociated from grammatically determined readings, on the one hand, or from considerations of fact and belief, on the other.[68]

Chomsky is clearly not referring to the English *sentence (16)*, but

(16) I am not against *my father*, only against the *labor minister*

rather to an utterance of *(16)*, as he says, "spoken recently by a radical Brazilian student". Moreover, Chomsky is not interpreting the utterance just with respect to the knowledge that an ideal speaker-hearer of English has about the semantic structure of English, but rather also with respect to obviously extragrammatical knowledge that the speaker in question is the son of the labor minister. We are thus led, again, to the conclusion that Chomsky's views about the interpenetration of grammatically determined semantic structure and extra-grammatical considerations of fact and belief are based on a confusion of competence and performance, in the present instance, on a confusion of the meaning of *sentences* in the language with the natural construal of their *utterances* in context. Mistakenly taking the natural construals of utterances to be the meanings represented in readings, Chomsky takes meanings as inseparably bound up with extra-grammatical fact and belief, and hence, as matters to be treated outside sentence grammar. To correct the mistake requires no more than drawing the same competence/performance distinction Chomsky originally created. If it is drawn, the situationally specific information that Chomsky reads into the grammatical meaning of sentences like *(16)* can be sharply distinguished from its grammatically determined meaning.

Other places in Chomsky's writings exhibit the same confusion between the meaning of a sentence in the language and the meaning of a use of a sentence in a context:

Suppose I say: *The temperature is dropping*. Nobody knows what that means without extralinguistic presuppositions. Does it mean that the temperature was lower five minutes ago? [original: *était moins élevée il y a cinq minutes*] Perhaps. But if I say *The temperature is dropping* while thinking that we are headed for a glacial epoch, the sentence is true even if the temperature has risen locally. Thus, for the simplest sentences, it is impossible to establish truth conditions, at least outside of the context of language use. And even so it would be necessary to distinguish fixed beliefs, temporary beliefs, etc.[69]

It is obvious that nobody knows what a *use* of *(17)* means without the

(17) The temperature is dropping

extra-linguistic presuppositions that inform us about the context in which it is used. One cannot even tell whether the use makes a statement, or, say, a request (e.g., to have the addressee put on warmer clothes), without such information. But it is plainly false that nobody knows what the English sentence *(17)* means. The meaning of the sentence is simply that the temperature at some location is lower at the time of the utterance point than at some time in the past relative to the utterance point and has been declining from this point to the utterance point.[70] This is what *(17)* and its French translation "La température baisse" both express in their respective languages.

Chomsky is also mistaken in claiming that "it is impossible to establish truth conditions" for sentences like *(17)* in isolation. A use of *(17)* makes a true statement if, and only if, the temperature at the location specified in the use is lower at the utterance point than it was at some time in the past and has declined from that point to the time of the utterance. Of course, such a truth condition alone is unlikely to be the natural construal of a use of the sentence. A natural construal of a use of *(17)* will undoubtedly reflect a significant contribution from the context of use. Generally, the information in a *statement* is not exhausted by the information in the meaning of the sentence used to make it. In the case of a sentence like *(17)*, the context can be expected to determine the relevant location, time of utterance, and so on. Thus, once we distinguish the meaning of *sentences* from the meaning of their *uses,* these is absolutely no reason here to think that sentences in isolation do not have truth conditions. Clearly, *(17)* does not have a *truth value* in isolation, but truth conditions and truth values are different things.[71]

Chomsky's confusion over sentences and uses of sentences can be further documented by another example in the same discussion of semantic representation:

Everybody believes, it's a fact, that truth conditions are linked to semantic representations. However, the question is far from being simple. John Austin gave some interesting examples on this subject. Let's take the sentence: *New York is two hundred miles from Boston.* Is it true or false? If you are asking in order to know how much time it would take you to get there by car, it would be true. But if you have only ten gallons of gas, if I know that your car gets 9.8 miles per gallon and if you want to know if you can go from Boston to New York without stopping, then the sentence is false if the real distance is 193 miles, etc.[72]

The confusion has here reached an extreme. Why should there be a question of whether *(18)* is true or false? If the real distance is two

(18) New York is two hundred miles from Boston

hundred miles, it is true, but if the real distance is 193 miles it is false. No ifs, ands, or buts. The question only arises because Chomsky is not, contrary to what he indicates, addressing himself to the English sentence *(18)*, but to uses of the sentence in various possible contexts. One of the contexts would modify the meaning of the sentence so that the utterance meaning of a use of it would be

(19) New York is approximately (roughly, almost, etc.) two hundred miles from Boston.

while the other would modify it so that the utterance meaning of a use of it would be

(20) You cannot get to New York in your car with the gas you now have without stopping for more because the distance from Boston to New York is exactly two hundred miles.

Chomsky conflates the question of the contextual construal of tokens of *(18)* with the question of the meaning of *(18)* in English, and then draws conclusions about the latter on the basis of how one has to go about answering the former.

One final illustration of Chomsky's confusion over the competence/performance distinction in semantics is an argument for the Extended Standard Theory that he presents in various places.[73] The most recent presentation of the argument is this:

"Beavers build dams" is true, but does not imply that all beavers build dams, only that beavers are dam-builders: dam building is characteristic of the species. But "dams are built by beavers" is, I think, naturally understood to imply that all dams are built by beavers, and is thus false . . . there is an interaction of "structural meaning," grammatically determined; "connotation" of certain types of verbs; and certain factual judgments. . . . it is clearly not the case that each datum comes marked, on its face, with an indication of the considerations that determine its status and range of interpretation.[74]

Chomsky's claim that "Beavers build dams" means that dam-building is characteristic of the species is wrong. The sentence "Beavers build dams but dam building is not characteristic of the species" is not contradictory. The point is clearer when one switches to examples like "Human beings build torture chambers but torture chamber building is not characteristic of the species." Moreover, Chomsky's claim that "Dams are built by beavers" implies that all dams are built by beavers is too strong. The sentence "Dams are built by beavers and dams are built by engineers" is not contradictory, and the sentence "All dams are built by beavers" is not redundant.

The construal Chomsky places on these sentences is a natural construal of them in many situations. The passive sentence is, as he remarks, "naturally understood to imply that all dams are built by beavers." But, as the counterexamples show, natural construals are not reliable guides to the literal meaning of sentence types. Chomsky confuses the literal meaning of these sentences, which is a matter of language, with their natural construal, which is matter of use.

Once semantic competence is distinguished from semantic performance, it is plausible to say that the sentence "Beavers build dams" means that the construction of dams is one thing that beavers do (among perhaps others)—just as it is plausible that the sentence "Human beings build torture chambers" means that the construction of torture chambers is one thing human beings do. If we turn now from sentences to utterances, it is also plausible to say that a "natural understanding" of utterances of "Beavers build dams," due to our extragrammatical knowledge of beavers, is, as Chomsky says, that dam building is characteristic of the species. Similarly, in the light of the competence/performance distinction, it is plausible to say that the English sentence "Dams are built by beavers" is synonymous with the active sentence, but that Chomsky's gloss is reasonable as a construal of utterances of the passive.[75]

Chomsky's new conception of sentence-grammar. Semantic skepticism achieves official status in Chomsky's new model of sentence grammar:[76]

$$(D) \text{ Sentence Grammar:} \xrightarrow{B} IPM \xrightarrow{T} SS \xrightarrow{SR\text{-}1} LF$$

$$\left\{ \begin{array}{c} SR\text{-}2 \\ \text{Other Systems} \end{array} \right\} : \quad LF \longrightarrow \text{``meaning''}$$

The new model presents a "picture of the general nature of grammar and its place within the system of cognitive structure"; Chomsky explains:

The rules of the base *(B)*, including the rules of the categorical component and the lexicon, form initial phrase markers *(IPM)*. The rules of the transformational component *(T)* convert these to surface structure *(SS)*, which are converted to logical forms *(LF)* by certain rules of semantic interpretation *(SR-1;* namely, the rules involving bound anaphora, scope, thematic relations, etc.) This much constitutes grammar.[77]

To place grammar within the system of cognitive structures generally, Chomsky goes on to say:

The logical forms so generated are subject to the further interpretation by other semantic rules (SR-2) interacting with other cognitive structures, giving fuller representations of meaning.[78]

Chomsky's explanation of the new conception of grammar leaves no doubt that meaning, in the sense of what determines semantic properties and relations of sentences like synonymy, analyticity, and semantic anomaly, is excluded from grammar: he says that "grammar" is intended to designate sentence grammar ("What we have been calling "grammar" in the preceding discussion is actually sentence grammar") and that meaning falls outside the domain of sentence grammar (see diagram *(D)*). And note the remark "It would be reasonable to say that the theory of grammar—or more precisely, "sentence grammar"—ends at this point," the point directly after *SR-1* rules produce the structures called "logical form".[79]

At another place where essentially the same diagram as *(D)* appears, Chomsky says, "The rules *SI-1* are rules of sentence-grammar, while the rules of *SI-2* are in general not".[80] The same exclusion of meaning from grammar is expressed in Chomsky's most recent formulation of his thesis of "absolute autonomy of formal grammar", which says that the theory of linguistic form "includes an interesting concept of 'grammar' and 'structure', perhaps all linguistic levels *apart from semantic representation*".[81] And, defending this thesis against counter-arguments of Montague grammarians and generative semanticists, Chomsky writes:

It seems to me fair to conclude that although there are, no doubt, systematic form-meaning connections, nevertheless, the theory of formal grammar has an internal integrity and has its distinct structures and properties, as Jespersen suggested. It seems to me reasonable to adopt the working hypothesis that the structures of formal grammar are generated independently, and that these structures are associated with semantic interpretations by principles and rules of a broader semiotic theory.[82]

Thus, recalcitrant boundary problems, formerly described as unresolvable without "a deep analysis of systems of semantic rules, on the one hand, and systems of belief, on the other", are now suddenly resolved. All the puzzling questions of delimitation are answered in one fell swoop: the boundaries of grammar include quantificational structures in the sense of *SR-1* rules and exclude meaning together with belief about the world and other pragmatic factors of concern only in a "broader semiotic theory". But Chomsky does not provide arguments to justify fixing the limits of grammar in this way. We find no arguments to show that bound anaphora, scope, thematic relations, and such things are free of entanglement with pragmatic factors like beliefs about the world while synonymy, lexical ambiguity, analyticity, and such things are not.

In the remainder of this section, I will examine some of the consequences of Chomsky's new conception of grammar *(D)*. I will exhibit the drastic results of excluding meaning from grammar and show that they undermine Chomsky's new conception. I will first discuss the consequences for linguistic theory and then turn to those for logical theory.

Contemporary linguistics is a stage of the linguistic tradition because there is a continuity of explanatory goals in the study of grammar that links the work of linguists today with that of the Port-Royal grammarians, Panini grammarians, and Aristotle. These goals, which center around understanding the structure of natural language, constitute the subject's identity conditions.

Among the central explanatory goals of grammar is the explanation of ambiguity in natural languages. It is as difficult to imagine grammar without the goal of explaining ambiguity as it is to imagine it without the goal of explaining well-formedness. Yet, as a consequence of Chomsky's exclusion of meaning from grammar, the new conception of grammar abandons the goal of explaining ambiguity.

Exclusion of meaning from grammar restricts grammar to phonological rules, syntactic rules (base and transformations), a lexicon without representations of the senses of morphemes and other lexical items, and the *SR-1* rules (which on pain of contradition cannot themselves provide an account of the senses of lexical items, since then grammar does not include "all linguistic levels apart from semantic representation"). This means that grammars do not address themselves to the polysemy of morphemes and other lexical items. But, since the meaning, and hence the ambiguity, of syntactically complex constitutents is a function of the sense of the lexical items that make them up, grammars under *(D)* offer no account of the ambiguity of words, phrases, and sentences.

One might be tempted to suppose that things are not as bad as all this because Chomsky's conception of sentence grammar can still explain examples like "Flying planes can be dangerous", "He dislikes old men and women", and other syntactically based ambiguity. While it is correct that sentence grammars on Chomsky new conception can assign expressions and sentences two or more distinct syntactic structures, such grammars cannot tell us when expressions or sentences with two or more syntactic structures are ambiguous. There is a difference between syntactic isomerism and ambiguity. This can be seen by noting that sentences with two or more syntactic structures like "John wrote a letter to a friend" and "It was done with an automated processing device" are not ambiguous.[83] Therefore, information about the senses of lexical items is necessary to determine when the two distinct syntactic structures of an isomeric sentence resolve into a single sense in the compositional meaning of the sentence. Without such information, grammars cannot account for these ambiguities of sentences. Chomsky's new conception of sentence-grammar thus sacrifices even the possibility of explaining the class of ambiguities that depend on syntactic derivation. This result is drastic enough to damn the new conception (D).

But in excluding meaning from sentence-grammar, (D) not only eliminates the possibility of explaining ambiguity, it also eliminates the possibility of explaining a host of other grammatical properties and relations. The relation of 'possible answer' has to be thrown out of grammar because its explanation presupposes the use of aspects of meaning. Without semantic representations and a notion of synonymy defined over them, possible answers cannot be distinguished from irrelevant remarks. The question "Does your stomach hurt?" has as one of its possible answers "Yes, my tummy hurts" as well as "Yes, my stomach hurts", but not "Yes, my head (foot, etc.) hurts". One cannot make do with a purely syntactic notion of constituent equivalence.

Take one more example. Thematic relations like 'agent of', 'recipient of', 'instrument of', etc. also cannot be specified in the grammar without information there about meaning, in particular, information about the meaning of verbs and other major constituents in construction with subjects and objects. This dependence of accounts of thematic relations on accounts of the meaning of such constituents is a persistent theme of all studies of them.[84] But, given the boundary drawn in (D), which puts the meaning of such constituents outside sentence grammar, the goal of accounting for thematic relations has to be abandoned, too.[85]

The arguments just presented show that accepting Chomsky's new conception of grammar (D) requires us to write off a number of traditional explanatory aims of linguistics. This is surely a reason for rejecting it. But essentially the same arguments establish the even stronger reason that (D) is incoherent. (D) stipulates that sentence-grammar contains a component LF whose explanatory goals include thematic relations, bound anaphora, and presumably focus controlled relations like 'natural answer', but (D) also stipulates that the boundaries of sentence-grammar exclude meaning.[86] As we have shown above, thematic relations cannot be dealt with if meaning is excluded. Further, bound anaphora cannot be handled as Chomsky wants to handle it without using meaning relations. For example, without meaning relations, the coreference of the underlined constituents in *"Tom's only sister* likes coffee and *his only sibling* likes donuts" cannot be distinguished from the disjointness of reference (of the underlined constituents) in *"Tom's only sister* likes coffee and *his only brother* likes donuts." Furthermore, standard cases of nominal/ pronominal coreference and disjoint reference depend on meaning relations. For instance, it is possible for the subjects of the two clauses in "Someone came in the front door and he went out the back door" to corefer but not for the subjects of the two clauses in "The woman came in the front door and he went out the back door". Finally, the same considerations that show that the notion of 'possible answer' cannot be handled without meaning also show that the notion of 'natural answer' cannot be handled without it. Thus, Chomsky's new conception of sentence-grammar is in the position of both requiring sentence-grammars to account for a set of properties and relations and precluding them from doing so.

We turn now to logical theory. The most significant issue in the philosophy of logic on which *(D)* bears is the traditional controversy between extensionalists and intensionalists over the nature of the logical form of sentences in natural language. Extensionalists hold that only the logical particles "and", "or", "all", "not", etc. together with certain aspects of the syntactic structure of sentences determine logical form, while intensionalists hold that word meaning generally, together with syntax, determines logical form. The issue is whether logical form in natural languages is like quantificational form in the familiar versions of standard logic, as, for example, Quinians claim, or whether this conception is too narrow to do justice to the logical structure of natural languages.

The argument against extensionalists, in particular Quine, has been that their account of logical form rests, ultimately, on an arbitrary distinction between a vocabulary of logical words and the rest of the vocabulary of the language. No satisfactory difference between the so-called "logical vocabulary" and the so-called "nonlogical vocabulary" has been made out either on an ordinary intuitive basis or on a theoretical basis. Pretheoretically, there is no logical distinction between standard examples of implication like the one from "Spassky can beat Fischer if anyone can but Spassky can't beat Fischer" to "No one can beat Fischer" and allegedly nonlogical cases like "Spassky had a nightmare about Fischer" to "Spassky had a dream about

Fischer" or "Spassky persuaded Fischer that Fischer shouldn't play" to "Fischer believed he shouldn't play". Theoretically, the attempts to provide a relevant difference have been completely unsuccessful.[87] The logical/nonlogical distinction, then, amounts to listing words like "not", "all", "and", etc. under the heading "logical vocabulary" and words like "nightmare", "dream", "persuade", "believe", etc. under the heading "nonlogical vocabulary".

Further, we can argue that the logical structure of the words listed as "logical vocabulary" so interlaces with the logical structure of those listed as "nonlogical vocabulary" that no complete theory even of logical form in the narrow sense is possible if one sticks to the notion that the logical form of sentences is determined solely by their "logical vocabulary". Consider the following example. Extensionalists are committed to constructing a theory of the logical form of sentences in natural language which fully represents their quantificational structure. Thus, they are required not only to formalize the standardly treated quantifiers "all" and "some" but also such quantifiers as "many", "few", "most", "several", "nearly all", "seventeen", and so on. Moreover, they will also have to account for the grammatical structures that make a word of the language a quantifier in one sentential context but not another. What makes a word a quantifier is not an inherent feature of the word itself but the role it plays in a sentence. For example, "all" and "seventeen" are quantifiers in "All God's children have wings" or "Seventeen of God's children have wings" but not in "Most of all humanity is good-natured" or "Only two of the seventeen survivors lived". In the quantifier role, a number word is used to express how many of the objects referred to by a term are asserted to have a certain property or relation, whereas, in the non-quantifier role, a number word is used no differently from any other modifier of a nominal. Thus, in the sentence "Only two of the seventeen (many, etc.) survivors lived", the number word "seventeen" ("many," etc.) modifies the nominal "survivors", functioning semantically to help pin down the set of objects that the subject of the sentence refers to in the manner of ordinary modifiers such as "starving" or "sun-burned" in "Only two of the starving (sun-burned) survivors lived".

Now, the quantifier position in sentences is a syntactic position that can be recursively expanded: there is no upper limit on the length of the quantifier expression that can occur in the position, for example, "The number of survivors equal to the sum of five plus seven lived", "The number of survivors equal to the sum of five plus seven plus the square root of twenty five lived", etc. Moreover, there is no word of the language that does not occur as part of the quantifier in a quantifier position in sentences. For example, the words "bachelor" or "nightmare" occur as part of the quantifier in "A number of survivors equal to the number of bachelors who have had a nightmare survived". Therefore, there can be no account of the full quantificational structure of natural languages if the so-called non-logical vocabulary are excluded from making a contribution to logical form.

Quinians will reply that a logic of two quantifiers is logic enough for us. Such a "spare" logic is to be marked off from the "lusher" systems that try to account for the full range of quantifiers in natural language by a number of metatheorems about consistency, etc. But, rather than a rebuttal, this reply merely reasserts the arbitrary distinction between logical and nonlogical vocabulary, this time taking the form of a distinction between logical and nonlogical quantifiers. The claim to mark off the "spare" logic on the basis of metatheorems, even if correct,[88] would no more justify counting the "lusher" systems as nonlogical than would theorems about tautologies justify counting systems of predicate calculus as nonlogical.

Thus, Chomsky's skepticism is confronted with a dilemma. Given that the distinction between logical and nonlogical vocabulary is arbitrary and untenable, all meaningful words in a natural language must be accorded the same logical status. Therefore, either all such words are treated as Quine treats the logical vocabulary or as he treats the non-logical vocabulary. Both choices abandon (D), but the first abandons skepticism, too. The question, then, is whether the price of taking the second choice—total exclusion of logical structure from sentence-grammar—is too high to make hanging on to skepticism reasonable.

There seems no doubt but that the price is too high. The total exclusion of semantics and logical structure from grammar not only sacrifices long standing goals of grammar, such as explaining ambiguity, thematic relations, pronominal relations, etc., but also denies that grammatical structure plays any role in the logical inferences people make beyond the trivial matter of providing conditions for assigning phonetic tokens to syntactic types. The choice of saying that no meaningful word makes a logical contribution and hence no sentence has a logical structure constitutes a throwback to the conception of grammar in American structuralism.

Chomsky is not always clear about his account of logical form. Sometimes he explains logical form as the set of grammatical phenomena that the SR-1 rules he has developed up to that point can be expected to handle.[89] But, by and large, he takes the development of his SR-1 rules to aim at an account of logical structure in essentially the sense of classical logic. This program can only be understood as an attempt to develop an account of the logical structure of sentences that will explain the applicability of logical principles in the narrow sense of classical logic's quantification theory. Chomsky says, "I use [logical form] to refer to those aspects of semantic representation that are strictly determined by grammar, abstracted from other cognitive systems" (other cognitive systems including meaning, speaker's beliefs, and so on),[90] and he takes the analyses of quantificational structures which are given by *SR-1* rules to justify classical logic against the claims of non-standard logics like Montague's. Chomsky writes:

The rules *SI-1* apply to an enriched surface structure, including trace, giving an analysis in terms of quantifiers and bound variables. Further rules of *SI-1* (those of anaphora) assign these representations a specific range of more explicit representations within *LF*. These considerations again seem to me to support the classical logical analysis over the revision suggested by Montague, if we take these as theories with empirical import.[91]

It seems clear, then, that Chomsky is claiming that "enriched surface structure" and *SI-1* rules vindicate "classical logical analysis" in the controversy over whether such analysis is too narrow, and that, therefore, support the extensionalist side in the controversy about logical form in natural language. Indeed, the extensionalist's distinction between "logical vocabulary" and "non-logical vocabulary" is mirrored in Chomsky's distinction between the elements in "enriched surface structure" to which *SI-1* rules apply, on the one hand, and the meanings of nouns, verbs, adjectives, and so on outside grammar within the "broader semiotic theory", on the other.

I will make a few comments on this claim. First, it is hard to see that Chomsky's new conception of sentence-grammar supports "classical logical analysis" when the new conception also fails to offer any reason for the distinction between logical and nonlogical vocabularies. The arbitrariness associated with the logical/nonlogical distinction in classical logic cannot be removed by an equally arbitrary logical/nonlogical distinction in contemporary grammar.[92]

Second, there is actually no convergence here between the needs of logic, even logic construed narrowly as in classical logic, and the resources of sentence-grammar on Chomsky's new conception. The new conception is both too broad and too narrow an account of logical form. It is too broad because the conception treats features of sentences having nothing to do with matters of logic as if they were part of logical form (understood so that something is a matter of logical form just in case the difference between its presence and absence is the difference between the presence and absence of implications). For example, as Langendoen points out,[93] sentences like "Mary gave Bill a present'' and ''Bill, Mary gave a present'' or sentences like ''Amy gave BILL a car'' and ''Amy gave Bill a CAR'' are represented as different in logical form by Chomsky, while classical logic treats the members of such pairs as the same in logical form. Another set of examples proving that Chomsky's conception (D) is too broad are synonymous sentences that are not natural answers to the same question, such as ''The house is above the stream'' and ''The stream is below the house''. Clearly such cases have the same implications.

Chomsky's new conception also gives too narrow an account of logical form. The conception has to get out of the inconsistencies noted above, resulting from the boundary between the grammatical and the non-grammatical being drawn in such a way that, while *SR-1* rules are grammatical rules and *SR-2* rules are not, *SR-1* rules are responsible for phenomena that cannot be handled without access to *SR-2* rules. To restore consistency, Chomsky would have to drop the explanation of ambiguity, referential relations, and thematic relations from the goals of sentence-grammar. This, however, significantly increases the separation between Chomsky's account of logical form and the real notion, since these grammatical phenomena play an unquestionably important role in determining the implication relations between sentences. For example, the representation of an ambiguous sentence is the representation of it as expressing distinct propositions, each of which is subject to different logical laws. For another example, thematic relations play the crucial role in logical form of relating terms to their proper argument places in predicates; without them, the output of *SR-1* rules would represent a jumble of terms and predicates rather than a structured proposition. Therefore, the account of logical form that Chomsky's enriched surface structure and *SR-1* rules provide fails in both directions, and thus captures no pretheoretically significant notion of logical structure.[94]

Chomsky's arguments against compositionality. One might suspect that even a fully adequate reply to Chomsky's skepticism about meaning would fall short of an exoneration of the theory of meaning sufficient to enable us to base arguments for an ontological position on that theory. Chomsky is a linguist, and prominent anti-intensional arguments are found also in philosophy; so perhaps these arguments would be left unanswered by confining our attention to Chomsky. This is not the case. Chomsky, in fact, buttresses his skepticism with the three main philosophical arguments against the theory of meaning. Thus, a full and adequate reply to Chomsky's skepticism will take care of anti-intensional arguments in philosophy as well.

One of these philosophical arguments is the attack on compositionality initiated by Mates and then employed by Davidson to motivate abandoning intensional analysis of logical form for a purely extensional analysis based on Tarski's truth definition.[95] The other two philosophical arguments are the one Putnam has constructed from alleged counter-examples to there being a class of analytic truths and the one Quine has constructed against semantic properties and relations serving as the basis for a scientific theory of language. I will reply to the first of these three arguments in this section and the next two in the final section.

There are two versions of the principle of compositionality. One, which we might call the *fundamental principle*, says that the meaning of a sentence is a function of the meanings of its constituent lexical items and its syntactic structure. The other, which we might call the *cyclic principle*, says further that the compositional process moves progressively outward from the most deeply embedded constituents of a sentence. I will suppose the cyclic principle for the purposes of the present discussion because it is the strongest, the one I have tried to explicate, and the one Chomsky's arguments are directed at.

Chomsky has recently used two arguments against the claim that meaning is compositional.[96] One is expressed as follows:

. . . consider such sentences as *everyone agrees that if John realizes that p, then he realizes that—*, where the space is filled either by *p* itself or by an expression *q* distinct from but synonymous with *p*. No doubt the truth value may change, as *q* replaces *p*, indicating that any difference of form of an embedded sentence can, in certain cases at least, play a role in the statement of truth conditions, hence, presumably, the determination of meaning. It remains to be determined whether there is some interesting subclass of such cases in which differences of deep structure suffice to account for the meaning differences, as the standard theory would require.[97]

The mistake in this argument is the assumption that the problem lies with compositionality rather than with the condition for substitution into opaque contexts. Chomsky makes the assumption, I think, because, since Frege, people have become accustomed to supposing that *the* intensionalist principle for making valid inferences when substituting into an opaque context is that synonymous expressions may be substituted *salva veritate*. But Frege's is neither the only intensionalist principle nor the most desirable one. In order to exonerate compositionality, I shall set out an alternative intensionalist principle that avoids the problem Chomsky raises that semantic equals added to semantic equals does not seem to yield semantic equals.[98] My plan is to begin with the grounds on which an intensionalist might be dissatisfied with Frege's principle, then revise Frege's principle, and finally show that the revised principle automatically handles the problem that Chomsky raises.

Frege's principle has one particularly undesirable feature for the intensionalist. It fails to capture a class of inferences that intensionalists are committed to as much as they are committed to the class it captures. For example, an inference like that from "I believe that I had a nightmare" to "I believe that I had a dream" which depends not on synonymy but on meaning inclusion is outside the scope of Frege's principle. To capture such implications, it is necessary to replace synonymy with semantic entailment (analytic inclusion) in the substitution conditions.[99] This change, however, requires a further change in Frege's principle, since the principle resulting from a direct replacement countenances invalid inferences like that from "Sam doubts that there are bachelors at the country club on family night" to "Sam doubts that there are males at the country club on family night."

The problem is that no account has been taken of the special class of opaque contexts that I have called "translucent contexts".[100] Such a context is the locus of an operation performed on the meaning of the constituent occurring in the context (e.g., "that there are bachelors at the country club on family night") by the meaning of the constituent creating the context (e.g., "doubts"). The operation changes the object of the propositional attitude from that expressed in the meaning of the embedded constituent to a function of both meanings. "Doubts" creates a translucent context: the meaning of the constituent "there are bachelors at the country club on family night" is changed by the negative component in the meaning of "doubts" to make the object of Sam's doubt the truth of the disjunction that either there are humans or adults or single people or males at the country club. Thus, the source invalidity of the inference from "Sam doubts that there are bachelors at the country club on family night" to "Sam doubts that there are males at the country club on family night" occurs at a level of the compositional process higher than the level at which Frege's principle for substitution imposes its semantic condition. Frege's condition held between clauses; the correct condition must hold between sentences. It is necessary, then, to make the further revision that the semantic condition that replaces synonymy, (*viz.*, semantic entailment) apply after all relevant compositional operations. The new intensionalist principle for substitution into an opaque context in a sentence S_i is that the substitution result in a sentence S_j such that S_j is semantically entailed by S_i. That is, the relation between the senses of S_i and S_j is that S_j's sense is analytically included in S_i's. Application of the definition of semantic entailment to full sentences automatically distinguishes the valid inferences involving opaque contexts from the invalid ones.

If Chomsky is correct about the meaning of "realize," in that reference can be made to "any difference of form of an embedded sentence," then "realize" also creates a translucent context, and its contribution can be handled on our theory. Let us take the meaning of "realize" to be something like what Chomsky is assuming: someone's realizing that p is that person's seeing that p depicts a real state of affairs. That is, the contribution that "realizing that p" can make to the truth conditions of a sentence differs from the contribution that "realizing that q" can make because of differences in the form of the sentences p and q. Someone can realize that p but fail to realize that q, even though p and q express the same proposition (and thus depict the same state of affairs), because realizing is a relation between a person, a particular sentence, and the state of things. In a nutshell, what Jane realizes when it's true that "Jane realizes that she has no indoor swimming pool" is different from what she realizes when it's true that "Jane realizes that she has no natatorium" because the object of the propositional attitude is a function of both the meaning of the complement sentence and the form of the sentence to which "realize" makes reference.[101]

Although Frege's principle permits the inference from "Jane realizes that she has no indoor swimming pool" to "Jane realizes that she has no natatorium", our new intensional principle does not. The former sentence does not semantically entail the latter because the former asserts that Jane sees that "Jane has no indoor swimming pool" reflects how things are, while the latter asserts that Jane sees that "Jane has no natatorium" reflects how things are. Since the cyclic version of compositionality predicts the differences Chomsky's argument is based on, he is mistaken in thinking that cases like "realize" offer an argument against compositionality.

Chomsky's second argument against compositionality runs as follows:

In ["the boys have living parents" and "unicycles have wheels"], plurality is, in a sense, a semantic property of the sentence rather than the individual noun phrases in which it is formally expressed. "Unicycles have wheels" means that each unicycle has a wheel, and is thus true, though "each unicycle has wheels" is false.

In these relatively simple examples, . . . it seems plain that the syntactic structures are not a projection of the semantics, and that the relation between "the world of ideas" and the syntactic system is fairly intricate. As the "plural sentences" show, even a principle of compositionality is suspect. . . . We cannot simply assign a meaning to the subject and a meaning to the predicate . . ., and then combine the two. Rather, the meaning assigned to each phrase depends on the form of the phrase with which it is paired.[102]

This argument, too, rests on a false assumption about compositionality, in this case, that compositionality ignores the syntactic microstructure of constituents. The fundamental principle says that the meaning of a sentence is a function of the meaning of *all* its constituents and *all* aspects of their syntactic structure.[103]

Here is one way in which a compositional theory can handle Chomsky's judgments that "Unicycles have wheels" is true while "Each unicycle has wheels" is false.[104] The subjects of the plural sentences are plural, collective, noun phrases, whereas the subjects of the sentences with "each" are not. The subjects of the sentences with "each" have semantically distributive quantifiers, whereas the subjects of the plural sentences do not. The "each" sentences can be glossed "Each separately (individually) has wheels".[105] There is, moreover, an ambiguity in the predicate "have/has wheels" between the senses 'is wheeled' and 'has more than one wheel'. The interpretation of the plural-collective noun phrases involves reference to objects as members of a class (or kind), while the interpretation of singular-distributive noun phrases involves reference to objects separately (individually), but "each" is also a universal quantifier, referring exhaustively over the full range of the objects in question. Accordingly, the subjects disambiguate: the plural-collective subjects select the predicate for classes or kinds, namely, 'is wheeled,' while the singular-distributive select the predicate for individuals, namely, 'has more than one wheel.' Thus, a compositional theory sensitive to the syntactic microstructure of these sentences predicts that "Unicycles have wheels" says that unicycles are wheeled, and that "Each unicycle has wheels" says that individual unicycles have more than one wheel.

Putnam's and Quine's anti-intensionalist arguments. Chomsky writes:

A review of the arguments for inseparability of knowledge of language from belief and fact supports this line of reasoning, I believe. These arguments relate, or can be reduced to the "theory of significations of words," and thus, if correct, show only that that part of grammar that Jespersen called "the dictionary," which deals with "special facts," involves considerations of fact and belief. The conclusion, then, would be that a full dictionary cannot be distinguished in a principled way from an encyclopedia, while a grammar can be distinguished as a separate idealized structure, with certain aspects of dictionary entries as parameters. We might accept the legitimacy of the parametrized idealization, while agreeing with Hilary Putnam, for example, that "natural kind" terms such as "lemon," "water," "run," and so on, cannot be provided with "dictionary entries" that ignore matters of fact and belief. Then as Quine has argued, analyticity will not always be distinguished from shared belief.[106]

Such quotations make it clear that Chomsky sees the arguments of Putnam and Quine as supporting his conception (D) and intends his readers to so view them. Putnam's and Quine's arguments not only support the distinction (D) makes between grammar, a "separate idealized structure", and other cognitive systems, in which meaning is inextricably bound up with factual belief, their arguments supply an explanation for why meaning is bound up with factual belief. The explanation is that there is no such thing as the rationalist's sharply separated realm of propositions, but only the empiricist's uniformly contingent, empirical beliefs, including relatively stable criteria, stereotypes, stimulus meanings, and so on. Thus, meanings are bound up with factual belief because they, too, are factual belief. If Chomsky's endorsement of Putnam's and Quine's arguments were complete and unqualified, he would have a comprehensive skeptical position, including an explanation of interpenetration.

But Chomsky exhibits a certain unwillingness to take Putnam's and Quine's arguments to their logical conclusion. In a couple of places, Chomsky suggests that features of lexical items produce analytic connections, e.g., that "I persuaded him to leave" might analytically entail "He intends to leave".[107] Such suggestions, if serious, make Chomsky's overall writings on the subject inconsistent. Chomsky cannot adopt Putnam and Quine's arguments to support (D) and at the same time accept the possibility of genuinely analytic sentences, which are counter-examples to their arguments. Putnam's and Quine's arguments are general; they are not aimed at particular sentences like "Cats are animals" or "Bachelors are unmarried". Their arguments are intended to show that there are no analytic connections whatever, and no analytic-synthetic distinction however narrowly defined. Their arguments against the distinction between knowledge of meaning internal to a language and knowledge of extra-grammatical fact, if sound, leave no room for a marginal a priori connection here and there. On the other hand, if Chomsky's cases are examples of analytic sentences, then discussions of whether such cases like "Bachelors are unmarried" are analytic—whether such cases belong with analytic sentences like "Someone who is persuaded to leave intends to leave" or with synthetic sentences like "Someone who is persuaded to leave will leave"—are merely about matters of detail.

The gravity of the charge of inconsistency makes it worthwhile to take further pains to make sure that the charge is correct. Putnam and Quine address their arguments to the question of whether there is, in principle, an acceptable theoretical specification of the domain of meaning. Their arguments are designed to show that there isn't, because the notion of meaning is like the notion of witchcraft. On their view, nothing counts as an analytic connection, anymore than anything counts as an effect of witchcraft. Now, Chomsky's suggestion that "I persuaded him to leave" analytically entails "He intended to leave" parcels out particular sentences into the categories of the analytic and the synthetic: "Someone who is persuaded to leave intends to leave" is put in the former and "Someone who is persuaded to leave will leave" is put in the latter. Therefore, Chomsky's suggestion *presupposes* a legitimate domain of meaning. Hence, if Chomsky is right, Putnam and Quine are wrong. Even if there is only one case of analytic entailment, there is a scientifically acceptable domain of meaning. The size of the domain is not at issue. It matters not the slightest whether there are infinitely many analytic sentences, as intensionalists think, or very few, as Chomsky's remarks imply. There is only one even prime, but that's enough to put the lie to the notion that an even prime is a chimera.

Given the marginal nature of the "persuade"/"intend" case and the centrality of Chomsky's new conception of sentence-grammar to his recent work, it seems that the inconsistency should be resolved in the direction of agreement with Putnam and Quine's criticism of the analytic-synthetic distinction and their view of meaning as part of a homogeneous fabric of extra-grammatical, empirical beliefs about the world. Only with this resolution, moreover, can Chomsky provide an account of why meaning is bound up with general belief.

It might seem *prima facie* strange to find an exponent of rationalism like Chomsky appealing to the arguments of empiricists like Putnam and Quine. But, as we pointed out already, Chomsky's position is not really the full-blooded rationalism of the classical philosophical tradition but only the nativistic claim that what we know is not learned from experience but innate. Classical rationalism makes the qualitatively different claim that there are necessary truths and they form an ontological domain independent from the physical and psychological. Classical rationalism intersects with nativism in holding that some of these truths are known to us on the basis of our innate endowment. Thus, Chomsky is far closer to Quine of late than to rationalism.

Philosophers are sometimes puzzled about where, exactly, Chomsky and Quine differ on issues like how much of language is innate. Chomsky has, of course, criticized Quine's acceptance of Skinner's psychology.[108] But, then again, Quine's innate quality space and distance measure raises the question of whether Quine isn't in some sense just as strong a nativist as Chomsky.[109] The difficulty that philosophers have in answering this question has been due to the fact that *Word and Object* does not make clear how powerful an innateness claim Quine wants to make. Now, however, Quine has clarified the point by stating that the quality space and distance measure determine logical form up to the quantificational notion of logical form.[110] Given that Chomsky's new model *(D)* reduces the scope of logical form in grammar down to the quantificational notion of logical form, there is a perfect coincidence. Thus, the initial strangeness dissappears because Chomsky turns out not to be a rationalist in any sense that might bother Quine.[111]

There is an irony in Chomsky's appeal to the arguments of Putnam and Quine: both Putnam's argument and Quine's argument fail because of Chomsky's contributions. Putnam's fail because of Chomsky's competence/performance distinction; Quine's fail because of Chomsky's refutation of the structuralist's taxonomic theory of grammar. Thus, Chomsky's own methodological and theoretical innovations undercut the support that his new conception of sentence-grammar might receive from the philosophical arguments of Putnam and Quine.

Putnam's arguments in his principal anti-intensionalist papers are all variants of the following argument.[112] It could turn out that cats are actually robots that look and behave like feline animals; if so, the sentence "Cats are animals" is false; hence, the sentence cannot be analytic, for if it were, it couldn't be false. All of Putnam's arguments, whether about blue lemons, pencils that turn out to be organisms, machine-trees, water and twin-earth water, etc., are of this form. The problem with the argument is that it is a non-sequitur. Yes, it is certainly possible that the objects we have been picking out in our referential uses of "cat" could be robots and not feline animals. But this possibility does not decide whether "cat" means "feline animal". The fact that the objects that the citizens of old Salem had been picking out in their referential uses of "witch" turned out to be ordinary women obviously did not determine that "witch" does not mean "woman possessing supernatural powers by virtue of a pact with an evil spirit". Putnam's hypothetical circumstances have no more bearing on the truth or falsehood of "Cats are animals" than the actual circumstances about the accused women in old Salem have on the truth or falsehood of "Witches possess supernatural powers". But if such circumstances have no bearing on the truth or falsehood of "Cats are animals", their imaginability does not refute the claim that the sentence is analytic.

If it really turned out that cats are robots, electronic devices put here by ill-intentioned aliens, and we knew that every cat on earth was actually a robot, we would still tell our children that Puss-in-Boots is a fictional animal, just as we tell them that witches possess supernatural powers. We would *not* tell our children that Puss-in-Boots was a fictional robot device for electronic surveillance. The reason is that meaning relations are not relations to empirical fact but relations in language. Because the concept of animal is part of the concept of cat, it determines our characterization of Puss-in-Boots despite what may be the case in empirical fact. Putnam's claim that it is possible for the objects to which people actually refer in uses of "cat" to be non-animals, being about empirical fact, is irrelevant to the thesis about language that the concept of cat contains the concept animal as a part. The latter thesis does not claim that people cannot *use* words to refer to objects that do not fall under the meaning of those words.

Two questions remain: one is how meanings in languages are ascertained independently of the empirical facts about the world and the other is how people use words to refer to objects that do not fall under their meaning. Let us take them in order. Kant would have said that the linguistic relation between "cat" and "animal" is ascertained by thinking through the concept of a cat to see if the concept of an animal is contained therein. This rightly puts the emphasis on the *a priori* as a means of answering conceptual questions, but, as his critics pointed out, it relies on a metaphorical notion of containment and applies only to subject-predicate sentences.[113] But the shortcomings can be fixed up using Chomsky's framework of generative grammar and the distinction it draws between matters of language and matters of its use. If we embed the problem of analyticity in this framework by taking analyticity as one of the semantic properties and relations to be accounted for in grammatical derivations, then questions of the analyticity of sentences can be decided on the basis of judgments about the internal grammatical structure of sentences in just the way that questions about well-formedness or rhyme are decided in syntax and phonology. In this framework, Kant's metaphorical notion of containment is replaced by a formal relation between semantic representations and extension of the concept of analyticity to transitive verb sentences is straightforward.[114]

How could people all along have referred to robots with the word "cat" when *ex hypothesi* "cat" means "feline animal"? The problem that has to be overcome in answering this question was created for contemporary intensionalism by Frege who claimed, wrongly, that sense determines reference simpliciter. We have to abandon the lore of earlier intensionalism and use our conception of semantic theory in generative grammar to develop a conception of the relation between meaning and reference on which extra-grammatical beliefs enter into the fixing of reference in language use. Then, we can explain references to robots with "cat" (or to ordinary women with "witch") on the basis of certain false beliefs about the objects in question which, *because of* the linguistic facts about their meaning, disposes the language user to think that they fall under the meaning of the word. In the robot-cat case, people falsely believe that things that behave in certain animal-like ways are in fact directing their own movements. In the witch case, citizens of Salem believe in supernatural powers and evil spirits. Therefore, these cases are essentially the same as Donnellan's more prosaic cases of reference under a false description, such as, a myopic person's reference to a man with a walking stick under the false description "the man carrying an umbrella".[115]

What relation can meaning and reference have such that a description is false and yet is the description under which reference takes place? There is no answer if we assume, as Frege and other traditional intensionalists did, that there is a single notion of reference. But this assumption is wrong. There must be two notions, one that functions as the criterion for saying that the description is false, and one in accord with which robots, ordinary women, and the man with a walking stick are the object(s) referred to on the uses of language in question. The former notion, which I will call the "type reference", is one in which only the meaning of an expression in the language provides the information for determining the referent; the latter notion, which I will call the "token reference", is one in which, in addition to meaning, various beliefs of the speaker, etc. provide the information for determining the referent.[116] Cases of reference under a false description can thus be explained as cases in which the type referent, projected from the meaning of the expression, is not the token referent on the particular use in question because contextual factors, such as shared belief, true or false, knowledge of a predisposing disability (e.g., myopia), and so on, enable actual reference to succeed in spite of the false projection from semantic competence (and sometime, as with sarcasm, because of it). In the cases of "witch" and, on Putnam's hypothetical, of "cat", both words lack a type referent: witches do not exist in the actual world and cats do not exist in the possible world that Putnam asks us to entertain.[117]

Given the notions of type and token reference, the old question of whether meaning determines reference is seen as two separate questions: Does meaning determine type reference? Does meaning determine token reference? On my theory, meaning determines type reference but not token reference, since the latter is strongly influenced by extragrammatical beliefs, performance factors. What relation, then, does meaning, or conditions for type reference, bear to token reference?

We have already suggested part of the answer: the condition for the type referent(s) of an expression functions as a criterion for the literal uses of the expression (thus when token reference occurs under a false description). The rest of the answer requires an explanation of why speakers should need token reference over and above type reference. It is true that, restricted to type reference, we would be condemned to literalness, but there are people who are completely literal. Although their lives are less interesting, they get along. Why should we need token reference?

The only answer that seems plausible is this. In order to maintain the stability in our system of concepts and its grammatical correlation to sensible signs, meanings have to be abstract enough to withstand changes in belief, experience, etc. But this makes meanings too abstract for efficient reference to objects in communication. Consequently, a further mechanism, employing far less abstract identifying conditions, is needed to connect words and the world in practical life.[118] For example, the semantic concepts 'animal' (capable of self-directed movements) and 'possesses supernatural powers' in the meanings of "cat" and "witch" are too abstract to afford language users a quick and easy means to make referential identifications. Extragrammatical stereotypes (insofar as they correlate with the extension of semantic concepts) compensate for such abstractness.

Putting the two parts of the answer together, we get the theory that token reference is accomplished by semantic performance principles operating as a heuristic programming system. The conditions for type reference, determined by meaning, function as the *fail-proof procedures*. The heuristic programming system accesses the speaker's semantic competence to obtain dictionary entries and semantic rules that specify these conditions for type reference, and it uses them to decide questions of standard or literal use. The conditions for token reference, determined by extra-grammatical beliefs found to correlate sufficiently with the type reference,[119] function as *heuristic strategies*. The system accesses the speaker's general knowledge of the world to obtain beliefs, stereotypes, etc. suitable for expediting identification of the token referents of utterances.[120]

This theory gives content to the notion of a semantic competence/performance distinction by dividing the task of explaining referential acts into explaining the contribution of the speaker's knowledge of the semantic structure of the language and explaining the contribution of his or her extragrammatical beliefs, intentions, etc. Furthermore, in assigning different functions to semantic competence and semantic performance factors in acts of reference, the theory exhibits the independence and priority of semantic competence with respect to the use of words in speech.

It is by virtue of this independence and priority that questions of analyticity cannot be settled on the basis of empirical cases. Because such cases concern connections between language and the world, they are irrelevant to questions about the internal grammatical structure of the language.[121] But, since analytic connections are intragrammatical, they set prior limits on what cases are possible in the same way logical connections do: if "Cats are animals" is analytic, a world in which cats are robots is no more a possible world than one in which someone is not happy and yet everyone is happy. Chomsky's competence/performance distinction, his distinction between language and its use, blocks the argument of Putnam's that Chomsky appeals to in support of his semantic skepticism.

The irony is even deeper in Quine's case. Quine tries to establish the strongest possible skepticism, namely, that the central notions of the theory of meaning correspond to no reality. He argues for the claim that there is no fact of the matter in questions of meaning on the grounds that there is no possibility for a scientific theory of meaning. The notions of synonymy and analyticity are too hopelessly confused to provide the necessary identity conditions for meanings and propositions. But, as I shall try to show, Quine's argument that these semantic notions are too confused for use in scientific theorizing about language rests on a conception of the ways in which linguistic constructs might be explicated that is valid only within the structuralist approach to linguistics—the approach Chomsky refuted.

Quine's case against meanings, from the earliest statement to the most recent, depends on his argument that the notions of synonymy and analyticity are hopelessly unclear. His argument for indeterminacy of translation rests on it,[122] and without it, his opponent always has the option available of using these notions to construct a comprehensive, explanatory theory for the pretheoretic semantic domain in the hope that the theory will vindicate these notions. The specific points at which Quine's argument rests on the structuralist approach are, first, its assumption of having exhaustively examined the possible ways that the central notions in the theory of meaning might be clarified, and second, its use of taxonomic standards to obtain the conclusion that these notions cannot, in principle, be clarified sufficiently for use in scientific theorizing. The only proper kind of explication for linguistic concepts on Quine's assumption is a substitution test based on distributional features of sentences.[123] Quine's appeal to structuralist theory in this connection is explicit. Quine writes:

So-called substitution criteria, or conditions of interchangeability, have in one form or another played central roles in modern grammar [= the structuralist's taxonomic theory—the theory of Bloomfield, Bloch, Trager, all of whom Quine explicitly cites]. For the synonymy problem of sentences such an approach seems more obvious still.[124]

The question of the scientific acceptability of the theory of meaning is thus, with the help of taxonomic theory, brought down to the question of whether it is possible to formulate a substitution test which, when applied to a corpus, empirically separates synonymous expressions from non-synonymous ones or analytic sentences from non-analytic ones on the basis of an appropriate, non-circular distributional property.

Now Quine easily shows that the all such substitution tests will lead to vicious circularity. The corpus is not allowed to contain substitution contexts that are intensional (e.g., "Necessarily, _____") because this begs the question, but if there are only extensional contexts, there is no way to specify a property that is preserved when and only when an expression is replaced by a synonym, short of using a property like analyticity. The absence of any non-circular substitution test leads Quine to conclude not only that semantic notions like synonymy have not been adequately clarified but that they cannot be explained in the science of language, and hence cannot, in principle, be clarified.

But Quine's conclusion only follows assuming that the taxonomic framework can be relied on to present the full range of possibilities for explication and clarification of concepts in the science of language. If one does not accept that framework, circularity can be interpreted as showing that something is wrong with the use of substitution procedures to clarify linguistic concepts. Quine's argument can thus be turned around, becoming a *reductio* of the claim that substitution procedures are an acceptable standard of clarity.

Chomsky's linguistic revolution, as we saw in the early chapters, overthrows the entire taxonomic framework. Further, Chomsky's theory of generative grammar provides an alternative way of explicating synonymy and other central semantic notions and an alternative standard of conceptual clarity.[125] Chomsky's new theory replaces distributional analysis with the construction of formal characterizations of highly abstract systems of rules that themselves define linguistic notions and their indirect confirmation. The concern of scientific theorizing about language is no longer devising procedures for the step by step inductive generalization of linguistic concepts out of the utterances in a corpus but rather with characterizing, as Chomsky puts it, "the properties of the completed solution".[126] The use of substitution tests disappears entirely, replaced by methodological principles for evaluating systems of formal rules as the best means of predicting and explaining grammatical facts. Thus, the circularity Quine discovered in attempts to clarify semantic notions on the basis of a substitution test no longer counts against their acceptability: the circularity is a product of a data-cataloguing approach to scientific theorizing about language, not of an inherent confusion in semantic notions.

Chomsky's approach of characterizing abstract systems of formal rules and evaluating their predictions and explanations offers a way of clarifying semantic notions that, unlike lexicographical definition and rational reconstruction, does not rest on prior synonymy relations but explains them. Synonymy and analyticity are explicated on the basis of definitions which are part of a semantic theory (which is part of linguistic theory). Semantic notions are defined on the model of definitions of other grammatical notions in linguistic theory. Syntactic notions, for example, are defined relative to the concept of syntactic rule and the concept of an optimal grammar (characterized in terms of methodological principles), e.g., 'S is syntactically well-formed' is defined in terms of the existence of a derivation of S in an optimal grammar. Semantic notions can, in analogy, be defined relative to the concept of semantic rules and the concept of an optimal grammar, e.g., 'S_i and S_j are synonymous' is defined in terms of the semantic rules of an optimal grammar providing derivations for S_i and S_j that terminate in the same semantic representation.

This new way of explicating semantic notions explains them in the same way in which syntactic definitions explain syntactic notions. Such definitions of semantic notions assume semantic representations of senses, just as syntactic definitions assume syntactic representations of constituent structure. Relative to a system of semantic representations, semantic definitions reveal the compositional structures across sentences that are necessary and sufficient for synonymy, analyticity, and so on. Such definitions specify the structure of senses that constitutes a sense's having a semantic property or relation. Since theoretical definition in this sense is not a possibility for linguistics on the taxonomic theory, explication via theoretical definition does not appear among the ways of clarifying semantic notions that Quine considers.

Quine's famous thesis of indeterminacy of translation says that the question of the meaning of an expression or the absolute synonymy of expressions is indeterminate because there is no fact of the matter to examine in an attempt to choose between non-equivalent answers to them.[127] This thesis provides Quine with grounds for excluding meaning from logical form and it can provide Chomsky with the thus far missing rationale for his conception (D). Since the thesis claims that there is nothing that a semantic component of a grammar is about, Chomsky can use it to argue that representations of meaning are idle in a sentence-grammar. Without such an argument, Chomsky's conception of sentence-grammar *(D)*, inheriting the logician's arbitrary division of vocabularies into a "logical vocabulary" and "non-logical vocabulary", lacks an explanation of why the words baptised "logical", and only these, contribute to the logical form of sentences *in natural languages*. With Quine's thesis, Chomsky can argue that the logician's stipulated distinction can be replaced with a principled distinction that the logical vocabulary contains the words of a language whose translation is determinate while the non-logical vocabulary contains the words whose translation is indeterminate. Hence, inferences that depend just on the logical vocabulary can be given a special status, as Quine does,[128] by treating them as consequences of conventions that determine the limits of understanding. Inferences that at some point turn on the non-logical vocabulary receive the status of contingent relations.[129]

But Quine's thesis rests on Quine's claim that semantic notions like synonymy and analyticity cannot be sufficiently clarified to serve in a scientific theory of natural language. Quine himself points out that the difference between ordinary inductive risk in every science and the special indeterminacy of semantics is that there is a fact of the matter in legitimate sciences but no fact of the matter in semantics because there are no senses, meanings, propositions, over and above the sentences of a language, about which semantic claims may be right or wrong.[130] The only argument Quine gives for this difference is his earlier argument that semantic notions are too hopelessly confused to be part of a theory in linguistics.

Now the indeterminacy thesis is supposed to be established *a priori* and to thereby rule out the very possibility of scientific semantics in the classical sense. The case for indeterminacy cannot leave the classical semanticist with the response, "Well, it was also at one time not determined how one settled questions about atoms or when objects have the same atomic structure; semantics may have a promising future, too". But insofar as the indeterminacy thesis rests on Quine's early circularity arguments against synonymy and analyticity, and these collapse with the collapse of structuralism, there is no basis for not allowing the option of constructing a comprehensive, explanatory theory based on pretheoretic intuitions about meaning, and therefore, still no basis for Quine's and Chomsky's account of logical form.

Indeed, allowing such an option enables us to show how indeterminacy can be avoided even in the most extreme case of radical translation.[131] Since now there is no structuralist requirement that we have to define grammatical concepts in terms of inductive generalizations from a corpus, the concepts of analyticity and synonymy themselves may be used in constructing a theory of translation and in confirming its predictions on the basis of the judgments of speakers, particularly bilinguals, about synonymy relations, analyticities, etc.

Now, Quine is widely thought to have disposed of any such a "bilingual ploy" by pointing out that the bilinguals would be illicitly helping themselves to analytic hypotheses in making such judgments. But without Quine's arguments against the semantic properties and relations there is nothing illicit in the bilingual or the monolingual or the multilingual employing tacit hypotheses about semantic structure of sentences so long as the truth of their judgments can be checked in the course of theory construction in the same way that the truth of judgements about syntactic structure or logical structure is checked. We help ourselves to or make use of tacit hypotheses in judging syntactic fact or logical fact. Such tacit hypotheses are, on a Chomskian viewpoint, the competence a linguist is trying to construct a theory of. How can it be illicit to take account of consequences of the phenomena that one is trying to construct a theory of?

If the linguist can employ such evidence in the way that other scientists employ evidence, then the determination of synonymy, translation, analyticity, and so on faces at worst only the same garden variety inductive risk faced in other sciences. Hence, we can avail ourselves of evidence from bilingual speakers about whether, for example, "gavagai" is the same in meaning as "rabbit", "rabbit stage", or "undetached rabbit part". Linguists can ask bilinguals for their intuitive judgments about which, if any, of these English expressions is synonymous with "gavagai". Less crudely, linguists can ask for judgments about related phenomena, such as whether "gavagai" bears the relation to some expression (in either language) that "undetached finger" bears to "hand" in English. There are indefinitely many speakers available, a large number of different semantic properties and relations, and infinitely many sentences to ask about. Since we may assume, as other science do, that, with sufficient effort, the evidence will be adequate in enough cases, we may also assume that what is expressed in the hypotheses that best explain the evidence are the facts of the matter in the domain of meaning.

Notes

1. Frege 1967: 1–25.
2. The full argument for this will be presented in Smith and Katz, in preparation.
3. Fodor, Fodor, and Garrett 1975.
4. The discussion to follow is adapted with major revisions from Katz 1977b.
5. Fodor, Fodor, and Garrett 1975: 515.
6. It should be noted that the clause in *(A)* relativizing the notion of psychological reality to "appropriate idealizations" cannot be interpreted to include idealizations to competence. Such an interpretation would invalidate FFG's argument from psychological evidence concerning performance to conclusions about semantic competence, in much the same way that Chomsky's idealization to syntactic competence invalidates the argument from psychological evidence about the comprehension of multiply center-embedded sentences to conclusions about the well-formedness of such sentences. The expression "appropriate idealizations" must refer to the ones involved in constructing a performance model which does not have to reflect all the peculiarities of empirical situations from which its evidence is drawn, e. g., idealizations away from the particular subjects in an experiment, the stimulus materials, and so on.
7. Fodor, Fodor, and Garrett 1975: 516.
8. The omission of the operations that generate structural descriptions seems to be a matter of principle. (See Fodor and Garrett 1966) But this raises the further question of what can be the point of performance-oriented constraints on grammars if their imposition is arbitrarily restricted to just structural descriptions. One might guess that FFG leave out operations because, on the one hand, they think that the evidence now goes against the derivational theory of complexity, and, on the other, proposals for transformation-reduced grammars, though available, are not yet firmly enough entrenched. Thus, performance-oriented constraints that cover operations run the risk of ruling out too much of standard syntactic theory. But, if this risk is not taken, as it is not taken by FFG, we are left wondering why a distinction is made between what in grammars requires psychological credentials and what does not require them, when there is no relevant difference.
9. Fodor, Fodor, and Garrett 1975: 552–553.
10. Fodor and Garrett 1966: 152. Note that the notion of internal evidence used here by Fodor and Garrett is that of judgments of speakers about a sentence having a grammatical property or relation.
11. Fodor, Fodor, and Garrett 1975: 516.
12. Chomsky 1965: 3.
13. In a recent update of the position in Fodor, Fodor, and Garrett 1975, Fodor, Garrett, Walker, and Parkes 1980 acknowledge the problem raised in Katz 1977b with the use of chronometric data and provide non-chronometric data based on the Levelt paradigm for obtaining judgments of relatedness among constitutents of a sentence (on which subjects rank pairs of constitutents as to their respective relatedness). However, these new data do not improve their case against definition. First, the arguments in Katz 1977b against Fodor, Fodor, and Garrett's (A) are still not met. Second, questions concerning relatedness of constituents—concerning relatedness as such, with no clarification as to the nature of the relation(s)—are likely to reveal only syntactic relations, and syntactic relations are the only ones the Levelt technique is known to reveal. In particular, there is no reason to believe that relatedness questions can reveal semantic relations unless they are directly reflected in syntactic relations. Third, decompositional semantic relations tend to be more subtle and less accessible than others. Without doubt, the Fodor, Garrett, Walker, and Parkes subjects would fail to discriminate some semantic relations that could be discriminated by a Jespersen or J.L. Austin, but such failures hardly count against the existence of the semantic relations. The failures of the subjects to recognize semantic relations in these experi-

ments should be interpreted as showing also that the Levelt paradigm is a bad indicator of semantic relations.

14. Fodor, Fodor, and Garrett 1975: 517. These are two of the principal conditions, though there are others like compositionality and formal representability, and the conditions *(B)* and *(C)* are informative only relative to an account of what the semantic properties and relations in natural language are, how they are defined, and what the semantic structure of syntactically complex phrases is.

15. Fodor, Fodor, and Garrett 1975: 517.

16. Carnap 1956: 222–229.

17. Fodor, Fodor, and Garrett 1975: 518.

18. Fodor, Fodor, and Garrett 1975: 519.

19. Fodor, Fodor, and Garrett 1975: 519.

20. Katz 1977d: 130–131.

21. I owe this insight to Virginia Valian.

22. Fodor, Fodor, and Garrett 1975: 520–521.

23. This is a consequence of *(B)* and *(C)*. The negative element is required to be nothing more than the antonymy relation needed to explain why, for example, "bachelor" is incompatible with "married."

24. Fodor, Fodor, and Garrett 1975: 522.

25. Even in sentences with no appropriate constituent actually appearing in the scope of implicit negatives, extra computation is required to check that none of the constituents of the sentence fall under the scope of such special syntactic restrictions. I do not think the question can be taken much further. The whole matter becomes ethereal at this point because we have no idea of the computational time-scales of lexical look-up, syntactic processing, semantic processing, etc. We do not even know what kinds of examples were used.

26. I owe this point to Scott Soames.

27. FFG cannot escape this criticism by claiming that, on their account, the computation underlying the evaluation of *(4)* need refer only to the single meaning postulate (or proper subset of the meaning postulates for the item) that relates the item to the expression in question (e.g., that relates "bachelor" to "unmarried"). The analytic approach can similarly claim that this computation need refer only to the single semantic marker (or to the proper subset of markers) that relates the item to the expression.

28. J. A. Fodor 1968: 10.

29. The use of syntactic notions is legitimate insofar as it serves only to characterize the syntactic objects for which the definition is stated.

30. Chomsky 1965: 10–15.

31. Chomsky 1956: 12.

32. Fodor, Fodor, and Garrett 1975: 525. Fodor, Garrett, Walker, and Parkes 1980 rehearse the claims concerning this issue from Fodor, Fodor, and Garrett 1975 but make no attempt to reply to my criticisms of the claims in Katz 1977b. Thus, their criticism that there is a *"prima facie* parsimony argument" against definition on the grounds that "any argument whose validity can be expressed by an extended logic plus definitions can be equally expressed by an extended logic without definitions" (p. 271, fn. 9) has already been answered. My point was that, although an extended logic without definitions can express, that is, mark, valid arguments that turn on meaning, it cannot explain them adequately. If it were possible to argue as Fodor, Garrett, Walker, and Parkes do against definition (i.e., semantic representation), it would also be possible to argue in the same way against predicate logic. The same *"prima facie* parsimony argument" can be constructed against predicate logic, since any argument whose validity can be expressed by an extended sentential logic (i.e., one with meaning postulates expressed in terms of sentential constants) plus quantificational apparatus can be equally expressed by an extended sentential logic without quantificational logic (see Katz 1977a). Furthermore, it is hard to see that Fodor, Garrett, Walker, and Parkes'

argument would be convincing even if this reductio weren't available. For their argument can be directly turned on their position. That is, the argument can just as well be used to eliminate the meaning postulate extension of logic in favor of unextended logic plus definitions: any argument whose validity can be expressed by an extended logic plus definitions can be equally expressed by an unextended logic with definitions. This asymmetry makes their argument inconclusive.

33. Wittgenstein 1974: 247–249.

34. Frege 1953: 3e–4e.

35. Quine 1961a repeats Frege's two criticisms of the Kantian definition of analyticity and then makes the same gratuitous switch to the notion of logical truth as Frege did. See Katz 1979c:355–356, and especially, Katz, J.J., Murphy, J., and Stamos, P. in preparation.

36. Katz 1977a.

37. Smith and Katz, in preparation.

38. We could also have a meaning postulate saying that all events have causes.

39. Fodor, Fodor, and Garrett 1975: 526.

40. Fodor, Fodor, and Garrett 1975: 526.

41. Note also that the meaning postulate approach can, correspondingly, abandon the critical assumption. We can imagine a system of meaning postulates built out of a vocabulary of predicates that are extremely different in form from simple surface content words. Such a system would by hypothesis fail to explain the speed of sentence comprehension. Meaning postulates are not essential in the explanation because they have nothing to do with the number of computations required.

42. Bever 1970.

43. Fodor, Fodor, and Garrett 1975: 526.

44. Fodor, Fodor, and Garrett 1975: 526.

45. Fodor, Fodor, and Garrett 1975: 527.

46. Carnap 1956.

47. Redundancy rules are a clause of the projection rule. Their function is to expand the abbreviated lexical semantic representation to supply the predictable semantic markers for the rest of the semantic interpretation process. See Katz 1972: 44–47.

48. Quine 1961a: 20–48, 1965b: 48–56.

49. Chomsky 1959b, 1967b, 1968a.

50. I think, however, that his early skepticism never really disappears, though, of course, the reasons for it change. Chomsky has never taken anything less than a cautiously agnostic position on the prespects for a theory of meaning.

51. Chomsky 1977a: 147. Translation from the French by Virginia Valian (The italics are in the original).

52. Chomsky 1977a: 148.

53. Chomsky 1972a.

54. Chomsky 1975a: 23.

55. Chomsky 1965: 159–160.

56. Chomsky 1965: 3.

57. Chomsky 1965: 10–15.

58. I do not wish to claim that all verificationists would use this example or that it has no verification conditions whatever.

59. The idea that a language user can expect other language users to be trying to say what they have reason to think true is now a familiar part of pragmatics. See, for instance, Grice 1975.

60. Chomsky 1957: 13–17.

61. Chomsky 1957: 13–14.

62. A semantic representation only predicts the extension of a semantic property or relation relative to a hypothesis about its definition. This means that semantic explication at the two levels are interdependent and have to proceed in tandem—a point on which

Chomsky has often insisted in connection with other levels of grammatical representation.

63. Lakoff 1971: 329–340.

64. Chomsky 1972b: 120–121.

65. Chomsky 1972b: 121. Italics mine.

66. Chomsky 1972b: 121–122.

67. The main difference between Chomsky's position and Lakoff's is that the latter abandons formal grammar to accommodate what he thinks are unformalizable facts while the former preserves formal grammar by putting the theory of meaning outside sentence-grammar.

68. Chomsky 1972a: 67–68.

69. Chomsky 1977a: 149.

70. I am overlooking the nicety of whether the past point must be in the immediate past of the utterance point.

71. Katz 1972: 120–127.

72. Chomsky 1977a: 149.

73. Chomsky 1975b: 97–98: Chomsky 1977b: 39.

74. Chomsky 1977b: 39.

75. We can even explain Chomsky's gloss in terms of performance factors such as the highlighting of the topicalized constituent and the Gricean maxim that conversationally obligates us to say as much as is relevant in the context. See Grice 1975: 41–58.

76. I have reproduced Chomsky's diagram fully: the quotes around "meaning" in my reproduction appear in the original. They are, I take it, shudder-quotes. It should also be noted that the abbreviations "SR-1" and "SR-2" of the original diagram (Chomsky 1975b: 105) are changed in Chomsky 1977b to "SI-1" and "SI-2".

77. Chomsky 1975b: 105.

78. Chomsky 1975b: 105.

79. Chomsky 1975b: 104.

80. Chomsky 1977b: 195–196.

81. Chomsky 1977b: 41. Italics mine.

82. Chomsky 1977b: 56–57.

83. Katz and Bever 1976: 26.

84. Fillmore 1968: 1–88: Katz 1972: 77–87.

85. It has to be noted here that in Chomsky's most recent work (Chomsky 1980a: 54–55), he again changes his notion of sentence-grammar, this time dropping thematic relations from the status of logical form. Whether this move is in response to the arguments in Katz 1980a or for some other reason cannot be determined because Chomsky gives no reason for demoting thematic relations to the limbo of "part of some other faculty that provides 'common sense understanding' of the world in which we live" (Chomsky 1980a: 55). Given the argument that I am constructing, *viz.*, that many of the explanatory goals of linguistics are sacrificed, including ones central to Chomsky's own Extended Standard Theory, dropping thematic relations from sentence-grammar and banishing them to performance concedes my point. But, from the viewpoint of trying to determine what principled basis Chomsky might be using to decide boundary questions in connection with sentence-grammar and logical form, dropping such relations, just like that, is more than a little disturbing. The situation verges on incoherence when we read later in Chomsky 1980a that base-generated structures of a grammar "give the fundamental syntactic configurations that determine thematic relations and in this respect enter into semantic interpretation" (pp. 147–148). After so many changes, it is quite impossible to determine a general basis for his decisions about boundary questions, and hence to evaluate his claims, in various places, that such questions are to be decided in accord with his program. He often claims that one or another view of his about these questions will be vindicated in the long run by construction of theories with explanatory power, but, without a principled basis, the claims are empty. How would we know what

domain to construct theories of or whether a theory with explanatory power was a theory
of the relevant domain if we had no clear pretheoretical notion of the domain on which to
base principled decisions? The danger Chomsky runs in his claims about boundary
matters here, and in connection with his notion of "core grammar", is that those claims
will turn out to be unfalsifiable on their own terms.

86. Chomsky 1975b: 105: Chomsky 1977b: 195.

87. For example, Quine's attempt (Quine 1972b) to give an independent theoretical
characterization does not get off the ground. See Katz 1975a.

88. Katz 1975a.

89. Chomsky 1975b: 103–105.

90. Chomsky 1977b: 5.

91. Chomsky 1977b: 204.

92. This is not to deny that Chomsky's account of quantifier structure may be correct.
That doesn't matter. Intensionalists do not necessarily deny what such quantificational
accounts affirm, but rather they affirm things that those accounts deny.

93.. Langendoen 1978.

94. This conclusion comes close to Chomsky's occasional comments that logical form
in his sense (output of *SR-1* rules) encompasses structures that have nothing more in
common than that they result from the application of his syntactic and surface-
interpretive principles. See Chomsky 1975b: 103–105.

95. See Mates 1952: Davidson 1967. Davidson, in making the crucial step from a
'means that' form of semantic analysis to a '*s* is *T* if and only if *p*' form, motivates the
move as the only way he knows to deal with the difficulty that "we cannot account for
even as much as the truth conditions of [belief sentences and others containing intensional contexts] on the basis of what we know of the meanings of the words in them".
See Davidson 1967: 453–455. Davidson says this without argument, and in fact does not
even take the trouble to answer intensionalists like Church 1954.

96. Chomsky 1972a: 88: Chomsky 1977b: 30–31.

97. Chomsky 1972a: 88.

98. Katz 1972: 265–280.

99. Katz 1972: 265–277.

100. Katz 1972: 275–277.

101. I am not claiming that there is a global rule that introduces information about the
form of an embedded sentence into the semantic interpretation process at the verb phrase
level. There is no need to make so strong a claim. One can claim instead that the
reference to the sentence in an occurrence of "realize" is like the reference in the
meaning of words like "former" and "latter". There is, of course, a need to be careful
about the difference between the meaning of the sentence containing "realize" as its
main verb and the statement the sentence makes.

102. Chomsky 1977b: 30–31.

103. Katz 1972: 104–115.

104. Katz 1977d: 105–110, 127–128.

105. Vendler 1967: 76.

106. Chomsky 1977b: 36–37. Chomsky 1979: 141 refers approvingly to Quine's "rather
persuasive" criticism of the theory of meaning. See also Chomsky 1975b: 41–42.

107. Chomsky 1975b: 233: Chomsky 1980: 28–29. In the latter discussion it is unclear
how Chomsky's remark that he believes there are "certain analytic connections" is to be
taken, since he leaves it open what their status is and how questions about their logical
status are to be resolved.

108. Chomsky 1968b: 53–68.

109. Quine 1960: 83–85.

110. Quine 1975: 67–82.

111. Quine 1965b: 48–56.

112. Putnam 1962: Putnam 1970: Putnam 1975. Putnam's argument in the latter paper
is explicitly dealt with in Katz 1980b. Expansions of my reply there are in Katz 1975:

Katz 1977c; Katz 1979b. My reply to Putnam's more recent, more Quinian skepticism (e.g., Putnam 1976) will be found in Katz 1979c.

113. Quine 1961a.

114. Katz 1972: Chapter 4.

115. Donnellan 1966.

116. A fuller discussion of these notions may be found in Katz 1977c and Katz 1979b.

117. Normally, the type referent(s) include the token referent(s); for example, in the actual world, uses of "cat" token refer to type referents of "cat." Indeed, the ordinary language notion of a standard (referring) use of an expression is nothing more than the case where the token referent(s) coincides with the expression's type referent(s).

118. Katz 1977c: 47–55.

119. This is to say that another function of the conditions for type reference is to pin down the set of things with which extragrammatical beliefs must correlate in order for such beliefs to be good heuristic strategies.

120. Katz 1977c: 47–80.

121. Unless it can be assumed, as it obviously cannot be in Putnam's cases, that the referential connections are standard uses of the term.

122. This is argued at length in Katz 1972: 282–292. Briefly, my point is this. Quine claims that a parallel between the case of truth in semantics and truth in physics gives us false reassurance on the question of translational synonymy and meaning. (Quine 1960: 75). In the case of translational synonymy, he argues, there is no fact of the matter because there are no "linguistically neutral meanings", no meanings "over against their verbal embodiments". (1960: 76.) Now, the only arguments that Quine gives for there being no meanings are those from Quine 1961a and other papers around that time.

Thus it should be noted that Chomsky is quite wrong in claiming that Quine's indeterminacy thesis applies "not just to problems of meaning but to any theoretical move in linguistics, for example, the postulation of phrase boundaries". (Chomsky 1980a: 14) Chomsky confuses two different notions of indeterminacy. One is the true thesis, namely, that there is no fact of the matter in questions of meaning. The other is that theories are underdetermined by the available evidence. (Chomsky 1980a: 15) But, unfortunately, it is the latter that Chomsky bases his discussion of indeterminacy on. It is this notion on which he bases his claim that Quine's thesis is "true and uninteresting" (Chomsky 1980a: 15). Of course, it is true and uninteresting that empirical theories are underdetermined by the evidence. But, clearly, the same cannot be said about the thesis that there is no fact of the matter in questions of meaning. Quine's actual thesis is that semantics, like witchcraft, is not about anything, and consequently there isn't even evidence to undermine a theory.

123. Quine 1961a: 24–47. The other possibilities can be immediately dismissed: notational abbreviation because it rests on arbitrary stipulation; ordinary lexical definition and rational reconstruction (what Carnap called "explication") because they assume prior synonymy relations without explaining them.

124. Quine 1961b: 56.

125. Of course one might have found the flaw in Quine's argument and the proper theoretical model for semantics without Chomskian linguistics. Take mathematics. What non-circular property can be found to distributionally characterize the notion of numerical identity in terms of substitution of one number n for another number m in the context "$x + m + y$"? How might one distributionally characterize the notions of sameness of truth value or logical truth? This line of criticism is developed in Katz 1975b: 59–60.

126. Chomsky 1975a: 13–23.

127. Quine 1960: 72–79.

128. Quine 1960: 57–60.

129. Quine 1960: 57–60, 80ff.

130. Quine 1960: 75–78.

131. Quine 1960: 26–79.

V

Intermediate Platonism: Semantic Arguments against Conceptualism

Introduction

If there are analytic sentences, then there are necessary truths which owe their status solely to the grammatical structure of natural language, and accordingly, a theory of the grammatical structure of natural language must account for such grammatically based necessary truth. In the present chapter, I shall continue the criticism of conceptualism in linguistics by arguing that conceptualist theories of natural language cannot account for grammatically based necessary truth. Conceding that conceptualist theories of natural language are tame in comparison with nominalist ones, still, if conceptualist theories cannot account for analyticity, such theories fail, in absolute terms, to account for all grammatically determined properties and relations in natural languages.

The argument is, however, incomplete until we show further that this failure of conceptualist theories is not also a failure of all other theories. We have to show that a Platonist liberalization of nominalist and conceptualist constraints can account for grammatically determined necessary truth. This task is taken up in the last section of the present chapter.

Frege's Arguments and Their Linguistic Analogues

In this and the next section, I will show that the arguments developed in the nineteenth century reaction to psychologism in logic and mathematics, particularly by Frege and Husserl,[1] carry over against psychologism in linguistics. In this way, I hope to bring out the reasons for conceptualism's failure to handle grammatically based necessary truths in a number of different ways, and I also hope to link the arguments about language and linguistics with the nineteenth century arguments about logic. I wish to exhibit the underlying connections between the foundations of logic and of linguistics by way of indicating why there should be a common ontological approach to these disciplines.[2]

To show that Frege's arguments against conceptualism in logic carry over to linguistics requires us first to deal with an obstacle that Frege himself put in the path of such an application. Frege, of course, took a Platonist position on logic and mathematics, but he adopted a conceptualist position on language. Hence, we have to show that this asymmetry in Frege's positions is mistaken and can be eliminated without affecting the criticism he makes of psychologism.

Frege contrasts the case of language with the case of logic and mathematics in the course of his attempt to put his finger on the precise point at which the "psychologizers" of logic go astray. He identifies this point as the ambiguity with which the term "law" is used in discussions of logic and mathematics. He writes:

In one sense a law asserts what is; in the other it prescribes what ought to be. Only in the latter sense can the laws of logic be called 'laws of thought': so far as they stipulate the way in which one ought to think. . . . the expression 'law of thought' seduces us into supposing that these laws govern thinking in the same way as laws of nature govern events in the external world. In that case they can be nothing but laws of psychology: for thinking is a mental process.[3]

Then, Frege goes on to say that psychological laws

. . . give an average, like statements about 'how it is that good digestion occurs in man', or 'how one speaks grammatically', or 'how one dresses fashionably'.[4]

He refers to grammar once more, and says that the laws of logic are laws of truth which

. . . do not bear the relation to thought that the laws of grammar bear to language; [these laws of truth] do not make explicit the nature of our human thinking and change as it changes.[5]

For Frege, the laws of grammar only make explicit the nature of human linguistic ability "at present and relative to our knowledge of men".

Since Frege does not explain why he takes this position on

grammatical laws, we must infer his reasons from things he says about language generally. This, however, is not difficult. Frege's conception of grammatical laws for natural languages as descriptions of human thinking is central to his concern with the construction of a logically perfect language, a Begriffsschrift or conceptual notation.[6] A motivating assumption of this construction was the idea that natural languages are highly defective instruments for thought. Frege supposed that there were at least three principal defects or "imperfections" in natural languages. First, the grammatical structure of sentences can incorrectly reflect their logical structure, thereby obscuring and misleading inference.[7] Frege cites the "useless prolixity" of the subject-predicate distinction in natural languages as an example. Second, the grammatical structure of sentences allows ambiguity.[8] This, too, obscures and misleads inference. Third, meaningful, grammatically well-formed expressions can fail to have a referent.[9] Frege claimed:

The history of mathematics supplies errors which have arisen in this way. This lends itself to demagogic abuse as easily as ambiguity—perhaps more easily. 'The will of the people' can serve as an example; for it is easy to establish that there is at any rate no generally accepted reference for this expression.[10]

Such "imperfections" make it desirable to construct a logically perfect language for serious thought. Natural languages ought to be replaced for scientific purposes with a logically perfect language, a properly constructed "conceptual notation".

In the preface to the *Begriffsschrift,* Frege writes:

I believe I can make the relation of my "conceptual notation" to ordinary language clearest if I compare it to the relation of the microscope to the eye. The latter, because of the range of its applicability and because of the ease with which it can adapt itself to the most varied circumstances, has a great superiority over the microscope. Of course, viewed as an optical instrument it reveals many imperfections, which usually remains unnoticed only because of its intimate connection with mental life. But as soon as scientific purposes place strong requirements upon sharpness of resolution, the eye proves to be inadequate. On the other hand, the microscope is perfectly suited for just such purposes; but, for this very reason, it is useless for all others.[11]

Natural languages are naturally developed organs like the eye; a conceptual notation is an artificially developed instrument like the microscope. Natural languages have evolved for communication over a wide range of circumstances; a conceptual notation is a specialized instrument designed for the limited purposes of scientific inquiry. The defects of natural languages are the defects of a natural organ (like the eye's limited sharpness of resolution, susceptibility to visual illusion, etc.) and reveal its evolutionary origin. Frege's account of why natural languages should be replaced by a logically perfect language explains why he takes the conceptualist position he does on grammatical laws: the origin of these laws mark them as psychobiological in character. Such laws describe the functioning of a natural organ for human thought, while the laws of logic are ". . . boundary stones set in an eternal foundation, which our thought can overflow but never displace".[12]

Since Frege's conceptualist view of laws of grammar depends on his claims about the imperfections of natural languages, we have to show why these claims are mistaken in order to remove the obstacle to employing Frege's arguments against psychologism in logic and mathematics also against psychologism in linguistics. But, before we do, it is worth pointing out that Frege's discussion of imperfections, natural organs, etc. does not, strictly speaking, prove anything about the laws of grammatical structure *for a language*. We may grant what Frege says to be true of our grammatical competence, just as we might grant similar points about logical and mathematical competence. We can resist applying what he says to the language that the speaker's knowledge is knowledge of, just as Frege himself would resist applying analogous remarks to logic and mathematics themselves.

The first of the imperfections mentioned above contains an important element of truth about grammatical and logical form in natural language. Sentences in natural languages do not wear their logical character on their orthographic sleeves. But acceptance of this truth does not require us to also accept Frege's further claim that natural languages are somehow deficient. To establish a deficiency, it is necessary to go beyond the fact that sentences like "John is easy to please" and "John is eager to please" have the same surface grammatical form but different logical forms and that sentences like "A bachelor hit a spinster" and "An unmarried adult human female was hit by an unmarried adult human male" have different surface grammatical forms but the same logical form. It must be established further, as Wittgenstein once claimed, that

Language disguises thought. So much so, that from the outward form of the clothing it is impossible to infer the form of the thought beneath it, because the outward form of the clothing is not designed to reveal the form of the body, but for entirely different purposes.[13]

But no such suitably strong claim has been established by Frege, Wittgenstein, or anyone else. Moreover, Frege's theory about the nature of the grammatical form/logical form distinction in natural language, which strongly influenced Russell, early Wittgenstein, Carnap, and others in this tradition, is not the only theory—nor clearly the best. There is the earlier theory of the Port-Royal *Grammar* and *Logic*.[14] This theory introduces a distinction between *surface grammatical form* and *underlying grammatical form*. It suggests that the logical form of a sentence is its grammatical structure at the deepest level of its underlying grammatical form.[15] This theory even went so far as to set out forms of argument by which the underlying grammar of sentences can be inferred from facts about their surface grammatical properties and relations.

Thus, we can agree with Frege that such things as subject-predicate word-order have primarily stylistic significance—using the subject place in surface syntax as "a *special* place where one puts what he wishes the listener to particularly heed"[16]—without also agreeing that subject-predicate sentences confuse "conceptual content" with stylistic form or that the grammar of such sentences lack "everything necessary for a correct inference".[17] Further, we can absolve natural languages from the criticism that they are the source of "logical mistakes", for example, that *(1)* and *(2)* are about different peoples.

(1) At Plataea the Greeks defeated the Persians

(2) At Plataea the Persians were defeated by the Greeks

On the Port-Royal theory, knowledge of a natural language can provide as much a basis for avoiding such mistakes as knowledge of a Fregean conceptual notation.

Further, it is the users of a natural language who make "logical mistakes", not the language. Frege's complaint that natural languages are defective in their presentation of logical form confuses language with its use, blaming the language for careless errors of its speakers. Blaming English for the fact that the logical structure of its sentences is not explicit in their surface grammatical form would be like blaming the physical world for the fact that the atomic structure of physical objects is not directly observable.

This criticism also applies to Frege's complaints about ambiguity and referential failures. Natural languages exhibit ambiguities in almost every sentence, but users of natural languages are not thereby compelled to go astray. If someone's fallacious inference from

(3) George likes some old men and women

to

(4) George likes some old women

can be blamed on English, then someone's wrong turn can be blamed on the fork in the road. English contains the distinction between the senses of *(3)* in its grammatical structure, and knowledge of this structure provides everything required to avoid the fallacy.

If, in accord with the urging of a demagogue, someone takes the expression "the will of the people" to refer to something real, blame can hardly be put on English. Natural languages say nothing one way or the other about the existence of things except perhaps in such extremely restricted cases as contradictory noun phrases like "a married bachelor" or semantically anomalous ones like "a purple itch propounding falsehoods". (Even in cases like "the largest integer", language does not mark the fact that reference fails.) Hence, blaming the natural language for such "logical mistakes" is like blaming a musical score when one plays a sour note.

It is not even clear that it is possible to make the reconstruction of languages required to eliminate such "logical mistakes". Any significant reduction of their linguistic basis threatens to cripple them as devices for communicating, expressing, and recording thoughts in forms suitable to the broad range of purposes to which intelligent creatures put them. For example, it seems clear that eliminating the distinction between surface grammatical structure and deeper under-lying grammatical structure and making the former formally exhibit *all* features of the logical form of a sentence would produce sentences of such extremely complex orthography as to render the language largely unfit for almost all rational purposes.[18] Further, it is an open ques-tion whether sentence generating devices powerful enough to produce syntactic structures capable of carrying all thoughts expressible in natural languages do not automatically assign different syntactic structures to the same sentence over a wide range of cases. If am-biguity is a logical consequence of sufficiently powerful sentence generating rules, the elimination of ambiguity will require the elimina-tion of sentence generating rules that assign different syntactic struc-tures to the same expression,[19] and this could rule out languages with a stock of sentential structures rich enough to express our thoughts freely. Finally, only an omniscient being could avoid every possibility of a "logical mistake" stemming from the failure on the part of a grammatically well-formed, meaningful expression to refer. Only if the rules for generating well-formed, meaningful sentences are constructed on the basis of universal knowledge can it be guaranteed that no well-formed, meaningful expression will fail to denote. Ignorance of anything can lead to referential failure. If the knowledge that there are no human beings over a thousand feet in height is not available, then rules may be constructed to allow the non-referring noun phrase "human over one thousand feet in height" as well-formed and meaningful. Moreover, eliminating *ad hoc* all expressions that fail to refer, even if this were realistic, would soon restrict the range of propositions expressible in languages so that their users would be unable, *inter alia,* to entertain hypotheticals, that is, to speculate about counter-to-fact possibilities.

The confusions behind Frege's claim that natural languages are logically flawed undermine his program to construct a logically perfect artificial language to replace natural languages for purposes of scientific inquiry. But, as we have just seen, the idea of using such logically perfect artificial languages in order to avoid "logical mistakes" is both badly justified and a disaster in implementation.

I conclude, then, that Frege had bad reasons for thinking that natural languages have a psychobiological status, and hence there are no grounds in his work for putting them in a different ontological category from logic and mathematics. This removes the obstacle Frege put in the way of a uniform treatment of linguistics, logic, and mathematics.

We may now take our argument against conceptualism a step further by showing that language and logic are bound up in a way that makes it necessary to treat them in an ontologically uniform manner. In particular, the propositions between which the laws of logic hold are the senses of sentences in natural languages.[20] The identification of the propositions of logic with the senses of sentences in natural language underlies the conception of the relation between logic and language pictured in *(T):*

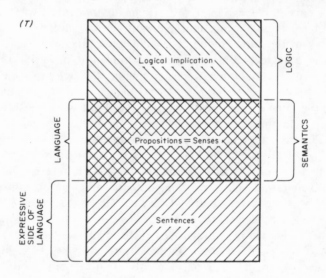

I will argue for this identification in the same way other identifications in science are argued for, namely, by showing that there is a correspondence between the cases at the two levels which holds without exception, and that the most economical explanation of the correspondence is to say that there is just one set of objects appearing under different aspects. The economy achieved consists not only in eliminating the need to posit another set of objects but also in eliminating the need to posit a mechanism of some sort to explain the correspondence. A familiar example of this kind of argument is the one on which science identifies water with H_2O.

The argument for the identification of senses of sentences and propositions involves a correspondence between linguistic cases and logical ones. For example, one point of correspondence is that the logician's distinction between sentences like

(5) Charity drinks procrastination

and

(6) Children drink prune juice

on which (6) but not (5) expresses a proposition, that is, enters into implication relations with other sentences, coincides with the linguist's distinction on which (6) but not (5) is meaningful, that is, has at least one sense. Another point of correspondence is that the logician's treatment of (3) as expressing more than one proposition, and hence as posing the danger of a "fallacy of ambiguity" to the unwary reasoner, coincides with the linguist's treatment of (3) as polysemous, that is, as having more than one sense. Still another point of correspondence is that the logician takes sentences like (1) and (2) to express the same proposition, that is, to function equivalently in argumentation, and the linguist takes them to be synonymous, that is, to have the same sense. One final example of a point of correspondence is that logicians treat expressions like "mortal" and "lives forever" as incompatible predicates while linguists treat them as antonymous, that is, as having opposite meanings.

These examples are illustrations, and no pretense is made to completeness. More illustrations could be given, but I see no point in continuing, since there is no prospect of establishing completeness. The aim here is to make the claim of a correspondence plausible.

In order to establish plausibility, it is necessary to show how apparent cases of failures of the correspondence can be dealt with. I will provide an example of this, showing that an apparent failure can be better accounted for as actually conforming to the correspondence.

The example I have chosen also illustrates the theoretical complexity in some cases of the correspondence.

It seems reasonable to say that the sentence

(7) I promise to eat a meal.

follows logically from the sentence

(8) I promise to eat breakfast.

But standard logic makes it look as if such semantic entailments constitute a failure of correspondence between senses of sentences and propositions of logic. For, although the correspondence does not require all logical implications to be semantic entailments, it does require all semantic entailments to be logical implications. But, since the notion of logical implication is defined in standard logic in terms of validity, only sentences that bear truth values can enter into logical implications. Since the senses of performative sentences cannot bear truth values, we seem to be faced with a failure of the correspondence in cases like the argument from (7) to (8) because such semantic entailments correspond to no logical implication.

However, I think the problem is with standard logic rather than with the correspondence. What prevents standard logic from counting such cases as implications is, first, its refusal to recognize the contribution of all meaningful words in the language to the logical form of sentences, and second, its related restriction of the notion of validity to truth. I have shown elsewhere that enriching the stock of logical forms by adding the logical structures of performative senses and introducing a new, and more abstract, concept of validity, which interprets the notion 'valid argument' extensionally but not narrowly in terms of just preservation of truth, naturally extends the scope of logic to encompass the full range of performative arguments like (7) to (8) without disturbing the treatment of statement arguments.[21] This extension converts what seems at first glance to be a failure in the correspondence into a further example of the correspondence.

It should be noted that the correspondence is between *senses* and propositions, and that nothing coarser grained than senses works. If we consider the various kinds of things that philosophers have tried from time to time to use in place of meanings or to reduce meanings to, we can see that they are all too coarse grained to provide a point for point correspondence. For example, Russell's extensions won't work because expressions and sentences with the same extension do not, like (1) and (2), function equivalently in argumentation. This perhaps needs no repetition, but it should be mentioned that the same point applies to the possible worlds semantics attempt to individuate propositions by their extensions in possible worlds. Essentially the same difficulties beset this attempt as Russell's. For example, (9) and (10), which have the same extension in every possible world, are clearly not the same proposition.[22]

(9) One plus one equals two

(10) A consistent formalization of arithmetic is incomplete

We can now turn to the explanation of the correspondence. We can either attempt to explain the correspondence by admitting the existence of two kinds of objects—senses in language and propositions in logic—and constructing a mechanism to account for why the behavior of objects of these two kind should correspond perfectly, or attempt to explain it by simply saying that propositions *are* senses of sentences. The latter explanation being far more parsimonous, is clearly preferable. It explains in the most economical way the fact that whenever and wherever there are particular logical features of sentences there are also isomorphic linguistic features. The reason is that they are the same features—seen from different perspectives—of one and the same objects. This explanation reduces the overall commitment of the theory of logico-linguistic structure: it is unnecessary to countenance two kinds of objects, propositions and senses of sentences, and to introduce a special mechanism to explain the correspondence between logical and linguistic features of sentences.

This step of identifying the objects described in a linguistic theory of meaning with the objects to which laws of logic apply extends the notion of 'logical implication' to include semantic implications. Semantic implications are those logical implications that express the inclusion of one logical form fully within another so that preservation of truth (for statement arguments) is solely a matter of the meanings of the sentences. The principles that Frege calls logical implications, and that are so-called in standard logic today, do not express the inclusion of one logical form within another (recall the discussion of the implication of (10)-(11) in Chapter IV) but represent implications that depend on deductive steps connecting the logical form of the conclusion to that of the premiss in a way that guarantees preservation of truth.[23] This difference does not, however, undermine the parallel between semantical laws and logical laws. The relations of inclusion of logical forms and deductive connection of logical forms both guarantee validity (though in different ways). Hence, semantical laws like the principle defining the relation between propositions on which one analytically entails another or the principle defining the conditions for analyticity are counterparts of logical laws like *modus ponens* which state deductive connections or conditions for logical truth. The semantical laws, like the logical laws, concern relations between propositions on which truths about implications depend. Therefore, we can claim that semantical laws, too, are, in Frege's sense, laws of (necessary) truth.

Once semantic implications are put on the same footing as logical implications, Frege's arguments against psychologism in logic are directly applicable to psychologism in linguistics. Frege's first argument is that the expression "laws of thought" is ambiguous and that the conceptualist's claim that the laws of logic or laws of thought are psychological rests on a failure to distinguish the different senses of the expression. "Laws of thought" can mean either the psychological laws concerning what people think or take to be true about how reasoning ought to proceed or the logical laws concerning what is true about valid reasoning. Such disambiguation shows the conceptualist to be wrong:

There is no contradiction in something's being true which everybody takes to be false. . . . If being true is thus independent of being acknowledged by somebody or other, then the laws of truth [logic] are not psychological laws.[24]

We have already noted a three-way ambiguity in the term "grammar", and hence, there is such an ambiguity in the expression "law of grammar". We distinguished *grammar₁* which refers to the speaker-hearer's tacit grammatical principles that determine language use, *grammar₂* which refers to a theory of these tacit grammatical principles, and *grammar₃* which refers to a theory of the language that the speaker-hearer's knowledge is knowledge of. Hence, parallel to Frege's objection to the psychologization of logic, we may construct essentially the same objection to the psychologization of grammar; namely, there is no contradiction in something's being true (say, some statement in grammar₃ correctly expressing a semantic law) which everybody takes to be false (say, the corresponding principles in grammar₁ and grammar₂ expressing claims incompatible with the semantic law); if being true is thus independent of being acknowledged by speakers, then the laws of grammatical truth are not psychological laws.[25]

This might seem at first glance to be an unfair criticism of Chomsky in light of the fact that he claims that a grammar is a theory of the ideal speaker-hearer's *perfect* knowledge of the language.[26] Since knowledge implies truth, and perfect knowledge complete truth, these tacit grammatical principles cannot imply anything but truths about the sentences of the language. Hence, there must be a contradiction in the notion of something's being true about the language which speakers's tacit grammatical principles take to be false.

If this objection were sound, the same line of argument would save the psychologizer of logic from Frege's criticism. It could be claimed that Frege's criticisms work only against a naive version of psychologism and fail against a more sophisticated version modeled on Chomsky's conception of linguistic competence. On such a version, the laws of logic are taken to be psychological principles constituting the ideal reasoner's perfect knowledge of implication, and there is nothing that can be true which the ideal reasoner takes to be false.

Invoking the notion of competence defined in terms of perfect knowledge cannot make the speaker's actual grammatical principles contain the whole truth about the language. The actual grammatical principles are the principles the speaker acquired in reaching fluency and which serve as the grammatical component of the speaker's performance system. These principles are whatever they are. They may make false claims about sentences; if so, what follows is just that there is no instantiation of perfect competence. There is nothing that is at the same time the psychologically real grammatical principles speakers employ in their use of language and perfect knowledge of the structure of the sentences of the language. But this is quite compatible with there being no contradiction in something's being true about the sentences which the *psychologically real* grammatical principles of the speaker imply is false.

Frege sought to drive home his claim that logical laws are not psychological laws as follows:

. . . . what if beings were even found whose laws of thought flatly contradicted ours and therefore frequently led to contrary results even in practice? The psychological logician could only acknowledge the fact and say simply: those laws hold for them, these laws hold for us. I should say: we have here a hitherto unknown type of madness. Anyone who understands laws of logic to be laws that prescribe the way in which one ought to think— . . . and not natural laws of human beings' taking a thing to be true—will ask, who is right? . . . The psychological logician cannot ask this question; if he did he would be recognizing laws of truth that were not laws of psychology.[27]

It may seem implausible for us to claim that here, too, there is a parallel argument to Frege's for distinguishing linguistics from psychology. Beings whose tacit grammatical principles do not correspond to those of English speakers, French speakers, etc. need not exhibit a new type of madness, they might, after all, just speak a new type of natural language or use another means of communication. If it turned out that porpoises communicate using a symbol system that does not strictly qualify as a natural language, we might take this as a significant aspect of their non-humanness but, surely, *not* as grounds for sending them off to an animal psychiatrist.

Although these considerations are no doubt right, they do not rule out a linguistic counterpart of Frege's argument. What they show is only that not all parts of a natural language can be compared to logic in the respect Frege's argument capitalizes on. Frege's argument capitalizes on the uniqueness of logical laws while these considerations make clear that the syntactic and sensible parts of languages are by no means unique. Thus, there can be a linguistic counterpart to the madness Frege describes, since none of these considerations challenge the fact that the semantic part of language is unique.

Frege not only supposed that there are no alternative logics; he also supposed that arithmetic is unique. But he didn't think that geometry enjoyed the special position of logic and arithmetic. The existence of alternative geometries represented to Frege the fundamental difference between logic and arithmetic, on the one hand, and geometry, on the other:

For purposes of conceptual thought we can always assume the contrary of some one or other of the geometrical axioms, without involving ourselves in any self-contradictions when we proceed to our deductions, despite the conflict between our assumptions and our intuition. The fact that this is possible shows that the axioms of geometry are independent of one another and of the primitive laws of logic, and consequently are synthetic. Can the same be said of the fundamental propositions of the science of number? Here, we have only to try denying any one of them, and complete confusion ensues.[28]

The uniqueness of arithmetic and the non-uniqueness of geometry have counterparts in the case of language thereby preserving the comparison between linguistics and mathematics. Language, too, has a unique portion and a non-unique one. The semantic side of a natural language parallels arithmetic and logic; the expressive side parallels geometry. If the identification of senses in language with propositions in logic is correct, then the uniqueness of logic guarantees the uniqueness of semantics. The uniqueness of semantics would also be a consequence of the effability of natural languages.[29]

Our overall conception of a grammar views it as a system like analytic geometry, except that, in the case of a grammar, the "geometrical objects" (the sentences) *express* the "arithmetical objects" (the senses), rather than, as in the case of analytic geometry, the geometrical objects being *represented in* arithmetical relations. Hence, different languages are different systems of expressive forms associated with an invariant semantic structure, in analogy to the way that different spaces are associated with the same arithmetic.

Thus, natural languages as a whole need not be compared with logic and arithmetic in constructing the counterpart of Frege's argument. We can compare natural languages exclusively in terms of their semantic side. Frege points out that the "psychological logician" is committed to saying of beings whose inference principles contradict the laws of logic "those laws hold for them; these laws hold for us", but that such tolerance is absurd because, by virtue of contradicting laws of logic, these beings are shown to have inconsistent inference principles, to exhibit "a hitherto unknown type of madness". Constructing the counterpart of this argument is straightforward. The "psychological linguist" is committed to a corresponding form of tolerance: beings whose semantic laws flatly contradict ours are ecumenically pictured as having laws that hold for them just as we have laws that hold for us. But, if their laws flatly contradict ours, then their laws claim that at least one analytic proposition is false, that is, their laws deny that some valid implication (holding by virtue of inclusion of logical forms). Such a parallel claim, however, is enough to establish, on the same grounds as Frege's conclusion, that we have run up against, if not "a hitherto unknown form of madness", then at least a novel variety of falsehood. Again, the conceptualist cannot even ask who is right without conceding the independence of the laws of semantics from psychology. Since the question obviously makes sense, the theory of the semantic structure of natural languages and the theory of the operation of the human mind must be different things. If the former theory were merely the theory of the tacit principles upon which we make inferences, then the question would make no sense.[30]

Husserl's Arguments and Their Linguistic Analogues

Husserl started out in mathematics under Weierstrass and Kronecker. From them, he received a sense of the centrality of arithmetic to mathematics as a whole. Husserl later became a student of Brentano. Under Brentano's influence he became a conceptualist, and he came to feel the need for a psychological clarification of the basic ideas of arithmetic. His first book, *The Philosophy of Arithmetic*,[31] attempts to provide psychological foundations for arithmetic. A year after the publication of *The Basic Laws of Arithmetic,* Frege employed its anti-psychologistic arguments in a review of *The Philosophy of Arithmetic* which devastates Husserl's psychologism.[32]

Husserl's response to Frege's criticisms, rare in intellectual history, was to fully acknowledge the force of the criticisms and give up his conceptualist position. He then set out to obtain a completely clear view of the controversy and work out the answers to the still open questions. He spent the following years in a comprehensive study of psychologistically and anti-psychologistically oriented writings on logic and mathematics. Husserl's considered opinion was that Frege was right.[33]

Husserl set out his own assessment of psychologism in logic and mathematics in the first volume of his second book *Logical Investigations*.[34] The work is a far more systematic critique of psychologism than Frege's, containing elaborations of undeveloped remarks of Frege's,[35] new and forceful arguments of his own, and an extensive critical survey of the then current versions of psychologism. We turn now to this book to see if its arguments can also serve as arguments against conceptualism in linguistics.

Husserl's arguments derive from a far more sophisticated and articulate conception of psychological laws than Frege's. In a passage that is an interesting anticipation of Chomsky's notion of an ideal speaker, Husserl writes:

Let us imagine an ideal person, in whom *all* thinking proceeds as logical laws require. Naturally the fact that this occurs must have its explanatory ground in certain psychological laws, which govern the course of the mental experiences of this being, starting from certain initial 'collocations'. I now ask: Would the natural laws and the logical laws in this assumed situation be one and the same? Obviously the answer is 'No'. Causal laws, according to which thought must proceed in a manner which the ideal norms of logic might justify, are by no means identical with those norms. If a being were so constituted as never to be able to frame a contradictory judgments in a unified train of thought, . . . this would not mean that the law of contradiction . . . [was a law] of nature explanatory of the being's constitution.[36]

Thus, psychological laws for Husserl express causally determined, exceptionless, connections in successions of events, stated with respect to an idealization similar to Chomsky's ideal speaker. Psychological hypotheses are prompted and justified by experience of such successions of events. Husserl notes that psychological hypotheses, unlike inductive hypotheses in the physical sciences, are vague and imprecise and cannot be made clearer and more precise without changing them explicitly to statistical generalizations. Husserl also notes that psychological laws contrast with logical and mathematical laws in that the latter but not the former are knowable *a priori*, apodictically evident, necessary, and completely exact as they stand.

On this conception of psychological laws, Husserl erects three principal arguments against psychologism. First, he argues that it is incomprehensible how the exact laws of logic and mathematics can be based on or develop out of laws of such vagueness and imprecision as those of psychology. He writes:

. . . only vague rules could be based on vague theoretical foundations. If psychological laws lack exactness, the same must be true of the prescriptions of logic. It cannot be doubted that many of these prescriptions are infected with empirical vaguenesses. But precisely the laws which are pointedly called 'logical', which as laws of proof make up the real core of all logic . . . are of absolute exactness.[37]

As it stands, however, this first argument is not compelling. The argument does not establish that such vagueness and inexactness are essential to psychological laws. It might be that such vagueness and inexactness are found only during a primitive stage of psychological investigation. A conceptualist might well reply that not all psychological laws are vague and inexact; logical and mathematical laws are the psychological laws that are exceptions to what is otherwise the rule in psychology for now but that in the future the rest of psychology will catch up. Husserl himself notes that nothing he says shows that perfectly exact psychological laws cannot be found, and he drops the argument.

Husserl's second argument is that psychological laws cannot provide foundations for logical or mathematical laws because the former are *a posteriori*—justified on the basis of experience—while the latter are *a priori*—justified on the basis of reason independent of experience. Husserl writes:

No natural laws can be known *a priori*, nor established by sheer insight. The only way in which a natural law can be established and justified, is by induction from the singular facts of experience. Induction does not establish the holding of the law, only the greater or lesser probability of its holding; the probability, and not the law, is justified by insight. Logical laws must, accordingly, without exception, rank as mere probabilities. Nothing, however, seems plainer than that the laws of 'pure logic' all have *a priori* validity. They are established and justified, not by induction, but by apodeictic inner evidence. Insight justifies no mere probabilities of their holding, but their holding or truth itself.[38]

Husserl observes that a natural law cannot be considered an "absolutely valid law". In the case of natural laws, we have "to treat it as an open *possibility* that such a surmise would fail to be confirmed by an extension of our ever limited horizon of experience"; and hence,

laws of thought, as causal laws governing acts of knowledge in their mental interweaving, could only be stated in the form of probabilities. On this basis, no assertion could be *certainly* judged correct, since probabilities, taken as the standard of all certainty, must impress a merely probabilistic stamp on all knowledge.[39]

The laws of nature, including the laws of thought, are *a posteriori* while the laws of logic and mathematics in contrast, are *a priori*. Laws of

logic and mathematics are proven by "apodictic inner evidence" and
no matter how "our limited horizon of experience" be extended,
nothing can disconfirm them. Laws of nature, including laws of
thought, cannot be so proven, since it is always possible to imagine an
extension of our experience in which even the most secure of these
laws turns out false. As Husserl summarizes:

The psychologistic logicians ignore the fundamental, essential, never-to-be-
bridged gulf between the ideal and real laws, between normative and causal
regulation, between logical and real necessity, between logical and real
grounds.[40]

Husserl's third argument runs as follows. If, as the psychologistic
logician claims,

the laws of logic have their epistemological source in psychological matters of
fact, . . . they must themselves be psychological in content, both by being laws
for mental states and also be presupposing or implying the existence of such
states.[41]

But

No logical law implies a 'matter of fact', not even the existence of presenta-
tions or judgments or other phenomena of knowledge,[42]

The psychologistic logician's claim is "palpably false". Logical laws
are not empirical. They are not laws *for* the empirical world. Such
laws, like the first and second laws of thermodynamics, imply the
existence of matters of fact. The first law of thermodynamics implies
that energy is conserved; the second implies that energy tends to be
increasingly less available. A psychological law such as the law of
effect implies that, other things equal, the pleasurable or satisfying
effects of a movement facilitates learning the movement. These are,
respectively, laws *for* physical processes like energy transfer and
psychological processes like learning. They express relations among
stages of such empirical processes. But a logical law, say noncontradiction, implies nothing about matters of empirical fact. Nowhere in
the empirical realm are there events, processes, etc. for which logical
laws are an account.

Moreover, laws of nature presuppose the existence of matters of
empirical fact as a condition of their justification as laws, of their
confirmation. The idea of scientific confirmation, according to Husserl,
is that of narrowing down the countlessly many theoretically possible
relations between the variables to a "certain factually delimited

sphere"—"the limits of unavoidable experimental error"—at which point we choose the simplest relation.[43] Thus, the scientific confirmation of laws of nature entails the existence of matters of empirical fact as evidence of their status as true laws. But scientific confirmation is inapplicable to a law of logic. Such a law

. . . is not one of countless theoretical possibilities within a certain factually delimited sphere. It is the single, sole truth which excludes all other possibilities and which, being established by *insight,* is kept pure from fact in its content and mode of proof.[44]

The question of what laws are laws *for* and the question of what laws presuppose are, according to Husserl, two sides of the same coin. The phenomena that a law is about and the phenomena that confirm it are one and the same. He uses this principle to complete his third argument:

The above considerations show how intimately the two halves of the psychologistic case hang together: that logical laws do not merely entail existential assertions of mental facts, but are also laws *for* such facts. We have just refuted the first half of their case. But . . . our refutation also covers the second half. For just as each law established empirically and inductively from singular facts, is a law *for* such facts, so, conversely, each law *for* facts is a law established empirically and inductively, and from such a law, as has been shown, assertions with existential content are inseparable.[45]

Husserl's first argument carries over to linguistics easily enough, since grammatical laws (principles of a generative grammar) have little of the vagueness and inexactness of psychological laws but are like logical and mathematical laws in expressing a particular, fixed relation between antecedent and consequent conditions. But this is of dubious significance since, as noted above, the argument has the unsupported assumption that psychological laws are not only at present vague and inexact but inherently so.

Husserl's second argument is really two arguments. One has to do with the apriority of logical and mathematical statements; the other with their necessity. Both carry over. Psychological truths are certainly *a posteriori:* we come to know them on the basis of observation, either introspection or perception. The psychological principle that the color of an after-image is the complementary color from its stimulus is known on the basis of a sample of observations of after-images and their stimuli. The principle is increasingly confirmed by larger and larger samples of positive instances of such complementarity and disconfirmed by the observation of a non-complementary relationship.

Semantic truths, in contrast, are *a priori:* we do not come to know them on the basis of inductive extrapolations from observational data. The analyticity of *(11)* and *(12)* is not established either on the basis of

(11) Nightmares are dreams

(12) If one succeeds in convincing Jones that his wife is dead, then Jones will believe that his wife is dead

self-observation or observation of the external world. *(11)* and *(12)* do not receive increasingly greater confirmation by piling up cases of nightmares that are dreams and cases of convincing Jones of the death of his wife that are cases of his coming to believe his wife is dead. It is as pointless to pile up positive instances as it is to attempt to refute *(11)* and *(12)* by finding negative instances. As we observed in the last chapter, a case of "nightmare" referring but not to a dream or of "success in convincing Jones that his wife is dead" referring but not to an event in which Jones comes to believe his wife is dead can only be reference under a false description.[46]

Semantic truths, like logical and mathematical truths, are grounded in intuition, what Husserl refers to as "insight" or "apodictic inner evidence". These intuitions concern no subjective state of the speaker (such as is reported in introspections) or physical state of the external world (such as is reported in perceptions), but the objective nature of sentences of a language. Such intuitions are acts in which a fact about the semantic structure of a sentence (or syntactic and phonological structure) can be fully certified at once. Thus, it makes no more sense to associate probabilities with analytic sentences than it does to associate them with, say, Goldbach's conjecture (to reflect the frequency with which even numbers have been found to be the sum of two primes). Of course, linguists, like mathematicians, may themselves become psychologically more certain of a statement as positive instances pile up, but such an attitude is subjective, about these linguists, while confirmation is an objective relation between the evidence and the hypothesis.[47]

The other part of Husserl's second argument distinguishes psychological truths from logical and mathematical truths on the grounds that the latter are necessary while the former are not. This argument carries over straightforwardly. Analytic truths are necessary, too. *(11)* and *(12)* are true in every possible circumstances: there is nothing that is even a possible example of a nightmare that is not a dream, nor anything that is success in convincing Jones that his wife is dead wherein Jones doesn't come to believe she is. In contrast, psychological truths can clearly be supposed false in some circumstances. The comparsion might be put as follows. Merely imagining a case in which the statement that an allegedly analytic sentences makes would be false *ipso facto* refutes the claim that the sentence is analytic, whereas no such "armchair" refutation is possible in the case of a psychological claim. In psychology, as in other empirical disciplines, claims are contingent, and refutation requires finding an actual counter-instance. Thus, just as Husserl's argument shows that logical truths cannot be psychological principles because they are necessary, so this argument shows that semantic truths cannot be, either, because they, too, are necessary.

Husserl's third argument must carry over since his second does and the third is a consequence of the second. But in order to make the argument stand on its own as well, we will have to construct an argument that semantic laws do not presuppose, or in general imply, the existence of mental or physical states or of any matter of empirical fact. The argument is as follows. Let us suppose that some analytic statement S logically implies a statement expressing a matter of empirical fact E, that is, $S \longrightarrow E$. Since E is a statement expressing a matter of empirical fact, it follows that $\Diamond$ (E is false). But, since for any logical implication $p \longrightarrow q$, if $\Diamond$ (q is false), then $\Diamond$ (p is false), it follows also that $\Diamond$ (S is false). On the other hand, S is analytic and from this it follows that $\sim \Diamond$ (S is false). Hence, we obtain the contradiction that that $(\exists S)($ $\Diamond$ $(S$ is false) & $\sim \Diamond$ $(S$ is false)). We conclude, then, that semantic laws cannot imply a matter of empirical fact. Now, insofar as laws of semantics imply no matter of empirical fact, they cannot be laws *for* matters of psychological fact, and hence, they cannot be psychological laws.[48]

On Necessary Truth in Semantics, Logic, and Mathematics

Conceptualist constraints on grammars preclude theories of natural languages that will be able to account for *all* the grammatically determined properties and relations of sentences. Since Platonism removes these constraints and does not replace them with any others, it allows linguistics to construct theories that can account for all grammatically determined properties and relations. This liberalization in itself is a powerful argument for Platonism. But the argument can be made stronger by showing that Platonism not only eliminates constraints that stand in the way of obtaining the best grammars but also provides linguistics an opportunity that neither of the other ontological positions can offer, the opportunity of completing the study of natural language by providng an explanation of linguistically necessary truth.

The explanation accounts for necessary truth in semantics, logic, and mathematics by exhibiting the dependency of such necessary truth on the existence of abstract objects. Such an explanation not only clarifies the notions on which these last arguments against conceptualism put such great weight and strengthens the case for Platonism but also provides a kind of transcendental argument for the existence of abstract objects. If the existence of necessary truth in semantics, logic, and mathematics is bound up with the existence of abstract objects—so that if there were no abstract objects, there wouldn't be necessary truths in these domains—then given that there are necessary truths in semantics, logic, and mathematics, there must be abstract objects.

Let us begin with a brief consideration of some of the accounts of necessary truths that one finds in the philosophical literature. These are addressed to the question of what it is about the nature of logical, mathematical, and semantic truths that enable them to be truth in all possible worlds.[49] This question, together with its epistemological corollary,[50] is well expressed in Dummett's remark:

The philosophical problem of necessity is twofold: what is its source, and how do we recognize it? God can ordain that something shall hold good of the actual world; but how can even God ordain that something is to hold good in all possible worlds?[51]

Dummett observes that a great many philosophers once greeted conventionalism as a "liberation".[52] Conventionalism is the doctrine that logic and mathematics are true by fiat, on the basis of conventions stipulated for the meanings of their terms. Conventionalism was greated as a liberation mostly by logical empiricists for whom it offered a much needed account of *a priori* knowledge. But since the honeymoon period when it formed the mainstay of logical empiricist thinking concerning *a priori* knowledge, its defects have become so painfully clear that few philosophers today take it seriously. Quine showed quite early that conventionalism is viciously circular because it uses the notion of logical implication without being able to explain it.[53] The notion of logical implication required to understand the application of logic to derive the infinity of logical and mathematical truths from a set of conventions cannot, on pain of infinite regress, be itself explained as a matter of convention. Further, it is quite impossible to comprehend how arbitrary command, no matter how authoritatively expressed, could by itself constitute the force of necessity that logical and mathematical truths carry. Commands can be disobeyed and replaced by other commands. How can mathematicians continue to pursue their work if they disobey the principle of non-contradiction or replace it with a stipulation that allows contradictions in their theories?

Constructivism, which is Dummett's solution to the problem of necessity, conceives of logical and mathematical entities as our creations, products of human constructions that began back in the dawn of civilization. This contrasts with the Platonist conception of such objects as objective, timeless, placeless entities that we discover and learn about. The Platonist attitude toward constructivism is that its "creation myth" leaves the problem no better off than do "convention myths" and asks us to swallow a number of implausible consequences. If we create mathematical and logical laws, couldn't we create different ones just as good? Why should mathematical and logical laws be necessary? The answers would have to be in terms of psychological limits on the creative process, but it seems hard to see how the arguments against conceptualist explanations of necessity in the individual case can be overcome by multiplying the number of individuals and spreading them out over the period of human history. It is also hard to accept the idea that mathematical and logical facts did not exist prior to our mathematical and logical Adams and Eves.

Another question that proves troublesome for constructivism is what meaning and truth in mathematics are. Since Platonism holds that mathematical and logical objects comprise a realm independent of us, they can make use of the same notions of meaning and truth in mathematics as in other sciences. The truth of the sentence "There are infinitely many primes" is a matter of whether there is a correspondence between its meaning and mathematical reality, in the same sense that the truth of the sentence "There are infinitely many people" is a matter of whether there is a correspondence between its meaning and demographical reality. But, insofar as constructivists take the very different position they do on the ontological status of mathematics and logic, they cannot take this version of the homogeneous view. They must either opt for a heterogeneous view or a different homogeneous one. Since heterogeneous views are always open to charge that there is nothing in the logical or semantic structure of sentences like "There are infinitely many primes" and "There are finitely many people" to warrant a radically different account of their logical or semantic structure, homogeneous views are preferable.[54]

Dummett is a constructivist who takes a homogeneous view. Homogeneity is obtained by adopting a use theory of meaning in general and treating the meanings of assertive sentences, in particular, sentences of logic and mathematics, verificationistically, as "the conditions under which we regard ourselves as justified in asserting a statement".[55] In fact, Dummett thinks that the homogeneity of his account of meaning is the source of the "strongest arguments" for constructivism:

The strongest arguments come from the insistence that the general form of explanation of meaning, and hence of the logical operators in particular, is a statement not of the truth-conditions but of the assertability conditions. We learn the meaning of the logical operators by being *trained* in their use, and this means being trained to assert complex statements in certain kinds of situation.[56]

Since he comes from the Wittgensteinian tradition, one can see why Dummett would think this. This tradition assumes that how we learn, or how it seems we learn, can be taken to directly reveal what it is we learn. But this assumption is mistaken in a way that makes the use theory of meaning not the ultimate justification for constructivism, as Dummett believes,[57] but its Achilles heel.

The fact that we may learn the meanings of words by being trained in their use (e.g., to make statements, ask questions, etc.) does not imply that meaning is use. The process by which we acquire knowledge of the meanings of words begins with an input of information and instruction to what may be represented as a "black box". Operations are performed on the input within the box, using unknown principles, and the end result is the output of grammatical rules, including, in particular, semantic rules. Now, assuming we have a clear idea of the input, if we wish to determine the character of the output (the nature of the semantic rules), we would have to be able to say something about the unknown language acquisition principles. Wittgensteinians seem to take them to inductively generalize the training in patterns of use that is assumed to constitute the input. Then, it is inferred that the semantic rules are rules of use. But this is a rather extreme empiricist view of language acquisition, and in the light of present knowledge a wholly gratuitous one at best. Most importantly, the Wittgensteinian approach puts the logical order of things backwards. We could not find out the nature of these language acquisition principles without first determining both the nature of the grammatical rules that are their product and the input to them. We cannot solve the language acquisition equation for the unknown inside the "black box" without having the values of the other two unknowns. Given knowledge of the input and output, we can pose the question of what kind of principles could obtain such an output on the basis of such an input in the time and under the conditions of actual language learning.

So, we have to have an idea of the output first. The prior question is what the fluent speaker's semantic rules are. And the prior question to this is what criteria are used to determine whether a theory of these semantic rules is correct. I shall argue that, by the criteria for evaluating theories of meaning, the theory that semantic rules are rules of use is incorrect.

To determine the criteria, we need do no more than look at the grounds on which theories of meaning have been criticized. Consider the theory that meaning is reference. This theory is standardly criticized for making false predictions about synonymy in cases of co-extensive expressions like "creature with a heart" and "creature with a kidney" and about meaningfulness in cases of expressions with a null extension like "the golden mountain". Similar criticisms, as we observed above in connection with (9) and (10), have been made of the theory that meaning is reference in possible worlds. The theory that meanings are mental associations of words is criticized for making false predictions about the degree of ambiguity words have. Words like "laundry", "husband", or "Hitler" are not nearly as ambiguous as an associationist theory would predict. This theory may also be criticized for saying that meaningful words like "how", "despite", etc. have no meaning, and nonsense words like Lewis Carroll's "slithy toves" have a meaning. The same criticisms are made of the related theory that meanings are mental images.[58] The point, I think, is by now clear: the criterion for judging theories of *meaning* is that they correctly predict sameness of *meaning*, *meaning*fulness, *meaning*lessness, multiplicity of *meaning*, and other semantic properties and relations. It could hardly be otherwise.

But, on the basis of this criterion, the theory that meaning is use fares no better than the theory that meaning is reference and the others. The most obvious facts about the semantic properties and relations of expressions and sentences of English count tellingly against this theory. For example, words like "bunny" and "rabbit", "piss" and "urine", or "Black" and "nigger" have the same meaning but clearly not the same use. Again, almost every word has an ironic use, so, for example, "perfect", "beauty", and "adore" can be used to say something is flawed, someone or thing is ugly, and someone hates someone, respectively, but clearly it is wrong to claim that the meaning of almost every English word has the sense of its antonym. In fact, it is quite rare to find genuine examples of words that are ambiguous between autonymous senses, e.g., "cleave". Again, there are expressions and sentences of natural languages that are so long or so complicated (e.g., that contain four hundred and sixty thousand center-embeddings) that they could never have a use, but nonetheless, are perfectly meaningful, for they are built up from meaningful components by operations, like conjunction, known to give meaningful results.

Strawson once propounded a natural version of the use theory of meaning in which the defining conditions for the meaningfulness of a referring expression is that it could be used to refer and the condition for the meaningfulness of an assertive sentence is that it could be used to make a true or false statement.[59] But expressions like "the largest integer" or "a complete and consistent formalization of mathematics", though meaningful, could not be used to refer and sentences like "The largest integer is prime" cannot be used to make a true or false statement on Strawson's account of statement-making. If we drop the natural version, are we to say that expressions that cannot—for logical reasons—be used to refer are just as meaningful as expressions that can be? Again, considering how rampant metaphorical uses of language are, how can a theory identifying meaning with use hope to specify the right degree of ambiguity of words and expressions? Or, for that matter distinguish between literally deviant expressions like "the cruel desert sun" and "the cruel desert sheik"?[60]

There is no end of such difficulties. The problem, as argued in the discussion of Chomsky in the last chapter, is that use is a product of more things than the grammatical meaning of the expression or sentence used. Our use of language depends on the various overtones, connotations, and associations words have for us: "bunny" has a childish tone, "piss" an obscene one, and "nigger" a pejorative one, but "rabbit", "urine", and "Black", which are synonyms, lack these special tones. Our use of language depends on the social conventions that together with such tones, connotations, and associations influence our use of words, but changes in these conventions do not change the language. Furthermore, the knowledge a speaker has that the audience cannot think an obviously ugly object that the speaker calls "beautiful" is something the speaker really thinks beautiful, or the psychological limitations on memory or speech processing, or the biological limitations on the life of the speaker, or the suspicion that Big Brother is listening can and normally do produce a variety of differences in use where meaning is constant, and can and do collapse a variety of differences in meaning into the same use.

Why do philosophers like Dummett adopt such a theory? I think the answer involves three principal factors. One, which was aluded to just above, is a kind of linguistic empiricism that requires a theory of meaning "to make the workings of language open to our view".[61] The previous quotation from Dummett continues, "We cannot, as it were, extract from this training more than was put into it".[62] If the theory of meaning were under a mandate to present language as wholly public in its acquisition and workings and if attaining linguistic fluency were like attaining a bank balance in a no-interest account, then the most plausible theory of meaning would be one which pictures the acquired semantic rules as maximally resembling the training in use that assumptively constitutes the teaching of language.[63]

The second factor is that Dummett thinks that he has refuted the opposed theory of meaning on which the meaning of assertions is given in terms of a specification of truth conditions.[64] Dummett has taken pains to examine one theory of meaning on which the proper task for the semantic analysis of language is to explain the grammatical association of concepts and propositions with expressions and sentences; he found such a "modest" theory wanting, but he then sweepingly rejects all modest theories in favor of his own "full-blooded" theory (i.e., one that gives a full theory of how language is understood).[65] The trouble with this as a justification of the use theory is that the particular modest theory that Dummett examines is Davidson's theory of interpretation, which, first, is hardly representative of all modest theories, and second, is not a theory of meaning at all.[66] Dummett overlooks other modest theories that *are* theories of meaning.

The third factor is the belief of use theorists that criticisms like those in Wittgenstein's *Philosophical Investigations* show that only a use theory can be a general theory of meaning because other theories cannot handle the large variety of non-assertive semantic structures in natural languages.[67] Since the meanings of words seem to enter into the meanings of assertive and non-assertive sentences in much the same way, one would be rightly reluctant to accept a theory that can say nothing about the meaning of questions, requests, promises, apologies, and so on. But Wittgensteinian criticism does not work against all theories of meaning that take meaning to be an aspect of grammatical structure and so not identifiable with use. The admitted success of these criticisms against the theories of Frege, Russell, and the early Wittgenstein is no measure of their success as general arguments against grammatical theories of meaning.[68]

The situation with respect to the problem of explaining the source of necessary truth in general, and in language, specially, is simply that nothing seems to work. Conventionalism is a paper-tiger; nominalism is a cure that is worse than the disease; formalism had the wrath of Gödel brought down on it; conceptualism's treatment of laws of logic, mathematics, and language as laws of psychology is an unsuccessful attempt to substitute natural necessity for logical necessity; constructivism, as a species of conceptualism, shares its failure and as well rests on a highly dubious theory of meaning; even theology, as Dummett observes, seems to hold no hope.[69] In this situation, one can follow Quine and claim there really is no such thing as genuine necessity, but if one is unwilling to go this far, if one acknowledges genuine necessity in these areas, then one ought to accept the one account of the meaning of logical, mathematical, and linguistic statements and of the reality such statements are about on which they can be necessary.[70]

The Platonist explains the necessity in logic, mathematics, and grammar on the grounds that the statements in these subjects are about abstract objects. The fact that logical, mathematical, and grammatical truths are necessary is exhibited as a consequence of the character of abstract objects. First, such objects have no temporal or spatial properties. Psychological and physical objects have temporal properties, and physical objects have spatial properties. (Psychological objects are thought of as not having spatial properties except what might be call positional properties in a phenomenological field.) Second, abstract objects are as objective as are physical objects, while psychological objects are subjective: no one person has a special relation to an abstract or physical object whereas a psychological object is the unique possession of the individual in whose consciousness it occurs. Frege discusses this characteristic.[71] Third, abstract objects are not only changeless in the sense of never being different at different times but are cohesive in the sense of having logically inseparable basic properties.[72] However the number two is conceived of, in whatever hypothetical circumstances it is considered, it must have the same mathematical properties, definitional and non-definitional alike.[73]

These characteristics—atemporality, aspatiality, objectivity, and cohesiveness—are, as it were, the features of the category of abstract object.[74] Given these characteristics, if a statement about an abstract object is true under one set of circumstances, it is true under all because none of the properties of the object, hence none of those by virtue of which the statement is true, can be different in different circumstances. Since the statement cannot fail to be true of the objects it is about in any possible world in which the objects exist, the statement is true in all such possible worlds and hence necessary. Worlds in which the objects of such a statement are supposed to lack the properties the statement asserts them to have will be impossible. Therefore, Platonism is able, where other ontological approaches to linguistics (mathematics and logic) are not, to give an account of how the truths of semantics (mathematics and logic) can be necessary.

Notes

1. Frege 1967 and Frege 1953 are the two main sources in English. Material relevant in this connection is also found in Geach and Black 1952. See also Klemke 1968; Dummett 1973, Husserl 1970.

2. This is related to the attempt I began in Katz 1979c to develop an alternative to both the old and new philosophies of science, what I called there "linguistic rationalism". The attempt will be continued in a number of further papers. The present book can be viewed in relation to this attempt as an argument that the rationalism of this alternative cannot be the mere nativism of conceptualist approaches to knowledge, but must rest on a Platonist ontology for at least the domains of language, logic, and mathematics.

3. Frege 1967: 12.

4. Frege 1967: 13.
5. Frege 1967: 13.
6. Frege 1972.
7. Frege's significance for contemporary analytic philosophy cannot be fully appreciated if one does not realize that, for better or worse, Russell, Wittgenstein, Carnap, et al. got their notion of the grammatical form/logical form distinction and much of their conception of a logically perfect language from Frege. See Frege 1972: 14.
8. Frege 1972: 112–113.
9. See Geach and Black 1952: 70.
10. Geach and Black 1952: 70.
11. Frege 1972: 104–105.
12. Frege 1967: 13.
13. Wittgenstein 1922: 61–63.
14. See Chomsky 1966a: 31–35.
15. In the actual Port-Royal grammar, underlying grammatical form does not go deep enough to encompass semantic structure, but the recent work on semantics in generative grammar has extended this earlier theory to encompass it.
16. Frege 1972: 113. Compare the discussion in Katz 1972: 414–434.
17. Frege 1972: 113.
18. I am assuming that "all features" means aspects of meaning, too, although a similar argument might be made with respect to quantificational structure.
19. It is logically possible that semantic rules could be added to remove senses to which multiple syntactic structures would otherwise give rise, but it is hard to imagine what they could be.
20. Many philosophers have an attitude toward meaning in natural language that could easily prevent giving this identity thesis a fair hearing. They think of linguistic meaning as essentially conventional while thinking of propositions, as Frege took senses, to be eternal logical objects. Accordingly, such philosophers will find this thesis to be prima facie implausible. This attitude is, for example, expressed in Tyler Burge's remark (Burge, 1979: 398–399) that Frege's notion of *sinn* is different from modern notions of linguistic meaning because "Frege was primarily interested in the eternal structure of thought, of cognitive contents, not in conventional linguistic meaning".

The attitude rests on two confusions. One is the confusion, on the one hand, between the correlation of the sensible signs speakers use with the mental structures they express with them, and on the other, these cognitive mental structures. The former, which reflects the customary linguistic practices in the community, is plausibly taken as a matter of convention; the latter, however, is not, at least not without serious argument to overcome the Chomskian view that such cognitive mental structures are not conventional but innate. The other confusion is the one that underlies the conceptualist view of language against which I having been arguing in this book. This is the confusion between natural languages and the speaker's knowledge of them. If this distinction is drawn, there is nothing implausible in identifying the abstract objects constituting the meanings of sentences and expressions in natural language with the elements in the "eternal structure of thought".

Burge, and I suspect many other philosophers of logic, have followed Frege in thinking that identifying the meanings of sentences and expressions in natural language with Fregean senses is a mistake because they seem to vary independently in the case of indexicals (Burge, 399–407). Burge quotes Frege's remark that "Words like 'here,' 'now' achieve their full sense always only through the circumstances in which they are used . . . and the sentence does not always express the same thought, because the words require supplementation to yield the complete sense, and . . . this supplementation can be different according to circumstances" (399). But not only does sense shift with circumstance so that the same linguistic meaning may be associated with different thoughts, different linguistic meanings, of, for example, "yesterday" and "today", may be associated with the same thought. These considerations, however, do not support the conclusion that it is a mistake to identify linguistic meanings and Fregean thoughts or *sinn*. What they show is that it is not possible, in general, to identify the thought expressed by a sentence in a given context with the linguistic meaning of the sentence. But the identification of linguistic meanings with senses does not require this, only that each linguistic meaning of a sentence is identical to some thought and each thought identical to some linguistic meaning. See my discussion of the relation between grammar and pragmatics (Katz 1977d and Katz 1980c) for an account on which the thoughts expressed in context are meanings of sentences in the language but under a different correlation between sentences and meanings from that in the language.

21. See Katz 1977d: 195–242.

22. See F. M. Katz and J. J. Katz 1977.

23. See Katz 1977a; Smith, G and Katz, J. J. in preparation.

24. Frege 1967: 13.

25. Just as everybody might take *modus ponens* to be false because their inferential competence contains a mistaken logical schema, so everybody might take the principle of analytic entailment to be false because their semantic competence contains a mistaken definition. Other ways in which the principles of grammarᵢ might differ from semantic laws are as follows. The speaker's tacit grammatical knowledge might contain a faulty projection rule, so that certain sentences are not assigned the right compositional meaning. Thus, such sentences could be ambiguous, redundant, analytic, etc. while speakers of the language take them to be unambiguous, non-redundant, synthetic, etc. This example runs along the same lines as some of those in Chapter V. Suppose G is the simplest grammar that handles all the facts about the structure of English sentences. G can be converted into another grammar G^* by adding a rule that scrambles the terminal strings in derivations exceeding n elements (or that blocks all derivations of sentences with more than m embeddings). Assuming n and m large enough, the effect of such an addition will never show up in speech. G and G^* are completely equivalent within the performance capacities of human speakers. But it is entirely possible that G^*, the grammar that does not handle all the facts, is actually the true grammarᵢ of English. (We may even come to learn this from neurological studies of the brain mechanism that serves as the grammatical component of the performance system for speakers of English; see Chomsky 1975b: 36–37. We may extend Frege's point to syntax by observing further that there is no contradiction in the speaker's tacit grammatical principles' characterizing certain extremely long ungrammatical sentences as grammatical or certain extremely complex grammatical sentences as ungrammatical.

26. Chomsky 1965: 3.

27. Frege 1967: 14.

28. Frege 1953: 20ᵉ–21ᵉ.

29. Katz 1978: 191–234.

30. It has been noted that G. E. Moore's attack on naturalism in ethics is part of the overall criticism of psychologism during the period. (See for example Chisholm 1960: 16). The well-known arguments in Moore 1956: ch. 1 are perhaps closer in spirit to this particular argument of Frege's than to other anti-naturalist arguments. For a general discussion of these questions across the areas of logic, language, ethics, etc., see Katz in preparation.

31. Husserl 1900.

32. Frege 1894. I wish to thank Linda McAlister for letting me see a draft of her translation of this review. An English translation now appears in Elliston and McCormick 1977: 314–324.

33. Husserl 1970: 179 (note 1).

34. Husserl 1970.

35. Compare the first of the arguments discussed below with the remark in Frege 1953:

38ᵉ: "It would be strange if the most exact of all the sciences had to seek support from psychology, which is still feeling its way none too surely.

36. Husserl 1970: 103. It is worth commenting in this connection on Edie's claim (Edie 1976: 45–71) that there is a "unity of purpose . . . behind the grammatical projects of Husserl and Chomsky". Edie claims that except for Chomsky's unfortunate lapse into "a relativistic psychologism of an almost Spencerian crudity" (61), Chomsky's aims are the same as Husserl's, namely, the construction of an aprioristic pure logical grammar. Edie's claim is, I think, completely wrong: it would be hard to find more disunity of purpose than one finds in the case of Husserl and Chomsky. There are three mistakes underlying Edie's claim. First, it underestimates the extreme importance of psychologism to Chomsky's project. The principal force behind Chomsky's work has been his concern with developing a psychologized linguistic theory. Second, Edie's claim fails to appreciate Chomsky's skepticism about just the semantic concerns that were central to Husserl's project. Third, Edie's claim mistakenly treats Chomsky's formal universals, not as biological impositions on human tacit linguistic knowledge —as Chomsky insists they be treated—but as a priori principles of pure logical grammar in Husserl's sense. Chomsky is no empiricist and he was responsible for ridding linguistics of statistical studies, but for him linguistics is a branch of empirical psychology with no aspirations to a priori knowledge.

37. Husserl 1970: 98–99.

38. Husserl 1970: 99.

39. Husserl 1970: 101

40. Husserl 1970: 104.

41. Husserl 1970: 104.

42. Husserl 1970: 104.

43. Husserl 1970: 106.

44. Husserl 1970: 107.

45. Husserl 1970: 107.

46. On the intended sense of "nightmare", not, for example, on the sense expressed when people say that their day at the office was a "nightmare".

47. I would like to try to sort out here the confusions in Quine's conception of my approach to semantics. One is his fault, one mine. I have already pointed out (Katz 1974: footnote 35, 317–318) that Quine simply misunderstood my claim to have answered his objections to Carnap. I agreed that Quine quite correctly criticizes Carnap's explication of analyticity for failing to say what analyticity is, but argued that my definition of analyticity (Katz 1972: 177–178) is not open to this criticism because it spells out the universal semantic structure that instantiates the property of analyticity in sentences. Quine somehow overlooks this and fastens on an empirical procedure mentioned in the course of one of my papers for eliciting analyticity judgments without using the term "analyticity". He then uses the fact that such a procedure, if proposed as a definition of analyticity, would be open to his criticism of Carnap to claim that my approach offers no proper explication of analyticity. (Quine 1967: 52–54.) The other confusion, the one that is my fault, is the construal of my approach as an empirical investigation. Though I take the blame for this construal, I still think it is going too far to conceive my approach as the same as Arne Naess's public opinion surveys. (See Quine 1972a: 448–449.) Not all empirical investigation is opinion polling.

48. Does the fact that $(\exists x)(Fx \vee \overline{F}x)$ is a logical truth show that Husserl was mistaken in thinking that the logical laws imply no matter of empirical fact? Not at all. There is no reason to suppose that the object whose existence is guaranteed by this logical truth is an *empirical* object. There does indeed exist something that is either F or non-F, but it is open to me to have it be an abstract object and this not only provides me with the extensional basis required but provides a better account of such necessary existence. Indeed, if we couple this logical requirement for an existent with the

arguments in the text showing that no logical law can imply a matter of empirical fact, we obtain an argument for the existence of abstract objects, since the requirement cannot be satisfied by any of the empirical objects in the psychological and physical realms. I want to thank Richard Mendelsohn and Alan Berger for raising the question and for discussing it with me.

49. On the strong notion of necessary truth, a proposition is necessary just in case true in all possible worlds, while on the weak notion it is necessary just in case it is true in all possible worlds in which the objects the proposition is about exist. The weak notion avoids complications and is as strong as is needed in the present connection. See Smith 1979.

50. Namely, what is the account of how we know necessary truths? This question is dealt with in the next chapter.

51. Dummett 1964: 494.

52. Dummett 1964: 494.

53. Quine 1964: 322–343.

54. Benacerraff 1973: 671–675.

55. Dummett 1964: 492.

56. Dummett 1964: 508.

57. Dummett 1964: 508.

58. See Katz 1981 for further discussion.

59. Strawson 1950: 184.

60. Note that the interpretation of such a metaphor is that the pain inflicted by the desert sun is like that inflicted by a human who is disposed to show no mercy, and further that such an interpretation makes no sense for non-metaphorical expressions like "the cruel desert sheik."

61. Dummett 1975: 100–101. The requirement on theories that they make "the workings of language open to view" is, when one stops to think about it, rather peculiar. Why should theories be responsible for the workings turning out to be surface phenomena? Why, aside from empiricist or behaviorist scruples, should we not allow the workings to be closed to view? If they are closed to view, they can still be discoverable on the basis of theoretical inference: atoms and deep syntactic structure are closed to view.

62. Dummett 1964: 508.

63. The alternative way of presenting the acquisition of meanings is as based on an innate conceptual space which potentially expresses them all, with the role of training or experience being the relatively minor one of associating vocabulary with points in the conceptual space. See Katz 1979c.

64. Dummett 1964: 492. Such theories are the homogeneous semantic account for Platonism, the principal rival of constructivism in the philosophy of mathematics.

65. Dummett 1975: 101–102.

66. For another modest theorist's view of Davidson's theory, see Katz 1975: 63–76.

67. Wittgenstein 1953.

68. In Katz 1977d I argue that such criticisms fail when theories of meaning abandon their commitment to the standard separation between logical and extralogical vocabulary and provide an account of the logical contribution of performative verbs and other performative structures to the meanings of sentences. See also Katz 1980c for a defense of the view that the distinction between meaning as part of grammatical form and matters of use can be strictly separated and extended beyond the constative portion of language to the performative portion.

69. I should also mention the view that necessity is relative to a body of knowledge. This view is expounded in a limited form by Putnam. It has been one of his themes since Putnam 1962. The view does not offer an account of genuine necessary truth. Genuine necessity cannot be reconstructed in terms of a body of beliefs, regardless of how broad

and compelling, that could, in principle, fail to be true, no matter how strong their confirmation. Relative necessity is only the notion of what must be true if some class of statements is true. But even here the "must" is watered down. For the truth of the class of statements cannot be taken to logically imply the necessity of the original statement insofar as the principles of logical implication themselves have to be understood as true only relative to some body of contingent statements. So if the statements to which some statement is relative are true, it still will not follow that that statement must be true.

70. This is a stronger claim than I need to make to argue that Platonism succeeds where it has been shown that conceptualism fails. But it seems to me correct to argue that, other things equal, one ought to accept an explanation of a fact one acknowledges if it is the only explanation of that fact.

71. Frege, in Klemke 1968: 519–535.

72. For example, for arithmetical objects, arithmetic properties; for geometrical objects, geometrical properties.

73. No question is begged even though cohesiveness uses the notion of necessary connection. The question at issue is not what necessity itself is but what makes truths of logic, mathematics, and grammar necessary.

74. These characteristics imply that members of the category of abstract object are universals in something like the traditional sense, while physical and psychological objects are particulars. But there is no implication about the relation between universals and particulars; no doctrine of exemplification follows. Further, it should be noted that things that are sometimes called properties of universals, e. g., being the cardinality of the set of Presidents of the United States, which depend on an exemplification relation, play no role in our account of the cohesion or individuation of abstract objects. Hence there are no grounds for criticizing this account of the permanence of abstract objects on the basis that the number 38 lacked the property of being the number of Presidents of the United States until Carter was elected.

VI

Advanced Platonism: Intuition

Introduction

We have argued that a Platonist interpretation of theories in linguistics is preferable to a conceptualist interpretation of them. Coupling this argument with Chomsky's argument against the nominalism of the American structuralist position, we obtain a general conclusion that a Platonist interpretation of theories in linguistics is *the* preferable interpretation. Both nominalist and conceptualist schemes impose constraints that derive not from the purely scientific commitment to provide the best account of the structure of sentences, but from a preconception about the object of study in linguistics, or from fears that too many theories may survive confrontation with the evidence even after pruning with Occam's razor. Without these constraints, we obtain grammars that save the phenomena that grammars are supposed to explain.

But an ontological position is not solely evaluated on the extent to which it enables us to save the phenomena. Ontological positions are also evaluated on the extent to which they fit into an overall philosophical system. Put another way, ontological positions are judged on the basis of their consequences for related philosophical issues. If the consequences for other philosophical issues were not a significant consideration in resolving issues in ontology, nominalism, with the risk it poses of sacrificing large portions of abstract sciences like mathematics, would never have had much philosophical appeal. Nominalism has enjoyed support from philosophers who fully appreciate the risks because, first, it has such broadly respectable a

192

philosophical basis (nobody but idealists deny the existence of physical objects), and second, it has a special attraction to empiricists.

Alternatively, Platonism would have been far more popular over the centuries had it not been for doubts about the respectability of its philosophical basis.[1] Platonism's ecumenical attitude toward ontological diversity poses no risk of sacrifice in abstract science while allowing issues concerning the mental and the physical to work themselves out as they may. Chief among these doubts is the fear that Platonism does not mesh with an acceptable epistemology.

Now, allowing for the fact that some of these doubts amount to little more than the aversion of empiricism to *a priori* knowledge, there are a number of real questions about how human beings can know truths about abstract objects. Furthermore, Platonists have themselves often contributed to the persistence of these doubts. One striking example in modern philosophy is Frege's neglect of epistemology throughout his expousal of unadulterated Platonism about logic and mathematics.

The present chapter attempts to mitigate these doubts as much as possible by developing an account of how humans obtain *a priori* knowledge of abstract objects. I do not expect that the account will, in its present form, free Platonism from all doubts about its epistemological foundations, but it ought to stimulate a reassessment of just how well-founded such doubts are. My intention is at least to dislodge the current supposition in philosophy that epistemology contains "knockdown" arguments against Platonic realism.

The Faculty of Intuition

Platonists invoke intuition to play essentially the same role in their account of *a priori* knowledge that perception and introspection play in accounts of *a posteriori* knowledge. Intuition is to provide an account of the source of the basic knowledge on which *a priori* knowledge in general is built. The Platonist's claim that intuition exists rests on the same considerations as the claim that perception and introspection exist, namely, first-hand experience with its operations, on the one hand, and the elimination of all other faculties as capable of supplying the knowledge in question, on the other.

People who have done some mathematics are personally familiar with mathematical intuition. Our certainty about a wide range of mathematical facts, even very many that can be proven, comes from intuition. For example, the fact that a cube has twelve edges, though provable, is certain for most of us because it is intuitively so. People without first-hand experience or people with doubts about the interpretation of intuition can examine the remarkable case of Ramanujan, an Indian postal clerk who discovered huge amounts of mathematics for himself without even a rudimentary knowledge of mathematical proof.[2]

Our grounds in first-hand experience dovetail with the fact that the other faculties are unable to provide *a priori* knowledge: neither of the other faculties that are sources of basic knowledge, perception and introspection, nor the faculties for constructing theoretical structures from cognitive raw materials, such as reason and memory, can explain how we know such truths. The former faculties inform us of particulars, while the latter presuppose basic knowledge.[3]

The critic of intuition may respond that invoking faculties that we know next to nothing about is a poor way of explaining something. I would agree if the explanation were of how we know this or that *a priori* truth. In specific cases, we want to see how the faculty operates in producing specific knowledge. But here the question is about the general way in which a class of facts is acquired. Moreover, to be consistent, the critic who makes this criticism of intuition would logically have to criticize introspection, and, to a lesser extent, even perception and each of our other faculties, too. Introspection is also a faculty that we know very little about, yet, except for the behaviorists, we are willing to accept introspection as a mode of obtaining basic knowledge, in spite of the fact that we know as little about the process by which we become aware of the color of an after-image or the intensity of a pain as we do about the process by which we become aware that a cube has twelve edges or that "Nightmares are dreams" is analytic. In both the case of introspection and intuition, our lack of knowledge about them is offset by the fact that we are acquainted with their operation and cannot expect to overcome our ignorance without acknowledging that there is a faculty we need to learn something about. In this spirit, let us look at some of the things that can be said about intuition, in particular, about the respects in which it is similar to and different from the two other faculties for acquiring basic knowledge, introspection and perception.

Introspection is a faculty for acquiring knowledge about the contents of our consciousness and perception is a faculty for acquiring knowledge about physical objects in the external world. On the Platonist view, intuition is a faculty for acquiring knowledge about abstract objects. This conception has led Fodor, Fodor, and Garrett to criticize the Platonist position in linguistics for being "virtually unintelligible".[4] They argue as follows. On the one hand, "a formal science like mathematics makes no claim for the psychological reality of the entities it describes", and on the other, "the intuitions of speaker-hearers [are taken by linguists] to be the data to which structural descriptions are required to respond"; furthermore, "this practice would be quite unwarranted unless speaker-hearers do have access to internal representations of sentences," and consequently, since "the primary data of linguistics are psychological data", Fodor, Fodor, and Garrett draw the conclusion that either "we use no psychological information, including intuitions, to constrain the grammar, or . . . we use all the pertinent psychological information to constrain it. However, the former alternative is not a serious option, since it would, in effect, limit the empirical data for linguistics to regularities in the corpus."[5]

Were this a sound argument, it would also be possible to prove that mathematics is "virtually unintelligible". The parallel argument runs as follows: Mathematics, too, traffics in intuitions. From the humble intuitions in Euclidean geometry to the sophisticated intuitions in topology, mathematics ultimately justifies its theories on the basis of intuitions that can also be said to provide the data to which descriptions of structure are required to respond. Further, this practice, too, would be unwarranted unless mathematicians have access to internal representations of mathematical structures. But, insofar as "a formal science . . . makes no claims for the psychological reality of the entities it describes", it can make no use of psychological information, no intuitions, to constrain its theories. Mathematics thus has no right to employ the intuitive basis it employs. Since no other is available, mathematics is unintelligible.

Since by parity of reasoning we have arrived at the absurd conclusion that mathematics is a dubious enterprise, both the original argument and its parallel must be rejected. The difficulty with them is their fallacious inference from the fact that a discipline does not make claims about psychological reality to the conclusion that its practioners cannot employ psychological data in the sense of the sort that intuition provides. The fallacy is due to an ambiguity of the expression "psychological data". "Psychological" can modify "data" in the manner of the construction "experimental data" and indicate the source of the data, or "psychological" can modify "data" in the manner of the construction "political data" and indicate what the data is about. Once we distinguish the *source sense* from the *import sense,* it is clear that Fodor, Fodor, and Garrett cannot validly infer that Platonist linguistics is "virtually unintelligible".

Perception, introspection, and intuition are mental faculties issuing in acts of apprehension. They differ principally in terms of the kind of object they enable us to apprehend. In perception, we observe the external world; in introspection, we observe our own thoughts, feelings, images, emotions, etc.; in intuition, we grasp numbers, sets, sentences, etc. Intuition is like perception: internal representations are the source of knowledge but do not represent something psychological. What is represented in both cases is something objective, in contrast to introspection, which is a matter of obtaining "mental meter readings". Though the source of an intuition is psychological, its import concerns objective matters of linguistic, logical, or mathematic fact.

Frege stressed the objectivity of the objects of intuition, saying they stand ". . . apart from everyone in the same way, where a possessor of the 'idea' is neither mentioned nor even tacitly presupposed."[6] There is a touching story about a visit of G. H. Hardy's to Ramanujan in the hospital that illustrates this point.[7] Hardy remarked on arrival that he had had a boring trip because of the dull number of his taxi, 1729. Ramanujan is reported to have scolded Hardy and pointed out that the number is quite interesting, being the smallest number expressible as the sum of two cubes in two ways. Now, the object of Ramanujan's intuition stood apart, in Frege's sense, from both men. It was a common object as much as if it had been Ramanujan's bed they were discussing. In contrast, had Hardy remarked about a pain of Ramanujan's the object would not, in Frege's sense, have stood apart; it would have been part of the content of Ramanujan's consciousness.

Intuition, introspection, and perception are similar in being faculties for acquiring new knowledge, in contrast to reason (which extracts conclusions contained in already available knowledge) and memory (which concerns the storage of information). Such new knowledge is specific to a particular ontological domain, again, in contrast with reason and memory which operate on any knowledge. Related to their providing new knowledge and their specificity, intuition, introspection, and perception provide the basic knowledge about, respectively, abstract objects, objects of subjective experience, and physical objects that lays the foundations on which reason erects the complex and general intellectual structures with which we are familiar from the advanced sciences. Reason itself cannot produce such foundations because, in applying equally to each domain of knowledge, it can say nothing specific about the foundations of any one. Reason, therefore, requires a starting point outside itself if it is to conclude something beyond truths of reason. Since each domain itself requires a starting point outside reason, the supposition that we can arrive at knowledge about the objects of a domain purely on the basis of inference leads to a vicious regress. Each proposition would have to be arrived at by inference from other propositions, themselves arrived at by inference from others, *ad infinitum*. Non-inferential faculties provide the starting points for investigation of their domains.[8]

Because the objects of intuition and perception stand apart from us so that no one is in a special epistemological position with respect to them, we can be straightforwardly contradicted by others when we make reports about those objects. But, in making reports about the objects of introspection, the experiencer cannot be contradicted, unless the situation is special and the normalcy of the circumstances somehow challenged.[9] This "privileged access", as it is sometimes called, is, as it were, the acknowledgement on the part of others that the reporter is the only person in a position to make a direct observation. Intuition enjoys no such privilege. Whereas there is a *prima facie* inappropriateness in contradicting another's report of an internal experience such as a pain, there would be nothing at all *prima facie* inappropriate about contradicting another report about one of his or her intuitions. Witness the fact that there is nothing inappropriate about Ramanujan's contradicting Hardy's statement about the number 1729; it is as if Hardy had failed to look closely enough to notice that what they were looking at was an interesting arboreal arrangement rather than a single tree.[10]

This brings us to the vexed question of whether intuitive judgments are certain, as Descartes held. He distinguishes "intuitus", a direct awareness of the essential nature of something, from "deductus", intuitus of necessary connection between premiss and conclusion and "enumeratio", a kind of wide lens deductio, a simultaneous awareness of an entire chain of logical connections rather than a series of successive awarenesses of the connections.[11] Descartes held that intuitus is a single, momentary act of infallible apprehension, in which the mind's eye sees the essential nature of its object.

But there are cases of fallible intuition. It once was intuitively clear that a curve is the locus of points satisfying equations that are continuous, hence differentiable, functions. But this certain intuition was later refuted by Peano's famous counterexample.[12] We can, of course, try to absolve intuition. Descartes distinguished intuitus from judgment and inference, taking truth and falsehood solely as features of judgment and inference. Intuition itself simply reveals an essential nature about which true or false assertions are made in judgment and inference. But such a rescue operation is a dubious matter in both theory and practice. It overlooks the fact that, even though truth and falsehood may not apply to intuition, the notions *veridical* and *illusory* do. The fact here is the same as with acts of perception. Here also, sure marks are required in order to guarantee that judgments correctly report what the mind's eyes has seen. Descartes's own attempt to provide such marks (clarity and distinctness) suffers from insufficient attention to explanation and from too diffuse a use,[13] but, more critically, Descartes's attempt raises the further question of how we tell when our apprehension is clear and distinct enough to guarantee veridicality. It passes the buck.

Given that intuition is a human faculty, it is hard to see why there should not be genuine instances of erroneous intuition. Descartes thought that mistakes due to inattention, turbidity, and confoundedness can be handled on his principle that whatever is clearly and distinctly apprehended is true, but, even if this is so, there are other sources of error in the operation of intuition that cannot be handled on this principle. For example, our view of an object of intuition may be colored by expectations about the object stemming from a theory that we cherish. Everyone who works in theoretical areas will have a number of examples of their own of how this can happen.[14] Again, our view may be colored by expectations stemming from preconceptions. In such a case, as in the previous one, our intuition may clearly and distinctly reflect the structure of something imposed on apprehension by such outside factors.

Consider the following illustration of the way expectations impose the wrong structure on the apprehension an object of intuition. Imagine a perfect sphere, say, the size of the earth. If you start at the North Pole and go one mile South, then one mile West, and then one mile North, you will return to the starting point. Question: is there another point on the surface of the sphere (as shown in Figure *1*) where you can

Figure *1*

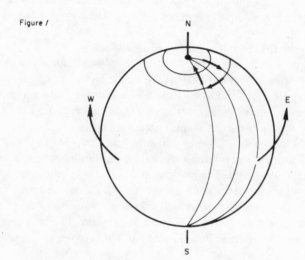

follow these instructions exactly and return to your starting point? Most people who have trouble with the problem expect that the path they will have to follow in going one mile south, one mile west, and one mile north is triangular. Indeed, the problem is set up to encourage this expectation. Then, they have the intuition that there is no point other than the north pole from which they can follow these instructions *taking a triangular path* and return to it. They are thus stumped because this intuition is misinterpreted as a demonstration that the conditions of the problem cannot be fulfilled. Once they realize that these conditions give them no reason to expect that the path will be triangular, they are on their way to a solution of the kind illustrated in figure 2.

Figure 2

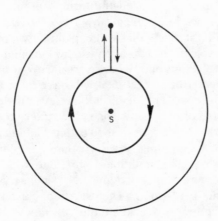

These examples may, of course, be quarreled with. But they raise serious questions about Descartes's position. I think they show that it is mistaken, but at least they show it to have failed to establish "sure marks". Thus, the questions they raise make it clear that one ought not wed oneself to the doctrine of the infallibility of intuition unless abandoning the doctrine will have intolerable consequences for theses we wish to hold on to. But this is not so in the present context. The infallibility of intuition is unnecessary for Platonism.

If we assume that intuition, like the other two faculties for providing basic knowledge, is fallible, we are not prevented from making any claim that we need to make to set out the Platonist position in this book. In particular, adopting the view that intuition is fallible does not preclude us from claiming that the truths of semantics, logic, and mathematics are necessary. Fallibility and certainty are epistemological categories, properties of the knower or the means of knowing, while necessity is a metaphysical category, a property of propositions. Even a Ramanujan might be mistaken in any one of his mathematical intuitions, but the necessity of the proposition that 1729 is the smallest number expressible as the sum of two cubes in two ways is not called into question by this possibility. Intuition need do no more than reliably exhibit the truth of such propositions under one set of circumstances.

The Epistemology of Intuitive Apprehension

Since the objects of intuition are atemporal and aspatial and hence not particular, how can particular acts of ours provide knowledge of such objects? We have thus far used the term "apprehension" as a kind of place-holder, and the problem now is to replace this label with a conception of what it labels that will explain how we can know things about abstract objects. Such a conception cannot be expected to be a full theory of intuition. We are very far from having reasonable hopes of that kind. But a great deal will have been accomplished, as will be clear in the course of the discussion, even if we provide nothing more than a sketch of how knowledge of abstract objects is possible.

One thing that will be accomplished is that Platonism will escape the dead end to which traditional Platonist theorizing about intuitive apprehension has led. The tradition from Plato to Gödel proposes a conception of intuition that extends the similarity between it and introspection and perception. The tradition conceives intuition on analogy to perception and makes intuitive knowledge depend on the knower establishing some form of direct contact with the objects of knowledge. In the *Meno,* Plato says, "The soul, then, being immortal, and having been born again many times, and having seen all things that exist, whether in this world or in the world below, has knowledge of them all." Gödel writes:

. . . the objects of transfinite set theory . . . clearly do not belong to the physical world and even their indirect connection with physical objects is very loose . . .

But, despite their remoteness from sense experience, we do have a perception also of the objects of set theory, as is seen in the fact that the axioms force themselves upon us as being true. I don't see any reason why we should have less confidence in this kind of perception, i.e., in mathematical intuition, than in sense perception, which induces us to build up physical theories and to expect that future sense perceptions will agree with them and, moreover, to believe that a question not decidable now has meaning and may be decided in the future.[15]

Even Husserl follows Plato's lead. It is, he claims,

. . . a fundamental error to suppose that perception (and every other type of the intuition of things, each after its own manner) fails to come into contact with the thing itself.[16]

The principal point at which my Platonism departs from traditional Platonism is in rejecting such perceptually inspired accounts of intuition. I think that the traditional claim that knowledge of abstract objects is knowledge by acquaintance cannot be reconciled with the nature of these objects. The difficulty is that perception demands a causal relation between perceiver and object perceived,[17] so that, if intuition were a form of perceptual acquaintance, then abstract objects, being outside space and time and being objective, could not enter such a relation. Being objective, abstract objects do not occur as a constituent of the conscious experience of a knower, and, being aspatial and atemporal, they cannot act on a knower through a causal process to produce a representation of themselves in the manner of sense perception.[18]

Failure to appreciate this difficulty renders a number of contemporary versions of Platonism incoherent. Consider, for example, Karl Popper's version. Popper claims that his conception of the "third world" is a contemporary form of the Platonist doctrines of Plato, the Stoics, Leibniz, Bolzano, and Frege.[19] Popper contends that there are "causal relations between the three worlds",[20] and says further that the objects in the third world are "of our making", that is,

According to the position which I am adopting here the third world (part of which is human language) is the product of men, just as honey is the product of bees, or spider's webs of spiders. . . . human language, and thus larger parts of the third world are *the unplanned product of human actions*, though they may be solutions to biological or other problems.[21]

If his conception of the third world is the realism of the tradition from Plato to Frege, how can there be causal relation between the third world and either of the other two? If the objects of the third world are "of our making"—as honey is the product of bees or webs the product of spiders—then Popper has to claim, inconsistent with realism, that numbers are contingent objects that didn't exist until humans came into existence. Further, he has to claim that numbers can be destroyed just as honey and the webs of spiders can. Popper seems not to appreciate the fact that objective entities with neither spatial nor temporal location cannot enter into causal relations.

Perhaps, however, we ought not take the references of Gödel and other traditional Platonic realists to perception so literally. Respect for the stature of these philosophers encourages us to reason as follows:

true enough, perception is a process in which the received information is a causal effect of an external stimulus (compare halluciation), but philosophers like Gödel could hardly have failed to foresee the crippling problem with modelling intuition on real perception. Although I am in sympathy with the motives behind this reasoning, the conclusion, if accepted, would leave us nearly as bad off as before. If we take the references to perception non-literally, we are then left with only a metaphor: we have a vivid but misleading expression of a similarity between intuition and perception. We know no more about intuitive apprehension than we do about what it is to *see* that one thing logically follows from another on the basis of the metaphorical extension of the visual sense of "see". The metaphorical construal of such references fails to clarify apprehension. The Platonist tradition thus presents us with a choice between two equally unattractive alternatives: an incoherent account of intuition, or none at all.

The rationalist tradition, however, contains an account of intuition that is not modelled on perception. Kant's account conceives of intuitive awareness, not as a causal effect of an external event, but as the effect of an internal construction. Kant distinguishes sharply between perception and introspection, on the one hand, which he calls "empirical intuitions", and (what we are calling) intuition, on the other hand, which he calls "pure intuition". Kant presents his conception of the nature of pure intuition in his discussion of the relation between philosophical and mathematical knowledge.

Philosophical knowledge is the *knowledge gained by reason from concepts;* mathematical knowledge is the knowledge gained by reason from the *construction* of concepts. To *construct* a concept means to exhibit *a priori* the intuition which corresponds to the concept. For the construction of a concept we therefore need a *non-empirical* intuition. The latter must, as intuition, be a *single* object, and yet none the less, as the construction of a concept (a universal representation), it must in its representation express universal validity for all possible intuitions which fall under the same concept.

. . . the mode in which reason handles [objects] is wholly different in philosophy and mathematics. Philosophy confines itself to universal concepts; mathematics can achieve nothing by concepts alone but hastens at once to intuition, in which it considers the concept *in concreto,* though not empirically, but only in an intuition which represents *a priori,* that is, which it has constructed, and in which whatever follows from the universal conditions of the construction must be universally valid of the object of the concept thus constructed.[23]

I will defend this conception as offering a coherent and plausible account. of intuitive apprehension. My defense will proceed in two

steps. First, I will try to clarify the abstruse aspects of Kant's conception by taking it to provide a general framework within which to
formulate specific theories of grammatical, logical, and mathematical
intuition, and by formulating a specific theory of grammatical intuition
within this framework. Second, I will try to anticipate the epistemological criticisms of this theory and provide satisfactory replies to
them.

It should be noted before formulating a theory of grammatical
intuition that the term "construction" will be understood here in a
different way from that in which it is understood in the philosophy of
mathematics known as Intuitionism and associated with the pioneering
work of L. E. J. Brouwer. The difference stems from Brouwer's
grounding of his intuitionism on Kant's apriority of time and hence on
abstraction from the experiences of

. . . the falling apart of moments of life into qualitatively different parts, to be
reunited only while remaining separated by time, . . . This intuition of two-
oneness, the basal intuition of mathematics creates not only the numbers one
and two, but also all finite ordinal numbers.[23]

In contrast, we ground our theory of intuition on Kant's conception of
pure intuition. Thus, Brouwer and the intuitionists take the numbers
one, two, etc. to be creations of human thinking and do not assume that
the totality of the numbers constitutes an objective reality in a well-
defined sense, whereas we take the numbers to be independent of their
intuitive representations and the totality of the numbers to constitute
an objective reality in a well-defined sense. In my theory of intuition,
construction produces objects of intuitive apprehension but these
objects are internal representations of abstract objects rather than the
abstract objects themselves. Again, Brouwerian intuitionists take construction to be a process producing the objects of mathematical knowledge, the numbers themselves. On my theory, an internal representation constructed in intuition corresponds to an abstract object outside
us or it does not correspond. If it corresponds, the intuitive judgment is
true, if not, false. Although with homogeneous intuitionists I hold that
truth is the same notion in all subjects, unlike them, I take truth in the
standard correspondence sense rather than in the verificationist sense
to which the Brouwerian notion of intuitive construction gives rise.
The epistemological questions that such a correspondence view raises
will be taken up when we turn to the epistemological criticism of
Platonism.

To flesh out the Kantian conception of pure intuition for the special
case of the apprehension of the grammatical structure of sentences, we
have to specify, as Kant puts it, "the universal conditions for the

construction'' of the concept of a sentence *in concreto*. The Kantian terminology is less formidable than it seems at first blush. A concept *in concreto* is a particular concept of something, e.g., a cube, the number seventeen, or the sentence ''They are flying planes'', in the form of a concrete object of intuition. The construction of a concept is the mental process of building the concept up out of its constituents. The conditions for such a construction are the features of the faculty of intuition that control and limit the operations in the assembly of a particular concept. Universal conditions are those that govern the construction of all of the concepts under a certain category. For example, the universal conditions for the construction of the concept of a sentence are the grammatical universals that specify the notion of possible sentence for language in general.

Our account of intuition relies on a nativism of the kind that Chomsky developed for the universal conditions for the construction the concept of sentence (natural language, etc.). These conditions must be sufficient not only for the construction of the abstract notion of a sentence of natural language but also for the concepts of 'English sentence', 'French sentence', etc. as well as their intuitive instantiations. Chomsky's theory that the human mind is equipped innately with a language acquisition device that enumerates the class of competence-grammars for natural languages and contains methods for choosing among these possible competence-grammars on the basis of primary linguistic data constitutes a sufficiently powerful form of nativism. In accepting this theory, we obtain a clear sense in which the universal conditions for the construction of the concept of a sentence in a natural language are in the mind of its speakers prior to their first experience with utterances of the language.[24]

Hence, one component of our conception of intuitive apprehension of grammatical structure is a nativistic theory of how speakers of a natural language acquire their knowledge of its grammar. But, although such an *a priori* source for the universal conditions is necessary, it cannot be the only component. As shown by our discussion in chapter III of the distinction between knowledge and its object, the special features of the psychological medium in which knowledge of a language is realized can lead to indefinitely many cases in which the mental representation of the grammatical structure of a sentence diverges from the grammatical structure of the sentence in the language. This is to say that we cannot expect that the tacit principles constituting a speaker's competence, as they stand, provide full and correct universal conditions for the construction of the concepts of the sentences of a natural language. There have to be further components in our conception of intuition to explain how intuition compensates for such possible misrepresentations of the grammatical structure of sentences.

The conception I am proposing contains two further components to compensate for the fact that such mental representations can, and probably do, contain errors of omission and comission about the structure of sentences of the language. One component corrects for such errors on the basis of an innate notion of the knowledge-of relation. Given the rich nativism we have adopted, we can suppose the faculty of intuition has access to this notion,[25] and given access, we can suppose that the faculty utilizes the distinction between knowledge and its object to compensate for misrepresentations of grammatical structure. For example, the faculty may employ this distinction to construct a more parsimonious grammatical system than the competence-system or to avoid features of competence representations that make false predictions about the structure of sentences.

The other component uses the innate idea of an abstract object to provide, as it were, the armature which intuition sculpts into the concept of a sentence *in concreto*. The idea of an abstract object specifies the ontological characteristics of the object that grammatical knowledge is knowledge of. Using both the 'knowledge-of' relation and the idea of an abstract object, the faculty of intuition can operate on principles reflecting the form tacit grammatical rules take in humans and depsychologize them, reconstructing representations of sentences as concrete concepts of abstract objects. These two further components seem sufficient, since they can rectify the respects in which a speaker's tacit rules misdescribe facts about the language and construct concepts of abstract objects that properly describe sentence structure.

Although I do not intend to go beyond sketching a conception of the faculty of intuition by attempting the more ambitious task of constructing a model of the operation of the faculty, something needs to be said about how the scope of the faculty develops with the increase of explicit knowledge about a subject. There are linguists, logicians, and mathematicians who have comparable tacit knowledge but differ significantly in the scope of their intuitions about abstract objects. This is a familar fact for those working in these fields. To some extent, such differences can be chalked up to differences in the operation of their faculty, in the way differences in intelligence are thought of as due to differences in the operation of this faculty in different persons. But not completely. There is a clear correlation between a new mastery of explicit theories in a discipline and increases in the scope of the faculty of intuition. When one attains a mastery of transformational theory or topology, one is able to intuit structural relations that one could not intuit before. As thus far sketched, our conception of intuition accounts for only intuitions based on tacit knowledge. Accordingly, we have to extend it by positing that explicit knowledge, knowledge of the kind acquired in scientific pursuits, constitutes another input to the faculty of intuition. Intuitions based on tacit knowledge come first ontogenetically but as soon as explicit knowledge is acquired it feeds back into the faculty of intuition.[26] Explicit knowledge thus provides a further basis for generating intuitions, especially about abstract objects we have come to know about within the context of advanced theories.

An actual model of the operation of the faculty of intuition would specify the operations on the principles of competence-grammars and show how the mental objects internally represented in a speaker's competence are transformed into concepts of abstract objects in intuition. Clearly, it is fanciful to think of providing such a specification and set of operating rules at this time. Fortunately, the present philosophical task calls for nothing so ambitious. It calls only for an explanation of how intuitive apprehension is possible, that is, for a coherent conception of how we can have inner representations of grammatical abstract objects without there having to be a causal relation of some sort between the subjective representation and the objective sentence. This, I claim, the above conception does. The conception characterizes actual intuitions as the result of projections from an *a priori* enumeration of systems of competence which corrects and depsychologizes complexes of grammatical information and casts them into concrete form as concepts of sentences modelled on the notion of an abstract object. The concepts of sentences *in concreto* that are projected reveal enough of the structure of sentences to our awareness for us to judge whether they have one or another grammatical property or relation. The knowledge of sentences acquired in this way is not mediated by contact between the knower and the known.

Contemporary epistemological criticisms of Platonism in mathematics have been almost completely directed against Gödel's Platonism. Gödel's Platonism, as we have seen above, is based on the perception model of intuition and thus presupposes some kind of causal contact with abstract objects. Benacerraf begins his influential criticism with the condition of adequacy that

. . . an account of mathematical truth, to be acceptable, must be consistent with the possibility of having mathematical knowledge: the conditions of the truth of mathematical propositions cannot make it impossible for us to know that they are satisfied.[27]

Gödel's Platonism, he then goes on to argue, fails this condition: ". . . what is missing is precisely what [the above condition] demands: an account of the link between our cognitive faculties and the objects known."[28] The human mathematician's "four-dimensional space-time worm does not make the necessary (causal) contact with'' abstract objects.[29] Benacerraf's form of the objection takes it to hold against any version of Platonism, claiming that Platonism generally suffers from incoherence because the very conditions for knowledge demand a link between ''our cognitive faculties and the objects known''.

The question that remains for us, then, is whether, having jettisoned the conception of intuition modelled on perception, we have eliminated the source of incoherence at the expense of relinquishing the possibility of mathematical knowledge. Can our conception of intuition (coupled with our supposition that mathematical truth is correspondence with mathematical reality) satisfy Benacerraf's condition on accounts of mathematical truth?

Benacerraf spells out the condition as follows:

It must be possible to establish an appropriate sort of connection between the truth conditions of p . . . and the grounds on which p is said to be known, at least for propositions that one must *come to know*—that are not innate.[30]

This demand seems reasonable enough. It is hard to see how one could have an account of mathematical truth consistent with the possibility of mathematical knowledge in which there is no connection between the grounds on which we claim to know mathematical propositions and their truth conditions. But our conception of intuition meets this demand, as can be shown in the following way. The truth conditions for a mathematical proposition are a function of its semantic structure. The truth conditions of ''Four is the sum of two primes'' say what property the number four must have for the sentence to be true. Now, if we construct a sufficiently articulated concept of the number four in intuition, we will be able to see that the concept is a concept of an object that is the sum of the two primes, and this shows us that the object satisfies the truth conditions of the proposition. Hence, the grounds on which we say that we know that the proposition is true are appropriately connected with the truth conditions for the proposition. So, Benacerraf's condition is met.

The advantage of this conception of intuition is apparent. It no more requires causal contact with abstract objects in its account of mathematical knowledge than it does in its account of mathematical truth (correspondence between what a mathematical proposition asserts and what is the case in mathematical reality). Benacerraf's epistemic condition on accounts of mathematical truth does not demand a ''link between our cognitive faculties and the objects known.''

Some critics of Platonism might insist that the connection is not acceptable unless there is a link between the mathematical objects the proposition is true of and the knower. You can't know the smell of a rose without having had an appropriate causal link to a rose. But, whereas one would certainly concede the point in the case of roses and other empirical objects, one is quite reluctant to do so in the case of numbers and other abstract objects. This reluctance is not just a matter of the extreme dissimilarity of the cases. In the case of empirical objects, the question of whether they have this or that property is contingent. Whether roses have a sweet fragrance or a fetid smell cannot be settled *a priori* because the space of possibilities includes both. Experience with roses is required to rule out the possibility of a fetid smell. But in the case of mathematical objects (logical objects, grammatical objects, *etc.*) the situation is otherwise. The question of whether they have this or that property is necessary. Whether four is the sum of two primes or not *can* be settled *a priori* because the space of possibilities does not include more than the one possibility. Since *a priori* methods alone suffice to determine what the one possibility is, experience is not required to know that four is the sum of two primes.

Note, moreover, that there is no argument on the part of the critic of Platonism to support the demand for a causal connection in every case of knowledge. It is perhaps because of the absence of such an argument that a careful philosopher like Benacerraf, although sympathetic to empiricism[31] and the causal theory of knowledge,[32] does not try to press the argument all the way.

Mark Steiner tries to obtain a refutation of Platonism's claim that we come to know basic truths in mathematics through intuition.[33] He distinguishes this doctrine from what he calls "ontological Platonism", the doctrine that mathematics is about "infinitely many real mathematical objects".[34] His aim is to refute the epistemological claim while accepting the ontological one.[35] To do this, he requires a theory of knowledge that makes mathematical knowledge continuous with empirical knowledge. Such a theory would, in the first place, be able to explain what is wrong with the appeal to a special faculty of intuition, and in the second, show why such an appeal is unnecessary—because there is a better account of how we know mathematical truths.

Naturally, Steiner appeals to Quine's holism. This theory pictures

The totality of our so-called knowledge or beliefs, from the most casual matters of geography and history to the profoundest laws of atomic physics or even of pure mathematics and logic, [as] a man-made fabric which impinges on experience only along the edges. . . . a field of force whose boundary conditions are experience. A conflict with experience at the periphery occasions readjustments in the interior of the field. . . . Having reevaluated one statement we must reevaluate others, which may be statements logically connected with the first or may be the statements of logical connection themselves.[36]

That Steiner thinks such holism meets his needs is clear:

The holist argues correctly that a single change in mathematical theory would result in wholesale chaos in scientific laws across the board. Applying the "maxim of minimum mutilation" to this situation explains why mathematical truth seems so certain.

One objection to holism, that it cannot account for the indubitability of mathematics, is thus inconclusive. The traditional doctrine of intuition attempted to bridge the gap between the human and the Ideal by postulating a special human faculty lodged in the soul. It attempted to reconcile the remoteness of mathematical objects with the firmness of mathematical knowledge. . . . . But intuition turns out not to be necessary for the reconciliation.[37]

Granting that a single change in mathematical theory could result in chaos throughout empirical science,[38] it is mistaken to think that the question at issue is why mathematical truth "seems so certain". This is the question facing philosophers like Mill and Quine who have already assimilated mathematics and logic to empirical science,[39] but it is not the question of whether they can be assimilated. If "certainty" means "sureness resulting from the removal of all real doubt in virtue of evidence or proofs", then all sorts of contigent matters can "seem so certain" and even be certain, for example, that John F. Kennedy's demise was not the result of having laughed himself to death at one of Calvin Coolidge's jokes. Thus, putting the issue of the acceptability of intuition in terms of explaining "why mathematical truth seems so certain" begs the question. The issue is not why such truth seems so certain but whether our knowledge of necessary truth can be explained on the basis faculties like perception, without invoking intuition. Platonists invoke intuition to explain our knowledge of necessary truth, justifying it, as I did above, by an inference to the best explanation. Assuming an empirical holism like Quine's, which eliminates all real necessary truth, intuition has already lost its epistemic role, without looking for an alternative explanation of mathematical certainty.[40]

For the Platonist, the faculty of intuition explains how we know objects with no possible causal link to sensation. Thus, Steiner is also mistaken in saying that the Platonist invokes intuition "to reconcile the remoteness of mathematical objects with the firmness of mathematical knowledge". Again, the formulation begs the question. Remoteness implies a continuous path: something remote lies a great distance away on such a path, but is, in principle, accessible in the same way as something close. The Platonist invokes intuition to reconcile the absolute inaccessibility of mathematical, logical, and grammatical objects to the faculties of perception and introspection with the fact of mathematical, logical, and grammatical knowledge.

The attraction of Quine's holism is, of course, that it denies that there is anything that we need to bring intuition in to reconcile. On Quine's picture of the totality of our knowledge and belief, it consists exclusively of contingent statements confirmed, directly or indirectly, in terms of sense perceptions of physical objects and their behavior. Conflicts with experience can, in principle, occasion reevaluations of *any* statement because all are contingent. But, attractive as this holism is to opponents of Platonism, it is irrelevant or incoherent and hence of little use to them.[41]

We are told that conflicts with experience "occasion readjustments" and "reevaluations" of statements within the total fabric of human knowledge, and also that no statement therein is immune from revision, and further, that reevaluation is necessary to accomodate conflict with experience. The necessity of accomodation is expressed by Quine's use of the term "must". Its appearance in Quine's argument is more than a little surprising. What is the nature of the compulsion? Since the Quinian position explicitly repudiates the idea of necessity, we might suppose that the modal is not used here with the force of logical necessity. But, then, Quine's general claim about the revisability of all statements, including logical and mathematical laws, collapses. Without the force of logical necessity behind the impulse to revise, conflicts with experience may be allowed to stand and revisions may be restricted as we choose. Quine can hardly mount an argument for the revisability of logical and mathematical principles without suitable force with which to back it up. On the other hand, if the modal is used with the force of logical necessity, that force is available because the reevaluation of statements is compelled on pain of contradiction. But this, presumably, makes the logical principle of noncontradiction immune from revision. Since logical principles, according to Quine, are "simply certain further statements of the system, certain further elements of the field", and "no statement is immune from revision", it follows that the principle both is immune from revision and is not immune from revision. This time Quine's conception of holism comes out incoherent.

We note that, if even this one principle is granted the status of an *a priori* necessary truth, the Platonist's rationale for invoking intuition is granted.[42] Also, the same assumption enables the Platonist to pay back the anti-Platonist in kind. An account of logical truth, to be acceptable, must be consistent with the possibility of having logical knowledge, and hence, the conditions of the knowability of logical propositions cannot make it impossible for us to know some *a priori* necessary truths. The anti-Platonist, in allowing only perception and introspection as sources of basic knowledge, makes it impossible for us to to know *a priori* that the truth conditions of a logical principle are satisfied in all possible worlds. Hence, the anti-Platonist's theory of logical truth makes logical knowledge impossible.

In connection with Gödel's remarks about the role of mathematical intuition in mathematical knowledge, Steiner writes:

This, of course, makes mathematical intuition hold up a lot, perhaps more than it can bear. We do not even know yet whether, even granted that sets exist, we could apprehend them, yet Gödel is making such intuition the cornerstone of his view of mathematical truth. How, indeed, are we to distinguish mathematical "intuition" from hallucination; what makes it "veridical"? We seem to be headed toward mysticism.[43]

Anti-Platonists ought not throw around the charge of mysticism. If Platonists are "headed toward mysticism", they will not be alone. Gödel says that he sees no "reason why we should have less confidence in . . . mathematical intuition than in sense perception, which induces us to build up physical theories and to expect that future sense perceptions will agree with them". Now, it is certainly true that there is no guarantee that inductive generalizations from the testimony of sense perception are reliable. The enduring objects and stable regularities that we choose (over emroses and counter-inductive projections) for our empirical theories are as much beyond the cognitions in which we form such concepts as abstract objects are beyond the cognitions in which we form concepts of them. Moreover, few philosophers today would hold out hope of justifying our practice of inductive projection.[44] But, in spite of the widely acknowledged failure on the part of philosophy to provide sure marks of the veridical in the case of empirical theories, hardly anyone would recommend Humean skepticism. But if we demand no philosophical guarantee in the exercise of our faculties of perception and understanding, why do Steiner and other critics of Platonism demand a guarantee in the exercise of our faculties of intuition and reason? If Platonists are open to the charge of mysticism because they make intuition the foundation of our knowledge of mathematics, logic, or grammar without offering a philosophical guarantee of its validity, then all of us, the critics of Platonism included, are open to the same charge, since no one has offered a philosophical guarantee for perception and understanding, although everyone makes them the foundation for empirical knowledge.

It might even be argued that empirical knowledge is in a worse position. It is often said that empirical science rests on faith in the orderliness of nature. This means that it must be taken on faith that inductive projections are being made in a world in which the objects and regularities are like our highly limited sensory evidence suggests, rather than in any of the infinitely many possible worlds with the same past experience but with very different objects and regularities. There is, then, a sense in which the sciences of the intuition do not rest on faith in something beyond us. In these sciences, reason replaces faith that empirical objects and regularities will be like our experiential concepts of them: no faith in nature is necessary because reason and intuition can establish a possibility as the only possibility.

Finally, the question Steiner asks about distinguishing hallucinatory from veridical intuitions does not arise on our conception of intuition as the inner construction of concepts of abstract objects *in concreto*. The possibility of Steiner's question is tied to Gödel's more traditional conception of intuition as a form of perception. The distinction between hallucination and veridical perception depends on the latter involving causal contact, and hence, application of the question to a conception of mathematical knowledge depends on the conception representing veridical apprehensions as involving causal contact with abstract objects. Thus, the conditions for such an application are not present in our conception of intuition.

One might still ask how we can be sure that the properties of an abstract object are really as intuition represents them to us. How do we *know* that the number four is the sum of two primes in mathematical fact as it is in our intuition of the mathematical fact? Here, however, the question at issue is not Platonism but skepticism. Empirical knowledge, as we have shown, has no advantage over *a priori* knowledge in encounters with the skeptic. Each will survive or succumb, not on the basis of its own special features, but on the resourcefulness of the philosophical believer in meeting the challenge of the philosophical skeptic.

The Linguist as Mathematician

Grammatical intuition provides us with basic knowledge about linguistic abstract objects. The source of an intuition is a psychological process in which the concept of an object is constructed *in concreto,* but the import of the intuition is an objective fact about the object internally represented. The construction is based on innate universal conditions for such constructions of three principal kinds, competence-rules expressing information about the grammatical structure of a language, a knowledge of the relation '*x* knows *y*', and knowledge of the characteristics of the category abstract object. The psychological process of constructing a concept is fallible, but, nonetheless, gives us knowledge.

Such knowledge, however, is confined to concepts constructed *in concreto*. To obtain knowledge of more general truths, we construct scientific theories using the basic knowledge that intuition provides. Such theories, on our view, are *a priori* systematizations of intuitionally arrived at facts. In linguistics, when such basic facts about the grammatical properties and relations of sentences are brought together under principles that explain them as consequences of the grammatical structure that the principles attribute to the language, we have a grammar of the language. When a system of such principles can be reduced to a minimal set from which the full set of evidence statements for the language follows and each fact about the language requiring a grammatical explanation can be explained with reference to the system, we have an optimal grammar of the language.[45]

Such *a priori* systematization plays an important role in compensating for the fallibility of individual intuitions.[46] The demand to bring all the intuitive judgments together within a coherent systematization is not only the force behind the resolution of unclear cases but also the force behind overturning judgments mistakenly accepted on the basis of mistakes in intuition. The demand stems, I think, from our ideal of a scientific theory which contains within it the general methodological canons that guide theory construction in the special sciences.

The conception of the faculty of intuition that we set out for the case of grammar can likewise be a general faculty, underlying intuition in mathematics, logic, and other *a priori* areas. To see that this is so requires nothing more than noting that we can substitute mathematical competence (i.e., the ideal calculator's knowledge of the natural numbers), logical competence (i.e., the ideal reasoner's knowledge of implication), and so on for grammatical competence in the relation 'x is knowledge of y', so that these systems of tacit knowledge, rather than tacit grammatical rules, provide the values of 'x'. The structure of the relation (i.e., the constaints that 'x is knowledge of y' imposes on its arguments) and the innate notion of an abstract object that provides the values of 'y' are common to all relevant competences. Thus, it seems reasonable to suppose a single faculty of intuition that operates on different competences to produce distinct sets of particular intuitive apprehensions about different sets of abstract objects.[47]

Thus, the Platonist's picture of the study of grammar differs radically from Chomsky's familiar picture of the linguist as psychologist. The Platonist's picture is of the linguist as mathematician. On Chomsky's picture, the linguist and the child in the language acquisition situation are facing essentially the same problem of discovering the tacit grammatical rules that adult speakers of the language use to communicate.[48] In contrast, on the Platonist picture, the task facing the linguist is entirely different. The linguist's task, like the mathematician's, is to construct a theory revealing the structure of a set of abstract objects rather than a theory of the empirical realization of knowledge of such objects. The linguist uses intuitive evidence only, no more thinking of using introspections, experimental findings, and neurophysiological correlates than would a number theorist or a logician. The linguist requires nothing more for an *a priori* systematization.

Various aspects of this "linguist as mathematician" conception call for discussion. One is the topic of elicitation that came up earlier in the discussion of Harris's and Chomsky's transformational theories. The notion of elicitation that results from this "linguist as mathematician" conception is different from the notion that appears in either American structuralist linguistics or Chomskian linguistics. American structuralism characterizes elicitation as a process of prompting verbal responses to acoustic stimuli. Chomsky characterizes it as a process of prompting introspective reports of conscious experience in the use of language. The Platonist, in contrast, characterizes it as a process of prompting speakers to exercise their grammatical intuition with respect to a particular sentence and thereby construct a sufficiently revealing concept of its grammatical structure for the informant to judge whether the sentence has a certain grammatical property or relation.

On the Platonist picture, elicitation as a general method is a practical necessity. Intuitions of an individual do not always reveal enough of the structure of a sentence to determine all of its grammatical properties and relations and an individual linguist could not count on amassing a large enough body of intuitive judgments to form a representative basis for theoretical systematization. If these conditions did not exist, a linguist who is a speaker of a language, cloistered in a study, could verify the facts of the language on the basis of his or her intuition alone, systematize these facts in the form of a theory, and check the predictive and explanatory adequacy of the theory, all without elicitation. Thus, even though linguistics is an *a priori* science and can, in principle, be done by an isolated linguist, in practice, a linguist finds it expedient to consult the intuitions of others (as also does the mathematician).

Linguists sometimes remark on the fact that their discipline is like mathematics in letting them work independently of other linguists and in freeing them of the often bothersome accoutrements of empirical science. I have heard it said that linguists fluent in the language they are studying carry their own laboratories, experimental apparatus, and subjects "in their heads". It is also normally assumed that linguists are entitled to be certain about their judgments of the structure of novel sentences in clear cases like the rhyme of the first and last words in "Bears have few cares", the syntactic well-formedness of "The house is red", and the ambiguity of "Flying planes can be dangerous", even though the judgments are based on a momentary intuition about a single sentence token.

This is an accurate picture, but what is often overlooked is how much at odds this picture is with the view of the linguist as a psychologist. If linguists were psychologists, the practices described, rather than being ordinary features of everyday research, would be examples of monstrous scientific irresponsibility. Such certainty about the structure of novel sentences, supported only by a pathetic sample with an n of one, would be nothing more than rank cocksureness. On the conceptualist picture, the linguist ought to collect a large representative sample of English speakers and set up carefully controlled situations in which to elicit judgments about sentence tokens and only then ought the linguist make statements about the grammar of sentences. The fact that this is a caricature of the actual study of grammar suggests that the conceptualist picture of the linguist as psychologist is a distortion.[49]

The Platonist's picture is thus more realistic. It accounts for why the grammarian does not depend on huge laboratories and extensive experimental apparatus and why a single clear case can warrant certainty. It is a measure of how influential conceptualism has become that recognition of the resemblance of linguistics to mathematics can be accompanied without a blush by the remark that linguistics thereby has it better than other empirical sciences. Few, if any, who express such pride in the fact that linguistics enjoys the lifestyle and certainty of mathematics, and at the same time, believe that linguistics can claim the status and significance of an empirical science, stop to wonder how such antithetical virtues can peacefully coexist in one discipline.

It may be objected, however, that there are certain less plausible aspects of the picture of the linguist as mathematician. It may be said, for example, that the practice of the grammarian and the mathematician are dissimilar in that the working mathematician, unlike the working grammarian, does not spend large amounts of time soliciting and collecting intuitions. Conversely, the grammarian does not make extensive use of formal deductive proceedures.

These are correct observations, but the differences they reveal are matters of degree, reflecting differences in the developmental stages of the two sciences, rather than matters of kind, reflecting differences in subject. Comparing linguistics today with mathematics today is somewhat like comparing logic today with logic at the time of Aristotle or mathematics today with mathematics at the time of Pythagoras. The precise study of logic and mathematics is, in the West, over two thousand years ahead of the precise study of language.[50] Given the relatively immature and unsettled state of grammar today, it is only to be expected that intuitions, which improve with use, will be far less clear and distinct in linguistics, thus requiring more cross checking between linguists, and that formalization, on which explicit proof procedures rest, will have progressed far less in linguistics.

Moreover, if we factor out the appeals to elicitation due to the comparatively enormous plurality of natural languages and the fact that very few grammarians speak more than a few of them and none speak even a sizable number, the differences in the practice of soliciting intuitions by linguists, on the one hand, and by mathematicians, on the other, are pretty much in line with what one would expect of branches of the same subject where the developmental differences are so large. This conclusion is further confirmed by the fact that linguists do not in fact make so very extensive a use of elicitation when they can rely on their own fluency as native speakers and that mathematicians make more use of the intuitions of other mathematicians than is popularly recognized. The linguist's soliciting tends to be done in borderline cases and from people who are thought to have an especially good ear. These are also the conditions under which mathematicians tend to consult the intuitions of other mathematicians.

It is misleading to compare the frequency with which deductive procedures are used in mathematics and logic with their frequency in linguistics unless one carefully distinguishes deductions within first-order theories from proofs of important metatheorems. Deductions within first-order theories play as important a part in linguistics as in logic and mathematics. Proofs of important metatheorems, on the other hand, are comparatively rare in linguistics. The reason is that, owing to the greater complexity of natural languages compared with first order mathematical systems and also to the far more primitive state of linguistics, that science lacks the comprehensive formalizations of first-order theories that are prerequisite for proving important metatheorems comparable to those that are the showpieces of modern mathematics. The ancient Greeks who proved that no rational number denotes the square root of two had a far easier job on their hands than the contemporary grammarian who wants to prove either that there are global syntactic rules or not. Compare questions of the completeness of logical systems with questions of the expressive power of natural languages.[51]

The comparison in terms of proof is misleading in another way. The tendency to conclude from this comparison that grammar and mathematics are fundamentally different puts too strong an emphasis on proof as *the* essential feature of mathematics. It is no doubt a critical feature, but if so strong an emphasis were justified, Hardy would have been foolish, which he surely was not, to classify Ramanujan with Gauss and Euler.[52]

Notes

1. As is made clear in the text, I do not make light of these doubts. But I wish to make clear that conceptualism is faced with equally serious doubts, even though, somehow, conceptualism manages to give the impression that it is metaphysically "trouble-free".

In chapter IV, I presented six principles characterizing the forms of conceptualism in linguistics. I discussed (P_1) - (P_5) but at the time ignored (P_6) because it does not enter into the issues between conceptualism and Platonism. But the conceptualists have to take a stand on (P_6) sooner or later. Otherwise their position is gravely incomplete: it does not tell us what exactly grammars and linguistic theory are about on their view that these theories are about something called "mental" or "psychological" or "cognitive" structures. Conceptualists are fond of saying that if grammars and linguistic theory are not about the mental (psychological, cognitive) it is not clear what they are about (cf. Fodor, Fodor, and Garrett 1975: 523). But the conceptualist, too, owes us an explanation. One does not have to be a behaviorist to think that these notions of the mental, the psychological, or the cognitive are none too clear.

Once conceptualists try to make clear what mental states and processes are, what first looks like a simple, easily understood, set of claims about what grammar and linguistic theory are about turns out to be as devilishly complex and confusing a tangle of metaphysical issues as anything in philosophy. For the conceptualist has to choose between a mentalist position which rejects (P_6) and a materialist position that accepts it, and then between versions of each. The choices cannot, moreover, be mere stipulations. In order to give a convincing answer to the question of what a grammar and a linguistic theory are theories of according to conceptualism, conceptualists will have to justify the choices as comprising, overall, a satisfactory solution to the mind-body problem. They will have to vindicate Cartesianism or some other notion of the mental (e. g., the intentional, the essentially private, etc.) or show us how to carry through the materialist program of reducing the mental to the physical. If there is a vindication of some notion of the mental, they will have to motivate a choice between monism, interactionism, parallelism and so forth. Here questions arise about how a non-material substance can cause physical movements, whether conservation of energy is violated, etc. If the original choice is for materialism, there will be the as yet unanswered "missing qualia" arguments, as well as all sorts of questions about the proper characterization of the reduction itself (identity with token states, functional states, etc.). The philosophical literature abounds with difficulties that will be more than child's play.

Therefore, remarks like Chomsky's, that ". . . much of the so-called 'mind-body' problem will be solved in something like the way in which the problem of the motion of the heavenly bodies was solved, by invoking principles that seemed incomprehensible or even abhorrent to the scientific imagination of an earlier generation" (Chomsky 1980a: 6), misconstrue the issue and convey to conceptualists a false sense of security. Such remarks misconstrue the issue because they represent it as an empirical matter. The impression given is that, although the principles are beyond us now, they are still continuous with present principles of empirical science in the way that Einstein's principles are continuous with Newton's. But this impression is wrong because the issue in the case of the mind-body problem is not empirical: it is philosophical. The various possible solutions to the problem—monisms like materialism or idealism, dualisms like parallelism or interactionism, etc.—are each completely compatible with any empirical facts about psychophysical correlations. The difficulties with each solution, e. g., the missing qualia problem, are philosophical, too. Hence, conceptualists are mistakenly led to think they can put their faith in the progress of science, which would be grounds for high hopes, whereas, in fact, they have to put their faith in the progress of philosophy— hardly grounds for high hopes!

2. See Hardy 1940.

3. The Platonist also has reason to think that attempts to explain away all *a priori*

truth, from the early attempts such as Schlick's attempt to treat them as tautologies to Quine's attempt to treat them as a special kind of highly central empirical principle, have been unsatisfactory.

4. Fodor, Fodor, and Garrett 1975: 523.

5. Fodor, Fodor, and Garrett 1975: 523.

6. Frege 1967: 16–17.

7. Hardy 1940: 37.

8. This characterization does not imply that the things directly knowable on the basis of these faculties are restricted to such initial premises. We may have intuitive knowledge and deductive knowledge of one and the same fact. There are, then, no grounds to suppose that the principles which we presently take to be the initial premises of a theory because of their intuitive plausibility are necessarily *the* initial premises. This point, among others, underlies Gödel's remark that the undecidability of Cantor's conjecture "from the axioms being assumed today can only mean that these axioms do not contain a complete description of that reality. Such a belief is by no means chimerical, since it is possible to point out ways in which the decision of a question, which is undecidable from the usual axioms, might nevertheless be obtained". Gödel 1964: 264–265.

9. For example, one might challenge the agent's honesty or question whether the agent succeeded in communicating what was intended.

10. There are cases in language where it is *prima facie* odd to contradict a speaker's report about the grammar of a sentence, namely, cases in which speakers are reporting on their own idiolects. But such cases are fundamentally different from cases of privileged access. Idiolect reports have only relative authority, possessed by virtue of the fact that those who make them are normally in a position like that of a native informant reporting on a language the audience does not know. The audience is thus in no position to contradict, not because of a special privilege of the speaker's but because of a special deficiency of theirs. Unlike the case of introspective reports, where, logically speaking, no one else can make the same direct observation, in the case of idiolect reports someone else can, in principle, have the same idiolect (i. e., the very same set of grammatical rules) and so make the same report.

11. Descartes 1955: 1–17.

12. Gardner 1976: 124.

13. See, for example, Keeling 1968: 173f; Kenny 1967: 225–249.

14. Theory can also influence us positively. It can sometimes inform us in a way that enables us to recognize features of an object that might otherwise go unrecognized. For an interesting discussion of such factors in the case of perception, see Hanson 1958: 4–30.

15. Gödel 1964: 271.

16. Cited in Chisholm: 1960: 20. I should also note here that Husserl finally grounds his account of such knowledge on what seems to me to be psychological assumptions that would have horrified the author of the *Logical Investigations*. (See Husserl 1962, where he seems to end up with nothing better than a phenomenological psychology to explain knowledge of essences).

17. Grice 1965: 461–2 contains a philosophical argument for the causal theory of perception.

18. This difficulty is at the bottom of much criticism of Platonism. See Benacerraf 1973: 671–675; also Putnam, to appear.

19. Popper 1972: 153.

20. Popper 1972: 155.

21. Popper 1972: 159–160.

22. Kant 1929: 577–578.

23. Brouwer 1913: 69.

24. This is roughly the same sense in which it is claimed that the general conditions for the construction of a novel sentence of a language are in the mind of the fluent speaker prior to the first occurrence of that sentence in speech.

25. Katz 1979c.

26. This extension we have given is possible because, on our view, tacit knowledge and explicit knowledge are the same except for the latter's being conscious and the former's not. See Graves, C., Katz, J.J., Nishiyama, Y., Soames, S., and Stecker, R. 1973; also Samet, J. 1980.

27. Benacerraf 1973: 667.

28. Benacerraf 1973: 674.

29. Benacerraf 1973: 671. Benacerraf's criticism is not escaped by attempting to construe abstract objects in ways that eliminate those of their features that make causal contact impossible. Maddy 1980, for example, "den[ies] that abstract objects cannot exist in space and time and suggest[s] that sets of physical objects do so exist". (Maddy 1980: 179, fn. 39) But abstract objects are by definition outside space and time. Therefore, these attempts may explain how such pseudo-abstract objects might be objects of perception and thus might solve the pseudo-problem about our knowledge of sets of physical objects located in egg cartons and elsewhere, but the attempts do *not* explain how genuine abstract objects might be objects of perception and thus do *not* solve the real problem about our knowledge of abstract objects. It may be that there is no solution to the problem Benacerraf raises, though I argue below that there is, but it is better for Platonists to honestly concede defeat than to claim victory without having even entered the competition.

30. Benacerraf 1973: 672.

31. Benacerraf 1973: 672.

32. Benacerraf 1973: 671.

33. Steiner 1975: 109–137.

34. Steiner 1975: 109f.

35. It should be noted that Steiner wishes to hold on to an emasculated form of the notion of intuition, principally, it seems, in order to appear to do justice to the use of intuition on the part of working mathematicians.

36. Quine 1961a: 42.

37. Steiner 1975: 130.

38. I have changed "would" to "could" because there are, obviously, changes in mathematics that would have minor results. Also, the holist is by no means the only one who takes empirical science to make wide use of mathematics and logic in order to elaborate consequences of theories, etc.

39. Quine 1965a: 100–125.

40. Steiner's phrase "lodged in the soul" implies that Platonism will commit us to some anachronistic soul psychology or spiritualism, but, as I have indicated above, there is no reason not to consider the faculty of intuition within the same framework within which we ordinarily view the faculties of perception and introspection. There is a tendency among the critics of Platonism generally to indulge in such remarks about intuition, reminiscent of the potshots behaviorists took at introspection not so many years ago, but no real arguments have been given to show why the study of intuition should be linked to one kind of psychology or outside of scientific psychology altogether.

41. The argument to follow is adapted from Katz 1979c.

42. Putnam now seems prepared to concede that there is at least one *a priori* necessary truth (Putnam 1978).

43. Steiner 1975: 122.

44. In Katz 1962, I extend Hume's skepticism to the Peirce-Reichenbach attempt to justify induction.

45. In the light of this chapter, this seems to be the proper place to reassess the earlier controversy between Cavell and Fodor and me. (Cavell 1958; Fodor and Katz 1963) Cavell had taken the position that the judgments of native speakers about their own language are incorrigible because native speakers' reports are expressions of self-knowledge. Fodor and I took the position that the judgments are completely corrigible

because they are about empirical phenomena in language use and introspection. Our view was that linguistics is based on evidence and theory construction of the type familiar in scientific psychology. I now think we were all both right and wrong. Cavell was right in resisting such a view of the native speaker's knowledge of his or her own language, but he was wrong in thinking that the native speaker's judgments about the language are incorrigible. Such judgments are, in the first place, not privileged in the sense of introspective judgments because they are not based on introspection, and in the second, revisable because intuitive judgments are fallible. An intuitive judgment may be revealed as in error because it cannot consistently fit into an optimal *a priori* systematization of the totality of intuitive judgments. Cavell ignored the claim of theoretical systematization, the grounds that overall coherence and methodology provide for revising cases that run counter to deep principles offering the prospect of comprehensive explanation. Almost everyone had the intuition that any condition defines a set, though, as Russell showed, this judgment about sets cannot be consistently fitted together with deep principles that systematize the most comprehensive class of judgments about sets.

46. This is not to deny that there are other ways, for example, better intuitions. See the discussion above.

47. It would be interesting at this point to compare my discussion of grammatical intuition with the discussion of mathematical intuition in Parsons 1980. The latter has, unfortunately, not been available long enough to make this possible. A few points are nonetheless worth mention. First, although Parsons uses Gödel's metaphor of perception in presenting his account of mathematical intuition, it seems to me entirely dispensable insofar as nothing in Parsons' account hinges on preserving the aspect of causal contact with the objects of knowledge. Second, Parsons' use of Brouwer's notion of two-oneness seems solely a matter of clarifying the idea of awareness of sameness of arithmetic structure, not a matter of appealing to Brouwer's conceptualism. Third, Parsons' point that generality in mathematical intuition is a matter of grasping sameness of structure under all construals of iterated application of operations of numerical addition (see Parsons: 151–158) is essentially the same as the one that I have made in connection with generality in grammatical intuition (see Katz 1966: 121–122, fn. 2, where it is argued that knowledge of the infinity of sentences arises from grasping the sameness of grammatical structure under all construals of iterated application of operations of syntactic addition).

48. Of course, on Chomsky's more recent "organ growth" metaphor, it is more natural in the case of the child simply to speak of it as growing a competence organ, but this hardly affects the present point about the task of the linguist.

49. No grammarian who is not under the spell of the psychologistic (or a social scientistic) view of linguistics would waste a moment gathering large samples of such data. This, of course, is not to deny that sociolinguistics does collect statistical data, and is right to do so. But it is the sociology of language, and its interests concern the discovery of what linguistic forms are found where, what forms are correlated with what social features, etc. Thus what linguists like Labov (see Labov 1972: 183–259) seem to have overlooked is that since sociolinguistics is the sociology of language, it is sociology, not grammar. Would Labov be prepared to claim also that the relation between the sociology or anthropology of mathematics (see Menninger 1969) bears on the study of numbers, sets, spaces, etc. in the same way he claims sociology bears on grammar?

50. Note the reversal of order of development compared to the order at the time of Panini; at that time linguistics was called "the science" because of its relatively high degree of formalization and systematization in comparison with the other special sciences.

51. See the discussion of expressive power in the next chapter for an account of how questions of completeness are viewed in grammar.

52. Hardy 1940: 33.

VII

Platonist Linguistic Theory

Introduction

To complete our argument for Platonism, we have to show that Platonism can treat the nature of linguistic universals better than conceptualism. This chapter presents Platonism's account of linguistic universals and compares it with the accounts of conceptualism.

Conceptualist accounts of linguistic theory are of two forms. One, that can be given by either competencists or performancists, takes linguistic theory to be a metatheory of grammars in which their common structure is represented. On this account, linguistic theory confines itself to expressing the universals of language. For the competencist, this means expressing the invariances in the sets of tacit competence principles for natural languages. For the performancist, this means expressing the invariances in the performance principles for language use from language to language. The other account, Chomsky's, takes linguistic theory to be a theory of the ideal language learner's initial competence to become an ideal speaker-hearer of any natural language given a sufficient exposure to its sentences. On this account, linguistic theory does not confine itself to expressing invariances, but contains whatever else is part of the innate conditions for language acquisition, the conditions which, to use the current metaphor, predetermine the process of growth of the "language organ" to its final, steady state.[1]

As we observed above,[2] this means that linguistic theory is taken to contain (i)-(v)

(i) a universal phonetic theory that defines the notion 'possible sentence'

221

    (ii) a definition of 'structural description'

    (iii) a definition of 'generative grammar'

    (iv) a method of determining the structural description of a sentence, given a grammar

    (v) a way of evaluating alternative proposed grammars

interpreted as, respectively, a technique for representing input signals, a way of representing structural information about these signals, a class of possible hypotheses about language structure, a method for determining what each such hypothesis implies with respect to each sentence, and a method for selecting one of the hypotheses allowed by the initial delimitation and compatible with the corpus to which the child is exposed.

Both conceptualist accounts of linguistic theory agree that a linguistic theory is at least a theory of linguistic universals (in the special conceptualist sense of common psychological structure) but Chomsky's says that it is also a theory of acquisition and claims that linguistic theory cannot be an adequate account of linguistic universals unless linguistic theory is a theory of acquisition.[3]

The choice of an ontological interpretation for linguistic theory depends completely on the choice of an ontological interpretation for grammars, since the ontological category for natural languages taken collectively cannot be different from the ontological category for them taken individually. Therefore, if we were only dealing with the first form of a conceptualist account of linguistic theory, we could rest our case against conceptualist interpretations for linguistic theory on the arguments already given against conceptualist interpretations of grammars. We could take linguistic theory to state the invariances in the grammatical structure of sentences over the full range of natural languages. But Chomsky's conceptualist account raises the question whether any form of linguistic theory can be adequate as an account of linguistic universals if it is not at the same time a theory of language acquisition. The next section takes up this question, and the following section takes up the claim that a linguistic theory must include *(iv)* and *(v)*.

Linguistic Universals and the Nature of Language

The notion of a linguistic universal in traditional linguistics is significantly narrower than simply the notion of something common to all languages. Linguistic universals are conceived as having this status in virtue of the nature of language itself and hence as revealing its nature. The question arises, then, of how to distinguish the narrower class of common characteristics of natural languages, the *bona fide* linguistic universals, from the broader class. Chomsky and Halle pose a version of this question:

General linguistics attempts to develop a theory of natural language as such, a system of hypotheses concerning the essential properties of any human language. . . . The essential properties of a natural language are often referred to as "linguistic universals". Certain apparent linguistic universals may be the result merely of historical accident. For example, if only inhabitants of Tasmania survive a future war, it might be a property of all existing languages that pitch is not used to differentiate lexical items. Accidental universals of this sort are of no importance for general linguistics.[4]

What conception of the nature of language can general linguistics use as a sound way of distinguishing essential from non-essential regularities in the domain of natural languages?

Chomsky and Halle give an answer based on their conceptualism. They say that: "The significant linguistic universals are those that must be assumed to be available to the child learning a language as *a priori*, innate endowment."[5] Given that, in their framework, linguistic theory is a theory of the ideal human language learner's initial competence, the significant linguistic universals or essential properties of language have to be those that our human biology imposes on any grammatical competence that we can acquire. The problem of "apparent linguistic universals" has a natural solution in terms of this answer: the regularity that existing natural language differentiates lexical items without using pitch must be counted as merely accidental if human beings are innately able to acquire grammatical competence in which pitch differentiates lexical items.

This solution is, of course, not open to us. Moreover, from a Platonist viewpoint, the solution is not even a solution to the problem of determining the genuine linguistic universals. The problem to which the Chomsky-Halle solution is addressed is the psychological question of what are the biologically specified regularities for the range of systems of grammatical knowledge available to human language learners, but the problem of determining the genuine linguistic universals is the non-psychological question of what are the essential properties of the languages that grammatical knowledge on the part of any intelligent creature is knowledge of.

The Chomsky-Halle proposal must be construed as claiming that only the first question, the psychological one, can have a significant answer for general linguistics, and hence, that general linguistics cannot obtain an adequate theory of linguistic universals unless it construes this theory conceptualistically, that is, as a theory of language acquisition. I shall argue not only that these claims are false because there is a perfectly acceptable answer to the non-psychological question but that this answer is clearly preferable as a conception of the nature of language and as an account of the genuine linguistic universals.

The problem of determining the genuine linguistic universals is more complicated than Chomsky's and Halle's account makes it look. There are, in fact, two distinct accidental/non-accidental distinctions involved in the understanding of linguistic universals. It is easy to see that the distinction that Chomsky and Halle have in mind—as their Tasmania example shows—is one in which an accidental property is not universal but seems so because of the deficient sample from which it is extrapolated. Their distinction is between the actual regularities across systems of tacit competence principles and the merely accidental regularities reflecting a skewed sample. Let us call this the distinction between pseudo-universals and significant universals.

The other accidental/non-accidental distinction is one in which accidental properties contrast, not just with properties validly induced from representative samples, but with essential properties, that is, properties such that their bearers would not be what they are without them. We call this the distinction between accidental and essential universals. The difference between these distinctions is exhibited by true regularities that are not essential properties, that reflect nothing about the nature of their bearers. For example, it is a true regularity that living hearts make beat sounds but the property of making beat sounds is not an essential property of the heart: a heart would not be a heart if it weren't a pump, but it might be a silent pump.

The Chomsky-Halle proposal fails to rule out this latter type of accidental property. The proposal, in effect, equates the essential with the innately specified. It can thus rule out pseudo-universals, as in their Tasmanian example, and also some universal, non-essential properties. But it can neither rule out all non-essential properties nor can it rule in all essential properties. Some innately specified non-essential properties will count as part of the nature of language and some non-innately specified essential properties will not count as part of the nature of language.

There are parallels for each of the arguments in chapter III. It is clearly possible for us to be genetically programmed for language acquisition in such a way that the competence grammars available are all less parsimonious than grammars not available but predictively and explanatorily equivalent to them. For example, the cognitive structures that determine the child's space of hypotheses about the adult competences in natural languages might require transformations using separate copying, deletion, and permutation operations, while more parsimonious hypotheses employing transformations using only copying and deletion are excluded. In this case, the Chomsky-Halle proposal would force us to say that the less economical principle, the one with the unnecessary permutation operation, reflects the real nature of language. Also, it is clearly possible for us to be genetically programmed, as certain calculators are designed, to use functions that compute the wrong values for cases that fall safely beyond the range of actual computations. For example, the cognitive structures that determine the child's space of hypotheses might require certain grammatical rules that scramble lines of derivations in cases falling beyond human performance capacities. In this case, the Chomsky-Halle proposal would force us to say that the linguistically absurd "scrambling rules" are essential to natural language: their proposal says that such biologically concealed grammatical discontinuities are an intrinsic part of natural language. In fact, such a case would show only that humans, perhaps in contrast to some other form of intelligent life, have imperfect knowledge of natural language.

Once the character of these difficulties is appreciated, it is clear that innate specification is not adequate.[6] The Chomsky-Halle proposal at its weakest comes to exclusion of evolutionary accident, the species parallel of historical accident such as in the Tasmanian case, and at its strongest to an undetermined form of biological necessity. But both fall short of the essentiality that is required for an adequate account of the nature of language. It is thus necessary for general linguistics to have another conception of the nature of language, one on which the properties conceived to be part of the nature of language are properties without which language would not be what it is.

It is reasonable to expect that the conception of the nature of language we are seeking can be developed in terms of universal features of the way that grammatical structure in natural languages systematically correlates senses with the sentences expressing them. Moreover, there is a closely related aspect of natural languages that has seemed to a number of philosophers to be of primary importance, namely, the capacity it affords speakers to express any of their thoughts.[7] Thus, one might put the question this way: what is it about the way that the grammatical structure of natural languages correlates senses with sentences that makes someone with knowledge of such structure, in principle, able to express any thought?

The simplest and most elegant answer is that the sense-sentence correlation is complete at both ends: there are sufficient sentences and senses so that, no matter what the performance capabilities of a speaker,[8] there will never be a case where the non-existence of a sentence or a sense is the reason why a speaker is unable to express a thought. In previous work,[9] I proposed and defended completeness at both ends in the form of what I called "the principle of effability":

(E) Each proposition (thought) is expressible by some sentence in every natural language.[10]

A number of philosophers who have agreed that natural languages are distinguished by their unrestricted expressive power have not supposed this to be an unmitigated blessing. Frege, as we have seen above, took such unrestricted power to be an essential aspect of natural language but one that leads to the imperfection that natural languages contain meaningful, well-formed expressions that fail to denote. Tarski took the unrestricted expressive power of natural languages to be their essential attribute and also to be their fatal flaw.[11] He saw their expressive power as the source of the Epimenidian paradox and hence as rendering natural languages incoherent. Like Frege, Tarski recommended abandoning natural languages for purposes of serious scientific investigation and replacing them with an infinite sequence of artificial languages whose member languages are incomplete about themselves but where such incompleteness is compensated for in the relative completeness of their successors.

We have already seen that Frege's criticism of natural languages for allowing the construction of non-denoting expressions stems from his failure to distinguish language from its use. The same is true of Tarski's criticism: his argument that natural languages are incoherent rests on an out-and-out confusion between language and features of its use. I will consider this point in some detail because of the light it sheds on the significance of the property of unlimited expressibility.

Tarski writes:

A characteristic feature of colloquial language (in contrast to various scientific languages) is its universality. It would not be in harmony with the spirit of this language if in some other language a word occurred which could not be translated into it; it could be claimed that 'if we can speak meaningfully about anything at all, we can also speak about it in colloquial language'.[12]

I am in complete agreement with this, and I shall subsequently argue that only in a theory of meaning along intensionalist lines, in which meanings are senses, is it possible to account for what Tarski calls "the spirit of [natural] language". But Tarski goes on to claim that

. . . it is presumably just this universality of everyday language which is the primary source of all semantical antinomies, like the antinomies of the liar or of heterological words. These antinomies seem to provide a proof that every language which is universal in the above sense, and for which the normal laws of logic hold, must be inconsistent.[13]

Spelling this out, Tarski says:

. . . no consistent language can exist for which the usual laws of logic hold and which at the same time satisfies the following conditions: *(I)* for any sentence which occurs in the language a definite name of this sentence also belongs to the language; *(II)* every expression formed from [*x* is a true sentence if and only if *p*] by replacing the symbol '*p*' by any sentence of the language and the symbol '*x*' by a name of this sentence is to be regarded as a true sentence of this language; *(III)* in the language in question an empirically established premiss having the same meaning as ['*c* is not a true sentence' is identical with *c*] can be formulated and accepted as a true sentence.[14]

In *Semantic Theory*,[15] I showed that it is not the universality of natural languages that is the "primary source of all semantical antinomies", but rather the assumption that condition *(II)* holds.

Unlimited expressibility or universality of natural languages enables us to form sentences that say of themselves that they are not true, but this, in and of itself, is unparadoxical. Paradox enters only when we go on to suppose that in forming such sentences we are forming sentences with a truth value. The true source of the Epimenides paradox in Tarski's formulation is the supposition that all sentences resulting from replacing the symbol '*p*' in the schema '*x* is a true sentence if and only if *p*' by an appropriate Epimenidian sentence and replacing the symbol '*x*' by a name of this Epimenidian sentence are automatically true statements. The contradiction Tarski obtains is thus a *reductio ad absurdum* of his assumption that condition *(II)* holds.

Nothing compels us to accept the thesis underlying condition *(II)* that meaningful, well-formed sentences of a language are *ipso facto* true or false. Being meaningful and syntactically well-formed has to do with conformity to the meaning and syntactic constraints on the construction of sentences in the language and not with the connections between language and the world that make a sentence either true or false. There is, here too, a confusion of language with extra-linguistic features of its use. Thus, instead of accepting *(II)*, we can just as well suppose that while some sentences resulting from the substitutions into the Tarski schema are true others, including the Epimenidian ones, are neither true nor false. This does not mean that they have some new truth value but rather that they are truthvalueless.

Logicians and philosophers are inclined to accept Tarski's supposition for the same reasons that inclined Frege to think that meaningful, well-formed expressions ought to denote. Indeed, Russell's theory of denotation, on which the meaningfulness and well-formedness of a sentence *is* sufficient for its statementhood is merely Frege's theory about the imperfections of natural languages with the Fregean ideal translated as linguistic reality.[16] I think that the confusion about linguistic and extra-linguistic matters leading to acceptance of *(II)* arises partly from this Fregean tradition and partly from the ambiguity in Tarski's use of the term "semantics" between a sense sense and a reference sense. Tarski takes the discipline of semantics to be the theory of reference. Semantics, he says, ". . . deals with certain relations between expressions of a language and the objects (or 'states of affairs') 'referred to' by those expressions."[17] However, meaning and synonymy are included under semantics so defined because Tarski thinks they can be explained in terms of satisfaction.[18] Since the attempt is in fact a failure, its acceptance by Tarski causes him to run the intensional and extensional senses of "meaning" together.[19] Thus, the unnoticed conflation enables Tarski to mistakenly think of the substitutions in the schema 'x is a true sentence if and only if p' as taking meaningful sentences and their names invariably into truths, whereas, in fact, the substitutions can only take statements (meaningful sentences that are either true or false) invariably into truths. The fallacy arises because "meaningful sentence" is open both to the intensional interpretation of a sentence that has a sense (isn't semantically deviant) and the extensional interpretation of a sentence that designates a truth value (to use Frege's terminology).

(II) fails because we can ask semantic questions about a language in two senses, an intensional sense in which such questions are about the sense structure internal to the language and an extensional sense in which such questions are about the external connections between a language and the world (*i.e.,* "certain relations between expressions of the language and the objects 'referred to' by those expressions"). Given the difference between these two kinds of semantic questions, we can distinguish two kinds of question about the completeness and consistency of natural languages. One is the question of whether a *language* can be complete and consistent; the other is the question of whether *a pattern of using a language* can be complete and consistent.[20] In these terms, we can distinguish the grammatical principle *(E)*—which is about the completeness of languages and says that there is no limit on the expression of thoughts either on the semantic side or on the expressive side—from the performance principle

(S) Each meaningful (assertive) sentence of a natural language can be used to make a true or false statement.

which claims that there is no limit on statement-making in the use of a natural language *(S)*, which I will call "the principle of statability", is not about natural languages but about what can be accomplished in their use. *(E)* is just about natural languages. Acceptance of *(S)* courts paradox, but acceptance of *(E)* does not.[21] Furthermore, rejection of *(S)* raises the problem of how to mark all and only the right sentence tokens as truth-valueless,[22] whereas rejection of *(E)* raises only problems about semantic properties and relations, e.g., about which sentences are semantically anomalous, which are translations into sentences of another language, and so on.

Separating effability from statability and freeing language from the charge of paradox has, I think, enormous significance. Everyone who has thought seriously about the semantic paradoxes has felt torn between the undeniable truth of the view that unrestricted expressiveness is "the spirit of [natural] language" and the apparently unavoidable consequence of logical paradox. On the one hand, it seems a clear and deep fact about natural languages that they provide us with the means to say anything, even such things as that what an Epimenidian sentence like

(s)   The sentence *(s)* on this page is not true.

asserts is true. But, on the other hand, there seems no way to secure the completeness of a particular language without paradox. Therefore, the separation of effability from statability and the exoneration of effability and language from the charge of paradox enables us to claim that unrestricted expressibility is "the spirit of [natural] language" without threat of inconsistency.

The special significance of this claim here is that we can use *(E)* to provide the principle that Platonism requires to construct an alternative conception of the nature of language and linguistic universals. We claim that the essential property of natural languages is that their grammatical structure constitutes an effable correlation of sentences with senses.[23] Thus, it is sufficient for something to be a linguistic universal that it is necessary for effability. Hence:

(LU)   A grammatical feature *F* is a linguistic universal if every natural language has *F* and a natural language could not be effable without having *F*.

(LU) characterizes the notion of a linguistic universal in a way that distinguishes them from properties that are merely accidental in the sense of both accidental/non-accidental distinctions drawn above.

We may illustrate *(LU)* with two features that are reasonably taken as linguistic universals and can be shown to be such on the basis of *(LU)*. The first is the feature of recursiveness. We may assume, for the sake of the present discussion, that there are only a finite number of rules in a grammar.[24] On this assumption, *(LU)* enables us to conclude that recursiveness is a linguistic universal. For if the syntactic rules were not recursive, the language would be restricted to finitely many sentences, and since a sentence has only finitely many senses, the language would be insufficient on the expressive side to express all of the infinitely many propositions.

The second features with which we may illustrate *(LU)* is what was referred to as the fundamental principle of compositionality in chapter IV. The formulation there was, strictly speaking, incorrect because it lacked a necessary qualification. The principle should say that the meaning of all the infinitely many sentences and other syntactically complex constituents of a natural language *except for a finite subset of them* is a function of the meanings of their constituents and their syntactic structure. The qualifications allows for idioms (syntactically complex expressions without compositional meaning). With this qualification, *(LU)* enables us to infer that compositionality is a linguistic universal. For suppose that a natural language is not compositional. Then there are infinitely many sentences whose meaning is not a function of the meanings of their constituents and their syntactic structure. In this case, there would be infinitely many propositions with no sentence of the language to express them.

Earlier we observed that Chomsky's and Halle's formulation of the problem of characterizing the "significant linguistic universals" was somewhat oversimplified insofar as it doesn't distinguish between the two accidental/non-accidental distinctions involved: on the one hand, the distinction between pseudo-universals (e.g., that pitch is not used to differentiate lexical items) and genuine universals, and on the other, the distinction between non-essential universals and essential universals. Thus, it seems possible for there to be features that are genuinely universal but not part of the nature or essence of language, the grammatical counterpart, as it were, of heart sounds. For example, on the basis of present knowledge about natural language, it is plausible to think that all natural languages contain both the syntactic category of word and the syntactic category of morpheme, but, in spite of this, the nature of language might allow a natural language to have just the category of morpheme (constructions out of morphemes form phrases or higher syntactic constituents).[25] It seems compatible with the partial specification *(LU)* that there be no syntactic category of word.

The possibility of such universal but not essential features is, however, ruled out for our conception of language because abstract objects have logically inseparable basic properties.[26] Given that a basic property (in this case a grammatical one) like having or not having the category word is a genuine universal, it is a property of language in general and hence logically inseparable from the other properties of language. Thus, such properties are essential.

But this doesn't mean that we must treat all properties of natural language in general on a par. Some are definitional, entering into our concept of the abstract object natural language, while others, no less inseparable, are not. For example, being the successor of one and being the only even prime are both logically inseparable properties of the number two, and having three angles and having three sides are both logically inseparable properties of triangles, but only the first property in each case is definitional.

(LU), being a sufficient condition for something to be a linguistic universal, leaves it open whether there are other features of the sentence-meaning correlation in natural languages that also determine linguistic universals. Since there is no reason to think this property alone defines natural language, completion of the definition of natural language, like the enumeration of the full set of linguistic universals, is matter for future studies.

It should be noted that such studies, from a Platonist viewpoint, cast their net wider than the class of natural languages. Platonism makes linguistics the study of languages generally. The analogy is in some respects misleading, but one might say that, on the Platonist view, linguistics is the study of natural languages and languages generally in the way that mathematics is the study of natural numbers and numbers generally. Note, however, that Platonism does not thereby dethrone natural languages from their supreme position in linguistics. On our view, natural languages are the consummate correlations of sentence and sense.

Let us return now to the main issue of this section. Two conclusions follow from what has been shown. The Chomsky-Halle solution to the problem of characterizing the significant linguistic universals is not the only solution. Also, their notion of universals as biologically necessary features of human linguistic competence is deficient in the same way that Chomsky's notion of grammatical principles as features of the ideal speaker-hearer's linguistic competence is.[27] Mere biological necessity allows linguists to prefer the worse theory over the better: it allows idiosyncratic aspects of human psychology to constrain the study of general linguistics in such a way that not all universal features of such systems will be essential to natural language and not all the essentials of natural language will be universal features of such systems. Thus, the Platonist alternative at the level of linguistic theory is preferable because it allows as linguistic universals just those features of natural languages which are necessary for them to be natural languages.

Linguistic Theory and General Scientific Methodology

In the previous section, we showed that linguistic theory is no less than a theory of linguistic universals. In the present section, we show that linguistic theory is no more than a theory of linguistic universals. In this way, we will establish the thesis of this chapter that linguistic theory is exactly a theory of linguistic universals.

In chapter II, we found *(i)-(iii)* to be unhappy formulations but nonetheless uncontroversial conditions on linguistic theory. *(i)* was found to express an overly narrow requirement on the notion 'possible sentence', excluding Sign as a natural language together with indefinitely many other possibilities (*e.g.*, a language whose expressive signs are drawn from an olfactory vocabulary). *(iii)* was found to make the separate conditions *(ii)* and *(i)* unnecessary.[28] Hence, with the necessary adjustments, this part of Chomsky's metatheory was found acceptable within a Platonist framework.[29] In contrast, *(iv)* and *(v)* were found controversial because their validity depends on the interpretation of linguistic theory as a psychological theory of the initial competence of the language learner. Given all this, on a Platonist metatheory, the components of linguistic theory reduce to a definition of the notion 'grammar of a natural language', and linguistic theory becomes simply a theory of the grammatical universals. Hence, the earlier arguments against *(iv)* and *(v)* may now be seen as arguments for the Platonist claim that the sole explanatory aim of linguistic theory is to capture all and only the grammatical universals of natural language.

These earlier arguments showed that it is incorrect to take a method for determining the logical consequences of hypotheses and a method for selecting a preferable hypothesis from those compatible with the available evidence to be parts of a theory in one of the special sciences.[30] Such methods are more properly regarded as belonging to the methodology of science generally. We did not assume that the conceptualist has to take such methods to be part of linguistic theory. The conceptualist may take them to be part of the methodology common to the sciences and take linguistic theory to contain instead special empirical principles describing the language learner's psychological or biological basis for deriving consequences of hypotheses and choosing a preferable one. But this alternative, too, was shown to lead to trouble. Which methods should the linguist use in constructing theories of natural languages, the empirical principles or the principles from general scientific methodology? What does the conceptualist advise if the empirical and *a priori* methods conflict? If conceptualists advise using the former, they will advise action contrary to good scientific practice (which is what the rejected principles codify) whereas if they advise using the latter, they will be advising action contrary to their own ontological position (since *ex hypothesi* the linguist will make choices counter to those of the language learner that led to internalizing the adult speaker's competence, the conceptualist will be agreeing that linguistics need not aim at discovering a theory of the adult speaker's competence). Either conceptualists remain loyal to their philosophy at the expense of adopting a program which is scientifically irresponsible or they remain loyal to scientific methodology at the expense of their philosophy.

Chomsky's early position contains an asymmetry that compounds the problem of choosing between his philosophy and good scientific practice. In connection with grammars, he advocates using the same biological methods that the child employs in testing and selecting among hypotheses, but in connection with theories of language, he advocates using general methodology. The source of the asymmetry is not hard to find. The original "little linguist" metaphor for the child is conversely a "big child" metaphor for the linguist, and such a metaphor suggests the first move. The second is pretty well dictated by the fact that the situation in the case of second level theories, theories of grammars, differs from that of first level theories, theories of languages, because there simply is no higher level acquisition process, no acquisition process whose output is the child's initial competence and which employs superevaluation methods that can be mimicked by the linguist in constructing a linguistic theory. Without such superevaluation methods, the only things left are the same methods from general methodology that other sciences employ. Thus, Chomsky writes that the status of an evaluation procedure for grammars

has often been misconstrued. It must first of all be kept clearly in mind that such a measure is not given a priori, in some manner. Rather, any proposal concerning such a measure is an empirical hypothesis about the nature of language. . . .

Perhaps confusion about this matter can be traced to the use of the term "simplicity measure" for particular proposed evaluation measures, it being assumed that "simplicity" is a general notion somehow understood in advance outside of linguistic theory. This is a misconception, however. In the context of this discussion, "simplicity" (that is, the evaluation measure m of (v)) is a notion to be defined within linguistic theory along with "grammar", "phoneme", etc. Choice of a simplicity measure is rather like determination of the value of a physical constant. . . . we regard an acquisition model for language as an input-output device that determines a particular generative grammar as "output", given certain primary linguistic data as input. A proposed simplicity measure . . . constitutes a hypothesis concerning the nature of such a device.

It is also apparent that evaluation measure of the kinds that have been discussed in the literature on generative grammar cannot be used to compare different theories of grammar.. . . . It is true that there is a sense in which alternative theories of language (or alternative theories in other domains) can be compared as to simplicity and elegance. What we have been discussing here, however, is not this general question but rather the problem of comparing two theories of a language—two grammars of this language—in terms of a particular general linguistic theory.[31]

If both first and second level theories are scientific theories, why should first level theories be chosen on the basis of an empirical hypothesis about the methods children use in acquiring their native language while second level theories are chosen on the basis of methods from general scientific methodology? If the choice of a linguistic theory from those that account for the second level evidence is based on simplicity "somehow understood in advance outside linguistic theory" (Occam's razor), how is it that the choice of a theory of a particular natural language from among those that account for the first level evidence is "an empirical hypothesis", "defined within linguistic theory along with 'grammar', 'phoneme', etc."? Conceptualist ideology notwithstanding, there is no relevant difference between first and second level theories to explain the asymmetry in the methods for their selection.

Moreover, the methods used to choose between competing first level theories ought to lie outside the area of competition. Since such methods provide the "rules of the game" in such selection, they ought not come from a philosophical approach underlying one rather than another set of first level theories. Such methods have to be bipartisan. If first level theories are chosen on the basis of a particular linguistic theory, and linguistic theories, in turn, are judged on the range of facts expressed in first level theories, how can research avoid the danger of self-fulfilling prophesy? How can there be the " 'competing theories', and 'pitting of one . . . against another', in an effort to discover which of several alternatives is valid", that Chomsky extolled in criticizing Harris? How can the confrontation of theories with fact be the crucible in which scientific truth is forged if partisan conceptions of linguistics determine our judgments of how well the theories account for facts?

Chomsky's early position is not, however, the only one taken in his writings. His writings are, in fact, inconsistent on the treatment of simplicity, particularly on the question of whether the simplicity principle in general scientific methodology applies to the choice of a linguistic theory. On the one hand, there are statements like the above quotation and like

Notice, incidently, that there is an interesting but poorly understood sense in which one can talk of the 'simplicity' or 'elegance' or 'naturalness' of a theory (of language, of the chemical bond, etc.), but this 'absolute' sense of simplicity has no clear relevance to the attempt to develop an evaluation measure (a simplicity measure) as part of a theory of grammar. Such a theory is an empirical hypothesis, true or false, proposed to account for some domain of linguistic fact. The 'simplicity measure' that it contains is a constituent of this empirical hypothesis. This distinction between 'simplicity' as an absolute notion of general epistemology and 'simplicity' as a part of a theory of grammar has been repeatedly emphasized . . .[32]

On the other hand, there are more recent statements like

. . . consider the question of whether the rules of a grammar should be un-ordered (let us call this linguistic theory T_U) or ordered in some specific way (the theory T_o). . . . There is no known absolute sense of "simplicity" or "elegance", developed within linguistic theory or general epistemology, in accordance with which T_U and T_o can be compared. It is quite meaningless, therefore, to maintain that in some absolute sense T_U is "simpler" than T_o or conversely. One can easily invent a general concept of "simplicity" that will prefer T_U to T_o or T_o to T_U; in neither case will this concept have any known justification.[33]

Chomsky switches from a position allowing an *a priori* notion of simplicity (albeit "poorly understood") that can be used to evaluate competing theories of language in general (in the same manner as we evaluate other scientific theories, *e.g.*, theories of the chemical bond) to a position that claims that there is no such notion, that even claiming there is one "is quite meaningless".

Chomsky provides no explanation of the switch. One might specu-late that he takes the latter view in order to eliminate the asymmetry, but the new view is at least as unattractive as the asymmetry. For without a notion of simplicity from "general epistemology" or general scientific methodology, it will be impossible to arrive at a rationally chosen best linguistic theory from among those that predict the second level evidence equally well. Chomsky's new position that no notion of simplicity is available for deciding between second level theories removes the asymmetry all right, but it is a Pyrrhic victory. If there is no way to choose between the indefinitely many linguistic theories that cannot be eliminated on the basis of evidence at the second level, then there will be no empirical simplicity measure to use in choosing among competing grammars, either. Such "empirical hypotheses", on Chomsky's position, are components of the linguistic theories and hence likewise inductively underdetermined. We will be left with indefinitely many "empirical hypotheses" and with linguistic theories which express, collectively, every conceivable picture of what the truth about language is (beyond the observations). Hence, linguistics could never arrive at a rational assessment of the nature of language.

Chomsky's claim that "there is no known absolute sense of 'simplicity' . . . developed within . . . general methodology" is open to two different construals. It can either mean that there is no pretheoretic notion of simplicity at all or that all attempts to explicate the pretheoretic notion have been unsuccessful. The first claim, however, is so outlandish it can be dismissed immediately. It would put all the sciences in the same fatal position that linguistics would be in without an *a priori* notion of simplicity in connection with inductive underdetermination. Every science would have to accept indefinitely many hypotheses each inconsistent with the others and none with a better claim to truth than others.[34]

The second claim, that attempts to provide an explicit theory of simplicity have made no significant progress, though perhaps true, is irrelevant to the issue here. We may distinguish a weak and strong form of the claim. Both concede the validity of a pretheoretic prohibition against multiplying theoretical apparatus beyond necessity (Occam's razor). The weak says that somehow progress has been negligible; the strong says that, for some reason, there can, in principle, be no progress.

Granting that, as things now stand,[35] nothing like an explicit distinction has been drawn between the simple and complex, still this has no relevance to the question of whether Occam's razor is the proper principle on which to choose between non-equivalent but empirically indistinguishable hypotheses. We do not stop using the distinction between virtue and vice, between beauty and ugliness, or between truth and falsehood because explicit formulations of them have thus far eluded our best efforts. The fact that we have no explication of a notion simply means that its use is, by and large, restricted to clear cases, and that we need to redouble our efforts at constructing an explication that can be used with unclear ones.

The strong form of the claim, if it were true, would imply nothing more than that an adequate explication to use with unclear cases is out of our reach. This does not mean that simplicity cannot be used to make all the practical scientific decisions we need to make. There is no possibility of a full formal explication of the notion of mathematical truth but this does not preclude the use of this notion to make the decisions we need to make in mathematics.

Chomsky's claim that "there is no known absolute sense of 'simplicity' . . . developed within . . . general methodology" embodies a deep confusion about the role of formal or explicit explication in science. Explication gives us the clearest of understanding of a practice, but the understanding is not necessary to the practice because the practice take place on the basis of tacit principles. This is clear from the example of language fluency itself. Since there is nothing to show that the informal, pretheoretic notion of simplicity, coupled with sophistication in areas of its application, is not all that is necessary to make the choices among theories left open by their predictive and explanatory success, even if Chomsky is right about the formal notion, his claim is irrelevant to questions about the actual methodology used in linguistics.[36]

One final point in connection with *(iv)* and *(v)*. Unless there is to be a still further asymmetry, the method for deriving structural descriptions of sentences, given a grammar, has to be treated in the same way that Chomsky currently treats the method for choosing the simplest grammar. Thus, Chomsky has to say that the former method, too, is "not given *a priori,* in some manner" but is "an empirical hypothesis about the nature of language" (in the conceptualist's sense); and he has to say further that these deductive methods are not based on "a general notion somehow understood in advance outside linguistic theory". But since generative grammars are formal deductive systems,[37] the algorithms for obtaining the class of derivations of a sentence will be part of the general logical theory for these systems. Hence, assuming symmetry in the treatment of *(iv)* and *(v)*, Chomsky's claim, that such algorithms are empirical and inside linguistics is not only false, but, taken together with the rest of what Chomsky says, it would *a priori* restrict the testing of theories generally to just those deductive methods (whatever they are) that children tacitly use in acquiring their linguistic competence.

This completes our argument for viewing linguistic theory as no more nor less than a theory of the nature of language. The nature of a natural language, on our hypothesis, is that it is a sentence-sense correlation with unlimited expressiveness. Linguistic universals are at least structural features of the correlation necessary for such expressiveness. The only evidential requirement that is imposed on linguistic theory is (D_6'). The methodological notions appearing in (D_6') come from the general theory of scientific methodology (or general epistemology). Simplicity, logical implication, and so on enter linguistics, as it were, from above. They are the normative principles that define impartial "rules of the game" for the competition between scientific theories. If more than one linguistic theory satisfies (D_6'), then the competition ends in a draw. The tied theories are counted equally correct because they are equivalent in the sense of *(EQ)*. If, by some chance, one linguistic theory were to coincide to a greater extent than the others with a psychological theory, this would have no more significance for linguistics than the coincidence of Riemannian geometry with physical theory has for pure mathematics.

Notes

1. Chomsky 1980a.
2. See Chapter II, discussion of *(I)-(V)*.
3. Chomsky and Halle 1968: 4.
4. Chomsky and Halle 1968: 4.
5. Chomsky and Halle 1968: 4.
6. Even if it were to be shown empirically that the innately specified coincides extensionally with the essential (however specified), this would not save the Chomsky-Halle proposal. Their proposal is an *a priori* claim and must, therefore, take the consequences come what may. If the good were to turn out to coincide extensionally with the pleasurable, this would not save the hedonist equation of the good with the pleasurable insofar as there might be (though, *ex hypothesi*, empirically there are not) good things that are not pleasurable and pleasurable things that are not good.
7. I am aware that expression of thoughts is by no means the only, or necessarily the most important, advantage that knowledge of a language confers on us. Wittgenstein, Austin, and their followers are right to criticize too narrow a reliance on the constative side of language. But there is no need to complicate our discussion here. The capacity that our knowledge of a language affords us to perform illocutionary acts depends, I think, on the same aspects of our grammatical knowledge on which the expression of thought depends. See Katz 1977d.
8. I wish to include all cases, even, for example, hypothetical cases of infinite beings (immortals) who have the time to express every thought.
9. Katz 1978: 191–234. In this work, I defend the principle of effability in ways that I cannot go into here, but I have learned from experience that I had better say something about its defense. Many people, on first encountering the principle, think of the "counter-example" of a tribe of moronic savages who speak a natural language, or of some early race of mankind like the ancient Hittites. How could anyone think their language, with its obvious limitations of scientific and technological vocabulary, capable of expressing any proposition? How could it express propositions about genes or black holes? The answer is that effability makes no claim about what the speakers of a language can express, so it does not matter that the speakers are moronic or primitive. Also, effability does not make any claims about the form of sentences expressing this or that proposition. Clearly, the languages in question, at the stage of development supposed, cannot express propositions about the theoretical entities of contemporary science *in the special terminology* developed for them in contemporary science, but this does not mean that such a language cannot express these propositions in any terms whatever. With no limitations on the length of sentences or their syntactic form, it is no longer clear that the language is incapable of expressing these propositions. See Katz 1972: 18–24; Katz 1979c: 359–364.
10. I should mention in this context that, assuming the identification of propositions with senses, *(E)* implies the intertranslatability of natural languages in the sense of *(I)*:

(I) For any pair of natural languages L_i and L_j, and any sentence S in L_i, and any sense σ of S, there is at least one sentence S' of L_j such that σ is a sense of S'.

The argument is straightforward. Select a pair of natural languages L_i and L_j; then select any meaningful sentence, S, in L_j. Let σ be one sense of S. By *(E)*, the proposition σ is the sense of some sentence S' in L_j. Since S and S' thus share a sense, they are translations. *(E)* therefore implies the strongest denial of Quine's principle of the indeterminacy of translation: *(E)* provides the most comprehensive foundations on which to base semantics of the kind for which Quine's principle of indeterminacy is the most trenchant form of skepticism.

Note further that *(E)* is stronger than *(I)*: *(E)* implies *(I)* but not conversely. *(I)* could be true with respect to a set of senses K of sentences which is only a proper subset of the propositions that are related under the laws of logic or are the potential products of rational thought. But if the senses of sentences in every natural language are drawn only from K, *(E)* would be false. Therefore, *(E)* makes a further claim about the completeness of the logical and expressive sides of natural languages, namely that the semantic structure of natural languages is complete with respect to the full range of objects to which laws of logic apply and that the expressive structure is complete with respect to the stock of senses semantic structure supplies.

11. Tarski 1956: 164–165; Tarski 1952: 13–49.

12. Tarski 1956: 164.

13. Tarski 1956: 164.

14. Tarski 1956: 164.

15. Katz 1972: 136–150; Katz 1979a: 91–126.

16. Russell 1919: 167–180.

17. Tarski 1952: 17.

18. Tarski 1952: 26 and footnote 20, p. 45.

19. See also Carnap 1946, page 55 for the definition of *synonymous* in terms of sameness of designation.

20. The first discussion to make this point is Herzberger 1965: 473–474.

21. The point can best be put in terms of the generalized diagonalization argument in Herzberger, forthcoming. Such an argument applies to concepts in the Fregean sense (i.e., rules for terms for determining, for each object in the universe, whether it is in the extension or not) or certain liberalizations thereof. But senses are not concepts in this extensional sense: they do not relate expressions of a language to things. Hence the diagonalization argument cannot apply in connection with *(E)* alone.

22. This question was a central concern of Herzberger and Katz, unpublished, which first set out the notion of groundedness. Now see Kripke 1975.

23. See Katz 1978: 209–220.

24. This is not usually a matter of controversy, but here it could be since Platonism does not have to assume that grammatical principles are finitely specifiable. Nonetheless, the assumption will be accepted here because I wish to leave the possibility open that an ideal speaker-hearer has *perfect* knowledge of the language (i.e., has an accurate internal representation of every rule of the grammar).

25. I want to thank D. T. Langendoen for the example.

26. See chapter V.

27. Chomsky 1975b: 29–30. Chomsky defines "universal grammar" as "the system of principles, conditions, and rules that are elements or properties of all human languages not merely by accident but by necessity—of course I mean biological, not logical necessity".

28. There is still a further point. Given a tolerance for redundancy in the formulation of the requirements on linguistic theory, why is there a separate condition requiring a universal phonetic theory that defines the notion "possible sentence" but no such explicit condition requiring a universal semantic theory that defines the notion "possible sense"? If there is such a condition for one of the interpretive components of the grammar, why not a condition for the other? The answer, I think, is that the omission reflects Chomsky's skepticism about meaning (even during the *Aspects* period when his support for semantics was stronger than at any other time).

29. There is a possible disagreement with *(iii)* that I have not taken up in the text because it is not directly involved in the Platonism/conceptualism controversy. *(iii)* requires that universals of language be stated as clauses in a definition of *generative grammar*. This is not necessary. Universals of language might also be expressed directly as statements about invariances in the structure of sentences in the union of the sets of sentences for each natural language. This is, in fact, just the approach taken in Johnson and Postal 1980: ch. 14.

30. It is important to bear in mind that "general scientific methodology" is used to refer to the actual principles of scientific method, not to someone's perhaps incomplete or mistaken explication of scientific method.

31. Chomsky 1965: 37.

32. Chomsky 1966b: 24.

33. Chomsky 1974: 48.

34. Chomsky's principle of restrictiveness does not get around this argument since there will always be indefinitely many equally restrictive hypotheses, indefinitely many more and more complex ways of keeping the child's hypothesis space to a minimum. Simplicity will be required to motivate the choice of the least complex of them.

35. For a general survey, see Sober 1975.

36. Note that it is the informal, pretheoretic notion of Occam's razor that is actually used in methodological arguments in linguistics. Chomsky himself used this notion in what is perhaps the most famous appeal to simplicity in the history of generative grammar. See Chomsky 1957: 43.

37. Chomsky 1959a: 137–167.

Bibliography

Aristotle. *Nicomachean Ethics*. 1145b 2–7.

Bell, E. 1937. *Men of Mathematics*. New York: Simon and Schuster.

Bellugi, U. and Klima, E. 1979. *The Signs of Language*. Cambridge: Harvard University Press.

Benacerraf, P. 1973. "Mathematical Truth", *Journal of Philosophy* 70: 661–679.

Bever, T. G. 1970. "The Cognitive Basis for Linguistic Structures", in J. R. Hayes (ed.) *Cognition and Language Learning*. New York: Wiley.

Bloomfield, L. 1933. *Language*. New York: Henry Holt.

———. 1936. "Language or Ideas", *Language* 12: 89–95.

Bresnan, J. 1978. "Toward a Realistic Model of Transformational Grammar", in M. Halle, J. Bresnan, and G. Miller (eds.) *Linguistic Theory and Psychological Reality*. Cambridge: M. I. T. Press.

Brouwer, L. E. J. 1913 "Intuitionism and Formalism", in P. Benacerraf and H. Putnam (eds.) *Philosophy of Mathematics: Selected Readings*. Englewood Cliffs: Prentice-Hall, Inc.

Burge, T. "Sinning Against Frege", *The Philosophical Review* 88: 398–432.

Carnap, R. 1946. *Introduction to Semantics*. Cambridge: Harvard University Press.

———. 1952. "Empiricism, Semantics, and Ontology", in Linsky, L. (ed.) *Semantics and the Philosophy of Language*. Urbana: University of Illinois Press.

———. 1956. *Meaning and Necessity*. Chicago: University of Chicago Press.

Cavell, S. 1958. "Must We Mean What We Say?", *Inquiry* 1: 67–93.

Chisholm, R. M. 1960. *Realism and Phenomenology*. New York: Free Press.

Chomsky, N. 1957. *Syntactic Structures*. The Hague: Mouton.

———. 1959a. "On Certain Formal Properties of Grammars", *Information and Control* 2: 137–167.

———. 1959b. "Review of *Verbal Behavior*", *Language* 35: 26–58.

———. 1962. "Explanatory Models in Linguistics", in E. Nagel, P. Suppes, and A. Tarski (eds.) *Logic, Methodology, and the Philosophy of Science*. Stanford: Stanford University Press.

———. 1963. "Formal Properties of Grammars", in R. D. Luce, R. R. Bush, and E. Galanter (eds.) *Handbook of Mathematical Psychology* 2: 323–418.

———. 1964a. "A Transformational Approach to Syntax", in J. A. Fodor and J. J. Katz (eds.) *The Structure of Language: Readings in the Philosophy of Language*. Englewood Cliffs: Prentice Hall.

———. 1964b. "Formal Discussion", in U. Bellugi and R. Brown (eds.) *The Acquisition of Language. Monographs of the Society for Research in Child Development* 29.

———. 1965. *Aspects of the Theory of Syntax*. Cambridge: M. I. T. Press.

———. 1966a. *Cartesian Linguistics*. New York: Harper and Row.

———. 1966b. *Topics in the Theory of Generative Grammar*. The Hague: Mouton.

———. 1967a. "The Formal Nature of Language", in E. Lennenberg, *Biological Foundations of Language*. New York: Wiley.

———. 1967b. "Recent Contributions to the Theory of Innate Ideas", *Synthese* 17: 2–28.

———. 1968a. *Language and Mind*. New York: Harcourt Brace and World.

———. 1968b. "Quine's Empirical Assumptions", *Synthese* 19: 53–68.

———. 1972a. "Deep Structure, Surface Structure, and Semantic Interpretation", in N. Chomsky, *Studies on Semantics in Generative Grammar*. The Hague: Mouton.

———. 1972b. "Some Empirical Issues in the Theory of Transformational Grammar", in N. Chomsky, *Studies on Semantics in Generative Grammar*. The Hague: Mouton.

———. 1974. "Chomsky Discussion" in H. Parret (ed.) *Discussing Language*. The Hague: Mouton & Co.

———. 1975a. *The Logical Structure of Linguistic Theory*. New York: Plenum Press.

———. 1975b. *Reflections on Language*. New York: Pantheon.

———. 1975c. "Knowledge of Language", in K. Gunderson (ed.) *Minnesota Studies in the Philosophy of Science VII: Language, Mind, and Knowledge*. Minneapolis: University of Minnesota Press.

———. 1976. "On the Biological Basis of Language Capacities", in R. W. Rieber (ed.) *The Neuropsychology of Language*. New York: Plenum Press.

———. 1977a. *Dialogues avec Mitsu Ronat*. Paris: Flammarion. Trans. *Language and Responsibility*. New York: Pantheon Books.

———. 1977b. *Essays on Form and Interpretation*. New York: North Holland.

———. 1979. *Language and Responsibility*. New York: Pantheon Books.

———. 1980a. *Rules and Representations*. New York: Columbia University Press.

———. 1980b. "Rules and Representations", *The Behavioral and Brain Sciences*, in press.

———. 1980c. "Discussion of Putnam's Comments" in M. Piattelli-Palmarini (ed.) *Language and Learning: The Debate between Jean Piaget and Noam Chomsky*. Cambridge: Harvard University Press.

Chomsky, N. and Halle, M. 1968. *The Sound Pattern of English*. New York: Harper and Row.

Chomsky, N. and Katz, J. J. 1975. "On Innateness: A Reply to Cooper", *Philosophical Review* 84: 70–87.

Church A. 1954. "Intensional Isomorphism and Identity of Belief", *Philosophical Studies* 5: 65–73.

Cooper, D. E. 1972. "Innateness Old and New", *Philosophical Review* 81: 465–483.

Davidson, D. 1967. "Truth and Meaning", in J. F. Rosenberg and C. Travis (eds.) *Readings in the Philosophy of Language*. New Jersey: Prentice-Hall, Inc.

Descartes, R. 1955. "Rules for the Direction of the Mind", in E. S. Haldane and G. R. T. Ross (eds.) *Philosophical Works of Descartes*. New York: Dover

Donnellan, K. 1966. "Reference and Definite Description", *Philosophical Review* 75: 281–304.

Dummett, M. 1964. "Wittgenstein's Philosophy of Mathematics", in P. Benacerraf and H. Putnam (eds.) *Philosophy of Mathematics*. Englewood Cliffs: Prentice Hall.

———. 1973. *Frege: Philosophy of Language*. New York: Harper and Row.

———. 1975. "What is a Theory of Meaning?", in S. Guttenplan (ed.) *Mind and Language*. Oxford: Clarendon Press.

Edie, J.M. 1976. *Speaking and Meaning*. Bloomington: Indiana University Press.

Elliston, F. and P. McCormick (eds.) 1977. *Husserl: Expositions and Appraisals*. Notre Dame: University of Notre Dame Press.

Feyerabend, P. 1965. "Problems of Empiricism", in R. Colodny (ed.) *Beyond the Edge of Certainty*. Englewood Cliffs: Prentice Hall.

Fillmore, C. J. 1968. "The Case for Case", in E. Bach and R. Harms (eds.) *Universals in Linguistic Theory*. New York: Holt, Rinehart and Winston.

Fodor, J. A. 1968. *Psychological Explanation*. New York: Random House.

Fodor, J. A. and Garrett, M. F. 1966. "Some Reflections on Competence and Performance", in J. Lyons and R. Wales (eds.) *Psycholinguistic Papers*. Edinburgh: Edinburgh University Press.

Fodor, J. A. and Katz, J. J. 1962. "What's Wrong with the Philosophy of Language?", *Inquiry* 5: 197–237.

Fodor, J. A. and Katz, J. J. 1963. "The Availability of What We Say", *Philosophical Review* 72: 57–71.

Fodor, J. D. 1977. *Semantics: Theories of Meaning in Generative Grammar*. New York: Harper and Row.

Fodor, J. D., Fodor, J. A. and Garrett, M. F. 1975. "The Psychological Unreality of Semantic Representations", *Linguistic Inquiry* 6: 515–532.

Fodor, J. A., Garrett, M. F., Walker, E.C.T. and Parkes, C. H. 1980. "Against Definition", *Cognition* 8: 263–367.

Frege, G. 1894. "Review of Dr. E. Husserl's *Philosophy of Arithmetic*", *Mind*, 81: 321–337.

———. 1953. *The Foundations of Arithmetic*. Oxford: Basil Blackwell.

———. 1967. *The Basic Laws of Arithmetic*. Berkeley: University of California Press.

———. 1968. "The Thought", in Klemke 1968.

———. 1972. *"Conceptual Notation" and Related Articles*. Oxford: Oxford University Press.

Graves, C. Katz, J. J., Nishiyama, Y. Soames, S., Stecker, R., and Tovey, P. 1973. "Tacit Knowledge", *The Journal of Philosophy* 70: 318–330.

Gardner, M. 1976. "In which 'Monster' Curves Force the Redefinition of the Word 'Curve' ", *Scientific American*, December.

Geach, P. and Black, M. 1952. *Translations from the Philosophical Writings of Gottlob Frege*. Oxford: Basil Blackwell.

Gödel, K. 1964. "What is Cantor's Continuum Problem?", in P. Benacerraf and H. Putnam (eds.) *Philosophy of Mathematics: Selected Readings*. Englewood Cliffs, Prentice-Hall.

Grice, H. P. 1965. "The Causal Theory of Perception", in R. Swartz (ed.) *Perceiving, Sensing, and Knowing*. Garden City: Doubleday Anchor.

———. 1975. "Logic and Conversation", in P. Cole and J. Morgan (eds.) *Syntax and Semantics: Speech Acts*. New York: Academic Press.

Hanson, N. R. 1958. *Patterns of Discovery*. Cambridge: Cambridge University Press.

Hardy, G. H. 1940. *A Mathematician's Apology*. London: Cambridge University Press.

Harris, Z. 1951. *Methods of Structural Linguistics*. Chicago: University of Chicago Press.

———. 1954. "Distributional Structure", *Word* 10: 146–162. Reprinted J. A. Fodor and J. J. Katz (eds.), 1964. *The Structure of Language: Readings in the Philosophy of Language*. Englewood Cliffs: Prentice-Hall.

———. 1957. "Co-Occurrence and Transformation in Linguistic Structure", *Language* 33: 283–340. Reprinted in Harris 1970. Page references in footnotes are to this latter version.

———. 1965. "Transformational Theory", *Language* 41: 363–401. Reprinted in Harris 1970. Page references in footnotes to this latter version.

———. 1970. *Papers in Structural and Transformational Linguistics*. Dordrecht: D. Reidel.

Hempel, C. 1950. "Problems and Changes in the Empiricist Criterion of Meaning", *Revue Internationale de Philosophie* 11: 41–63.

Herzberger, H. 1965. "The Logical Consistency of Language", *Harvard Educational Review* 35: 469–480.

———. Forthcoming. "The Incompleteness of Language",

Herzberger, H. and Katz, J. J. Unpublished. "The Concept of Truth in Natural Languages".

Hjelmslev, L. 1936. in *Proceedings of the International Congress of Phonetic Sciences*. Cambridge.

Husserl, E. 1900. *Philosophie der Arithmetik*. Halle: Max Niemayer.

――――. 1962. *Ideas: General Introduction to Pure Phenomenology.* New York: Macmillan.

――――. 1970. *Logical Investigations* 1. New York: Humanities Press.

Janda, A. 1978. *The Linguistic Analysis of the Honey Bee's Dance Language.* Ph. D. Thesis, Graduate Center of the City University of New York.

Johnson, D. and Postal, P., 1980. *Arc-Pair Grammar.* Princeton: Princeton University Press.

Joos, M. 1958. *Readings in Linguistics.* New York: American Council of Learned Societies.

Kant, I. 1929. *Critique of Pure Reason.* New York: Macmillan.

Katz, F. M. and Katz, J. J. 1977. "Is Necessity the Mother of Intension?", *Philosophical Review* 86: 70–96.

Katz, J. J. 1962. *The Problem of Induction and its Solution.* Chicago: University of Chicago Press.

――――. 1964. "Mentalism in Linguistics", *Language* 40: 124–137.

――――. 1966. *The Philosophy of Language.* New York: Harper and Row.

――――. 1972. *Semantic Theory.* New York: Harper and Row.

――――. 1974. "Where Things Stand with the Analytic-Synthetic Distinction", *Synthese* 28: 283–319.

――――. 1975a. "The Dilemma Between Orthodoxy and Identity", *Philosophia* 5: 287–298.

――――. 1975b. "Logic and Language: An Examination of Recent Criticisms of Intensionalism", in K. Gunderson (ed.) *Language, Mind, and Knowledge. Minnesota Studies in the Philosophy of Science* 7, Minneapolis: University of Minnesota Press.

――――. 1977a. "The Advantage of Semantic Theory over Predicate Calculus in the Representation of Logical Form in Natural Languages", *Monist* 60: 380–405.

――――. 1977b. "The Real Status of Semantic Representation", *Linguistic Inquiry* 8: 559–584.

――――. 1977c. "A Proper Theory of Names", *Philosophical Studies* 31: 1–80.

――――. 1977d. *Propositional Structure and Illocutionary Force.* New York: T. Y. Crowell, Harper and Row: paperback 1980, Cambridge: Harvard University Press.

――――. 1978. "Effability and Translation", in F. Guenthner and M. Guenthner-Reuter (eds.) *Meaning and Translation: Philosophical and Linguistic Approaches.* London: Duckworth.

――――. 1979a. "A Solution to the Projection Problem for Presupposition", in C.-K. Oh and D. Dineen (eds.) *Syntax and Semantics 11: Presupposition.* New York: Academic Press.

――――. 1979b. "The Neoclassical Theory of Reference", in P. A. French, T. E. Uehling, Jr., and H. K. Wettstein (eds.) *Contemporary Perspectives in the Philosophy of Language.* Minneapolis: University of Minnesota Press.

――――. 1979c. "Semantics and Conceptual Change", *The Philosophical Review* 88: 327–365.

――――. 1980a. "Chomsky on Meaning", *Language,* 56: 1–41.

――――. 1980b. "Fodor's Guide to Cognitive Psychology", *The Behavioral and Brain Sciences* 3: 85–89.

――――. 1980c. "Literal Meaning and Logical Form", *The Journal of Philosophy,* in press.

――――. 1981. "Common Sense in Semantics", *The Notre Dame Journal of Formal Logic,* in press.

――――. In preparation. "Sciences of the Intuition".

Katz, J. J. and Bever, T. G. 1976. "The Fall and Rise of Empiricism", in T. G. Bever, J. J. Katz, and D. T. Langendoen (eds.) *An Integrated Theory of Linguistic Ability.* New York: T. Y. Crowell, Harper & Row.

Katz, J. J., Murphy, J., and Stamos, P. "Semantics and the *Cogito*", in preparation.

Keeling, S. V. 1968. *Descartes.* London: Oxford University Press.

Kenny, A. 1967. "Descartes on Ideas", in W. Doney (ed.) *Descartes*. Garden City: Anchor.

Klemke, E. (ed.), 1968. *Essays on Frege*. Urbana: University of Illinois Press.

Kripke, S. 1975. "Outline of a Theory of Truth", *Journal of Philosophy* 72: 690-716.

Labov, W. 1972. *Sociolinguistic Patterns*. Philadelphia: University of Pennsylvania Press.

Lakoff, G. 1971. "Presupposition and Relative Well-Formedness", in D. Steinberg and L. Jakobovits (es.) *Semantics*. Cambridge: Cambridge University Press.

———. 1978. "Some Remarks on AI and Linguistics", *Cognitive Science* 2: 267–275.

Langendoen, D. T. 1978. "Review of *Essays on Form and Interpretation*", *Journal of Philosophy* 75: 270–279.

Lewis, D. 1969. *Convention*. Cambridge: Harvard University Press.

———. 1975. "Languages and Language", in K. Gunderson (ed.) *Language, Mind, and Knowledge*. *Minnesota Studies in the Philosophy of Science* 7. Minneapolis: University of Minnesota Press.

Mach. E. 1893. *History and Root of the Principle of Conservation of Energy*. Chicago: Open Court Publishing Company.

Maddy, P. 1980. "Perception and Mathematical Intuition", *The Philosophical Review* 89: 163–196.

Mates, B. 1952. "Synonymity", in L. Linsky (ed.) *Semantics and the Philosophy of Language*. Urbana: University of Illinois Press

Maxwell, G. 1962. "The Ontological Status of Theoretical Entities", in H. Feigl and G. Maxwell (eds.) *Scientific Explanation, Space and Time*. *Minnesota Studies in the Philosophy of Science* 3. Minneapolis: University of Minnesota Press.

Mayer, J. W., A. Erreich, and V. V. Valian, 1978. "Transformations, Basic Operations, and Language Acquisition", *Cognition* 6: 1–13.

McCawley, J. 1977. "An Interview with Professor James D. McCawley", *Forum der Letteren* (conducted by F. G. A. M. Aarts) 18: 231–251.

Menninger, K. 1969. *Number Words and Number Systems*. Cambridge: M. I. T. Press.

Montague, R. 1974. *Formal Philosophy*. New Haven: Yale University Press.

Moore, G. E. 1956. *Principia Ethica*. Cambridge: Cambridge University Press.

Osherson, D. 1974. *Logical Abilities in Children* 2. Potomac, Md.: Earlbaum.

———. 1975. *Logical Abilities in Children* 3. Potomac, Md.: Earlbaum.

———. 1976. *Logical Abilities in Children* 4. Potomac, Md.: Earlbaum.

Parsons, C. 1967. "Foundations of Mathematics", in P. Edwards (ed.) *The Encyclopedia of Philosophy* 5: 188–213.

———. 1980. "Mathematical Intuition", *Proceedings of the Aristotelian Society* 80: 146–168.

Partee, B. 1979. "Montague Grammar, Mental Representation, and Reality", in P. French, T. Uehling, Jr., and H. K. Wettstein (eds.) *Contemporary Perspectives in the Philosophy of Language*. Minneapolis: University of Minnesota Press.

Piaget, J. 1965. *The Child's Conception of Number*. New York: Methuen.

Popper, K. R. 1972. *Objective Knowledge: An Evolutionary Approach*. London: Oxford University Press.

Putnam, H. 1962. "It Ain't Necessarily So", *The Journal of Philosophy* 59: 658–671.

———. 1970. "Is Semantics Possible?", *Metaphilosophy* 1: 189–201.

———. 1975. "The Meaning of 'Meaning' ", in K. Gunderson (ed.) *Language, Mind and Knowledge*. *Minnesota Studies in the Philosophy of Science* 7. Minneapolis: University of Minnesota Press.

———. 1976. " 'Two Dogmas' Revisited", in G. Ryle (ed.) *Contemporary Aspects of Philosophy*. London: Oriel Press.

———. 1978. "There Is At Least One *A Priori Truth*", *Erkenntis* 13: 153–170.

———, To appear. "Philosophy of Mathematics: A Report". PSA Critical Research Problems Conference.

Quine, W. V. O. 1960. *Word and Object*. Cambridge: M.I.T. Press.

————. 1961a. "Two Dogmas of Empiricism", in W. V. O. Quine, *From a Logical Point of View*. Cambridge: Harvard University Press.

————. 1961b. "The Problem of Meaning in Linguistics", in *From a Logical Point of View*. Cambridge: Harvard University Press.

————. 1961c. "On What There Is", in W. V. O. Quine, *From a Logical Point of View*. Cambridge: Harvard University Press.

————. 1964. "Truth by Convention", in P. Benacerraf and H. Putnam (eds.) *Philosophy of Mathematics*. Englewood Cliffs: Prentice Hall.

————. 1965a. "Carnap and Logical Truth", in W. V. O. Quine, *The Ways of Paradox*. New York: Random House.

————. 1965b. "Necessary Truth", in W. V. O. Quine, *The Ways of Paradox*. Random House: New York.

————. 1967. "On a Suggestion of Katz", *The Journal of Philosophy* 64: 52–54.

————. 1972a. "Methodological Reflections on Current Linguistic Theory", in D. Davidson and G. Harman (eds.) *Semantics of Natural Language*. Dordrecht: D. Reidel.

————. 1972b. *The Philosophy of Logic*. Englewood Cliffs: Prentice-Hall, Inc.

————. 1975. "The Nature of Natural Knowledge", in S. Guttenplan (ed) *Mind and Language*. Oxford: Oxford University Press.

Rorty, R. 1967. *The Linguistic Turn*. Chicago: University of Chicago Press.

Russell, B. 1919. *Introduction to Mathematical Philosophy*. London: Allen and Unwin.

Samet, J. 1980. *Tacit Knowledge*. Ph.D. Thesis, Graduate Center of the City University of New York.

Sapir, E. 1921. *Language*. New York: Harcourt, Brace.

Shapere, D. 1966. "Meaning and Scientific Change", in *Mind and Cosmos: Essays in Contemporary Science and Philosophy* 3. Pittsburgh: University of Pittsburgh Press.

Smith, G. 1979. *Rigid Designation, Scope, and Modality*. Ph.D. Thesis. M. I. T.

Smith, G. and Katz, J. J. in preparation. "Intensionally Admissible Models: The Extensional Interpretation of Intensional Semantics."

Sober, E. 1975. *Simplicity*. Oxford: Oxford University Press.

Steiner, M. 1975. *Mathematical Knowledge*. Ithaca: Cornell University Press.

Strawson, P. F. 1950. "On Referring", in J. F. Rosenberg and C. Travis (eds.) *Readings in the Philosophy of Language*. Englewood Cliffs: Prentice-Hall, Inc.

Tarski, A. 1952. "The Semantical Conception of Truth", in L. Linsky (ed.) *Semantics and the Philosophy of Language*. Urbana: University of Illinois Press.

————. 1956. "The Concept of Truth in Formalized Languages", in J. H. Woodger (Trans.) *Logic, Semantics, and Metamathematics*. Oxford: Clarendon Press.

Turing, A. M. 1950. "Computing Machinery and Intelligence", *Mind* 59: Reprinted in A. R. Anderson (ed.) 1964, *Minds and Machines*. Englewood Cliffs: Prentice Hall.

Valian, V. 1979. "The Wherefores and Therefores of the Competence/Performance Distinction", in W. Cooper and E. Walker (eds.) *Sentence Processing*. Hillsdale: Earlbaum.

Vendler, Z. 1967. "Each and Every, Any and All", in Z. Vendler, *Linguistics in Philosophy*. Ithaca: Cornell University Press.

Wexler, K., P. Culicover, and H. Hamburger, 1976. "Learning-Theoretic Foundations of Linguistic Universals", *Theoretical Linguistics* 2: 215–253.

Wittgenstein, L. 1922. *Tractatus Logico-Philosophicus*. London: Routledge and Kegan Paul.

————. 1953. *Philosophical Investigations*. Oxford: Basil Blackwell.

————. 1974. *Philosophical Grammar*. Berkeley: University of California Press.

Index

Abstract objects, 6, 8, 12, 15, 181, 186, 189n, 191n
  contrasted with 'ideal', 55–6
  our knowledge about, 193, 201–9, 219n
  'transcendental argument' for, 180
  See also Intuition; Platonism
Ambiguity, 132–33, 164–66
American Structuralism, 17, 25, 50, 136
  notion of evidence in, 70
  philosophical views of, 2, 43
  See also Nominalism; Taxonomic grammar.
Analyticity, 5, 94–95, 169, 178
  and conceptualism, 115
  and logical truth, 104–14
  Putnam's arguments against, 143–49
  Quine's arguments against, 149–53
  See also A priori knowledge; Semantic implication.
Analytic philosophy, 7
Analytic/Synthetic distinction, 4, 143–44.
  See also Analyticity
A priori knowledge, 193, 208
Aristotle, 14, 19n, 132
Austin, J. L., 121

Bell, E. T., 92n
Benacerraf, Paul, 190n, 206–8, 218n, 219n
Berger, Alan, 189n
Berkeley, Bishop, 56
Bever, Thomas, 43n, 112, 157n
Bloomfield, Leonard, 17, 25–26, 31–33, 39, 43n
  his 'convenient fictions', 31, 80, 115
Bolzano, B., 201
Brentano, Franz, 173
Bresnan, J., 18, 20n
Brouwer, L. E. J., 203, 218n
Burge, Tyler, 187n

Carnap, Rudolf, 13, 19n, 109, 155n, 159n, 163, 187n, 189n, 239n
  and inductive logic, 22
  and meaning postulates, 113
Cavell, Stanley, 219n
Center-embedding, 108
Chisholm, Roderick, 188n, 218n
Chomskian revolution, 2, 24, 33–44
  and semantics, 150. *See also* Generative grammar
Chomsky, Noam, 4–6, 8, 19n, 20n, 22–4, 33–44, 92n, 149–59, 170–71, 174, 187n, 188n, 189n, 204, 213, 214, 220n, 221–22, 230–31, 238n, 239n, 240n
  as representative of conceptualism, 11, 18
  and Platonism, 46–48
  his 'demarcational nihilism', 84–85
  his skepticism about meaning, 115–30
  his new sentence-grammar, 130–34, 137–38
  on universals, 223–25
  and scientific methodology, 233–37
Church, Alonzo, 158n
Cognitive structures, 89–92
Competence/performance distinction, 49, 59
  and competencism, 53–54
  and the critique of psychologism, 170–73
  and skepticism about meaning, 119, 122–23, 126–30
  and semantics, 145, 148–49. *See also* Ideal speaker-hearer
Competencism, 41, 53–55, 99
Compositionality, principle of, 138–42
  as linguistic universal, 230
Computational functions, 62–63
Concept: two notions of the, 46
  'in concreto', 204
Conceptualism, 15, 17, 22–23, 60–61, 80, 115, 160